MICHIGAN
STATE PARKS

BUCKET LIST

ISBN: 9798758884041

Thank you for buying our book!
We hope you like it.

Your feedback is important to us, and we
would greatly appreciate it if you could take
a moment to share your thoughts by leaving
an online review.

Your review will not only help us improve as
an author but also assist other potential
readers in making informed decisions.

Once again, thank you for your support and
for considering leaving a review.

ABOUT MICHIGAN

Michigan is a state situated in the upper Midwest region of the Great Lakes in the United States. It shares land borders with Wisconsin to the northwest and Indiana and Ohio to the south. Additionally, it's connected to the states of Minnesota and Illinois, as well as the Canadian province of Ontario, through Lakes Superior, Michigan, Huron, and Erie. Michigan covers a significant area of nearly 97,000 square miles (250,000 square kilometers) and has a population of nearly 10.12 million, making it the 10th most populous state and the 11th largest in terms of area in the United States. Notably, it's the largest state in terms of area east of the Mississippi River. The state capital is Lansing, and its most populous city is Detroit. Metro Detroit is one of the most densely populated regions and boasts a significant metropolitan economy. The name "Michigan" is derived from a modified version of the original Ojibwe word "ᒥᓯᑲᒥ" (mishigami), which translates to "large water" or "large lake."

Michigan comprises two distinct peninsulas. The Lower Peninsula is shaped like a mitten and constitutes the majority of the state's land. The Upper Peninsula, often referred to as "the U.P.," is separated from the Lower Peninsula by the Straits of Mackinac, a narrow channel stretching five miles (8 kilometers) connecting Lake Huron to Lake Michigan. The Mackinac Bridge is the link between these two peninsulas. Michigan boasts the longest freshwater coastline of any political division within the United States, as it is surrounded by four of the five Great Lakes and Lake St. Clair. The state also boasts 64,980 inland lakes and ponds, and it ranks second in terms of water area among all U.S. states, with Alaska being the only exception.

The area now known as Michigan was originally inhabited by various Native American tribes over thousands of years. In the 17th century, French explorers claimed the region as part of the New France colony, when it was primarily populated by indigenous peoples. French and Canadian traders, settlers, Métis, and others migrated to the area, settling predominantly along the waterways. Following France's defeat in the French and Indian War in 1762, the region came under British control. After the American Revolutionary War, Britain ceded the territory to the newly independent United States.

The area was initially part of the larger Northwest Territory until 1800 when western Michigan became part of the Indiana Territory. The Michigan Territory was established in 1805, though some aspects of the northern border with Canada were not finalized until after the War of 1812. Michigan was admitted to the Union as the 26th state in 1837 and was admitted as a free state. It quickly became a pivotal hub for industry and commerce in the Great Lakes region, attracting immigrants from various European countries in the late 19th and early 20th centuries, with notable numbers coming from Finland, Macedonia, and the Netherlands. The 1930s witnessed an increase in migration from Appalachia and Black Southerners as part of the Great Migration, with many settling in the Metro Detroit area.

While Michigan has developed a diversified economy, it gained significant recognition as the epicenter of the U.S. automotive industry in the early 20th century, emerging as a major national economic force. The state is home to the three major U.S. automobile companies, all of which have their headquarters in Metro Detroit. Once known for its logging and mining industries, the sparsely populated Upper Peninsula now plays a vital role in tourism due to its abundant natural resources. In contrast, the Lower Peninsula is a hub for manufacturing, forestry, agriculture, services, and high-tech industries.

Michigan is a state overflowing with the beauty of unspoiled nature. It boasts the longest freshwater shoreline in the country, offering lake experiences akin to oceans. Visitors can savor golden beaches, indulge in a bounty of fresh farm produce, witness breathtaking sunrises and sunsets, and immerse themselves in countless recreational opportunities.

Michigan is home to over 100 public beaches, some of the world's tallest freshwater sand dunes, striking sandstone cliffs painted with multiple colors, and it hosts two National Lakeshores, along with the sole national marine sanctuary in the Great Lakes — the Thunder Bay National Marine Sanctuary in Lake Huron. Along the shoreline, you'll discover 129 lighthouses, a multitude of maritime museums, ten shipwreck-diving preserves, and historic military fortifications.

Detroit, known as "America's Great Comeback City," pays homage to its automotive legacy within the Motor Cities National Heritage Area and celebrates its music heritage at the Motown Museum. The city is also home to the renowned Henry Ford Museum, recognized as America's premier history attraction, and it boasts a thriving arts and culinary scene.

In Michigan, there's an array of recreational options, thanks to its lakes, campgrounds, wildlife refuges, and state parks and recreation areas. The state offers rivers for water sports and an extensive network of hiking, biking, snowshoeing, cross-country skiing, and snowmobiling trails weaving through 19 million acres of forests.

Michigan's waters are speckled with hundreds of islands. Isle Royale National Park in Lake Superior is a remote wilderness haven where wolves and moose roam freely. Mackinac Island, situated in the Straits of Mackinac, transports visitors to a 19th-century resort community, entirely free of automobiles, dominated by an 18th-century fort and the more than century-old Grand Hotel, which is the largest summer resort hotel in America.

The Upper Peninsula, covering 90 percent with forests, maintains its charm as accessible wilderness. There, you'll discover vast wildlife and waterfowl refuges, 150 waterfalls, iron and copper mines, and the Soo Locks, where ocean-going freighters make a dramatic 21-foot leap from Lake Superior to Lake Huron, all within a short drive of one another.

INVENTORY

- ☐ BEAR SPRAY
- ☐ BINOCULARS
- ☐ CAMERA + ACCESSORIES
- ☐ CELL PHONE + CHARGER
- ☐ FIRST AID KIT
- ☐ FLASHLIGHT/ HEADLAMP
- ☐ FLEECE/ WATERPROOF JACKET
- ☐ GUIDE BOOK
- ☐ HAND LOTION
- ☐ HAND SANITIZER
- ☐ HIKING SHOES
- ☐ INSECT REPELLENT
- ☐ LIP BALM
- ☐ MEDICATIONS AND PAINKILLERS
- ☐ SUNGLASSES
- ☐ SNACKS
- ☐ SPARE SOCKS
- ☐ SUN HAT
- ☐ SUNSCREEN
- ☐ TOILET PAPER
- ☐ TRASH BAGS
- ☐ WALKING STICK
- ☐ WATER
- ☐ WATER SHOES/ SANDALS

PARK NAME	COUNTY	EST.	VISITED
Algonac State Park	St. Clair	1937	
Aloha State Park	Cheboygan	1923	
Baraga State Park	Baraga	1921	
Bay City State Park	Bay	1923	
Belle Isle Park	Wayne	1845	
Bewabic State Park	Iron	1923	
Brimley State Park	Chippewa	1923	
Burt Lake State Park	Cheboygan	1921	
Cambridge Junction Historic State Park	Lenawee	1965	
Cheboygan State Park	Cheboygan	1962	
Clear Lake State Park	Montmorency	1966	
Coldwater Lake State Park	Branch	1988	
Colonial Michilimackinac Historic State Park	Emmet	1960	
Craig Lake State Park	Baraga, Marquette	1956	
Dodge #4 State Park	Oakland	1922	
Duck Lake State Park	Muskegon	1988	
Fayette Historic State Park	Delta	1959	
Fisherman's Island State Park	Charlevoix	1975	
Fort Wilkins Historic State Park	Keweenaw	1923	
Grand Haven State Park	Ottawa	1920	
Grand Mere State Park	Berrien	1973	
Harrisville State Park	Alcona	1921	
Hartwick Pines State Park	Crawford	1927	
Hayes State Park	Lenawee, Jackson, Washtenaw	1920	
Historic Mill Creek Discovery Park	Cheboygan	1978	
Hoeft State Park	Presque Isle	1922	
Hoffmaster State Park	Muskegon, Ottawa	1963	
Holland State Park	Ottawa	1926	

PARK NAME	COUNTY	EST.	VISITED
Indian Lake State Park	Schoolcraft	1932	
Interlochen State Park	Grand Traverse	1917	
Keith J. Charters Traverse City State Park	Grand Traverse	1920	
Lake Gogebic State Park	Gogebic	1930	
Lakeport State Park	St. Clair	1946	
Laughing Whitefish Falls State Park	Alger	1946	
Leelanau State Park	Leelanau	1964	
Ludington State Park	Mason	1927	
Mackinac Island and Fort Mackinac Historic Park	Mackinac	1895	
Maybury State Park	Wayne	1971	
McLain State Park	Houghton	1930	
Mears State Park	Oceana	1923	
Meridian-Baseline State Park	Ingham, Jackson	1967	
Mitchell State Park	Wexford	1919	
Muskallonge Lake State Park	Luce	1956	
Muskegon State Park	Muskegon	1923	
Negwegon State Park	Alcona, Alpena	1962	
Newaygo State Park	Newaygo	1966	
North Higgins Lake State Park	Crawford	1965	
Old Mission State Park	Grand Traverse	1989	
Onaway State Park	Presque Isle	1921	
Orchard Beach State Park	Manistee	1921	
Otsego Lake State Park	Otsego	1920	
Palms Book State Park	Schoolcraft	1926	
Petoskey State Park	Emmet	1969	
Porcupine Mountains Wilderness State Park	Gogebic, Ontonagon	1944	
Port Crescent State Park	Huron	1955	
Sanilac Petroglyphs Historic State Park	Sanilac	1971	

PARK NAME	COUNTY	EST.	VISITED
Saugatuck Dunes State Park	Allegan	1978	
Seven Lakes State Park	Oakland	1992	
Silver Lake State Park	Oceana	1920	
Sleeper State Park	Huron	1924	
Sleepy Hollow State Park	Clinton	1965	
South Higgins Lake State Park	Roscommon	1924	
Sterling State Park	Monroe	1935	
Straits State Park	Mackinac	1924	
Sturgeon Point State Park	Alcona	1960	
Tahquamenon Falls State Park	Chippewa, Luce	1947	
Tawas Point State Park	Iosco	1960	
Thompson's Harbor State Park	Presque Isle	1988	
Twin Lakes State Park	Houghton	1964	
Van Buren State Park	Van Buren	1966	
Van Riper State Park	Marquette	1956	
Warren Dunes State Park	Berrien	1930	
Warren Woods State Park	Berrien	1949	
Watkins Lake State Park and County Preserve	Washtenaw	2017	
Wells State Park	Menominee	1925	
Wilderness State Park	Emmet	1927	
William G. Milliken State Park and Harbor	Wayne	2004	
Wilson State Park	Clare	1920	
Young State Park	Charlevoix	1921	

COUNTY	PARK NAME	EST.	VISITED
Alcona	Harrisville State Park	1921	
Alcona	Sturgeon Point State Park	1960	
Alcona, Alpena	Negwegon State Park	1962	
Alger	Laughing Whitefish Falls State Park	1946	
Allegan	Saugatuck Dunes State Park	1978	
Baraga	Baraga State Park	1921	
Baraga, Marquette	Craig Lake State Park	1956	
Bay	Bay City State Park	1923	
Berrien	Grand Mere State Park	1973	
Berrien	Warren Dunes State Park	1930	
Berrien	Warren Woods State Park	1949	
Branch	Coldwater Lake State Park	1988	
Charlevoix	Fisherman's Island State Park	1975	
Charlevoix	Young State Park	1920	
Cheboygan	Aloha State Park	1923	
Cheboygan	Burt Lake State Park	1920	
Cheboygan	Cheboygan State Park	1962	
Cheboygan	Historic Mill Creek Discovery Park	1978	
Chippewa	Brimley State Park	1923	
Chippewa, Luce	Tahquamenon Falls State Park	1947	
Clare	Wilson State Park	1920	
Clinton	Sleepy Hollow State Park	1965	
Crawford	Hartwick Pines State Park	1927	
Crawford	North Higgins Lake State Park	1965	
Delta	Fayette Historic State Park	1959	
Emmet	Colonial Michilimackinac Historic State Park	1960	
Emmet	Petoskey State Park	1969	
Emmet	Wilderness State Park	1927	

COUNTY	PARK NAME	EST.	VISITED
Gogebic	Lake Gogebic State Park	1930	
Gogebic, Ontonagon	Porcupine Mountains Wilderness State Park	1944	
Grand Traverse	Interlochen State Park	1917	
Grand Traverse	Keith J. Charters Traverse City State Park	1920	
Grand Traverse	Old Mission State Park	1989	
Houghton	McLain State Park	1930	
Houghton	Twin Lakes State Park	1964	
Huron	Port Crescent State Park	1955	
Huron	Sleeper State Park	1924	
Ingham, Jackson	Meridian-Baseline State Park	1967	
Iosco	Tawas Point State Park	1960	
Iron	Bewabic State Park	1923	
Jackson, Lenawee, Washtenaw	Hayes State Park	1920	
Keweenaw	Fort Wilkins Historic State Park	1923	
Leelanau	Leelanau State Park	1964	
Lenawee	Cambridge Junction Historic State Park	1965	
Luce	Muskallonge Lake State Park	1956	
Mackinac	Mackinac Island and Fort Mackinac Historic Park	1895	
Mackinac	Straits State Park	1924	
Manistee	Orchard Beach State Park	1921	
Marquette	Van Riper State Park	1956	
Mason	Ludington State Park	1927	
Menominee	Wells State Park	1925	
Monroe	Sterling State Park	1935	
Montmorency	Clear Lake State Park	1966	
Muskegon	Duck Lake State Park	1988	
Muskegon	Muskegon State Park	1923	
Muskegon, Ottawa	Hoffmaster State Park	1963	

COUNTY	PARK NAME	EST.	VISITED
Newaygo	Newaygo State Park	1966	
Oakland	Dodge #4 State Park	1922	
Oakland	Seven Lakes State Park	1992	
Oceana	Mears State Park	1923	
Oceana	Silver Lake State Park	1920	
Otsego	Otsego Lake State Park	1920	
Ottawa	Grand Haven State Park	1920	
Ottawa	Holland State Park	1926	
Presque Isle	Hoeft State Park	1922	
Presque Isle	Onaway State Park	1921	
Presque Isle	Thompson's Harbor State Park	1988	
Roscommon	South Higgins Lake State Park	1924	
Sanilac	Sanilac Petroglyphs Historic State Park	1971	
Schoolcraft	Indian Lake State Park	1932	
Schoolcraft	Palms Book State Park	1926	
St. Clair	Algonac State Park	1937	
St. Clair	Lakeport State Park	1946	
Van Buren	Van Buren State Park	1966	
Washtenaw	Watkins Lake State Park and County Preserve	2017	
Wayne	Belle Isle Park	1845	
Wayne	Maybury State Park	1971	
Wayne	William G. Milliken State Park and Harbor	2004	
Wexford	Mitchell State Park	1919	

1. Algonac State Park
2. Aloha State Park
3. Baraga State Park
4. Bay City State Park
5. Belle Isle Park
6. Bewabic State Park
7. Brimley State Park
8. Burt Lake State Park
9. Cambridge Junction Historic State Park
10. Cheboygan State Park
11. Clear Lake State Park
12. Coldwater Lake State Park
13. Colonial Michilimackinac Historic State Park
14. Craig Lake State Park
15. Dodge #4 State Park
16. Duck Lake State Park
17. Fayette Historic State Park
18. Fisherman's Island State Park
19. Fort Wilkins Historic State Park
20. Grand Haven State Park
21. Grand Mere State Park
22. Harrisville State Park
23. Hartwick Pines State Park
24. Hayes State Park
25. Historic Mill Creek Discovery Park
26. Hoeft State Park
27. Hoffmaster State Park
28. Holland State Park
29. Indian Lake State Park
30. Interlochen State Park
31. Keith J. Charters Traverse City State Park
32. Lake Gogebic State Park
33. Lakeport State Park
34. Laughing Whitefish Falls State Park
35. Leelanau State Park
36. Ludington State Park
37. Mackinac Island and Fort Mackinac Historic Park
38. Maybury State Park
39. McLain State Park
40. Mears State Park
41. Meridian-Baseline State Park
42. Mitchell State Park
43. Muskallonge Lake State Park
44. Muskegon State Park
45. Negwegon State Park
46. Newaygo State Park
47. North Higgins Lake State Park
48. Old Mission State Park
49. Onaway State Park
50. Orchard Beach State Park
51. Otsego Lake State Park
52. Palms Book State Park
53. Petoskey State Park
54. Porcupine Mountains Wilderness State Park
55. Port Crescent State Park
56. Sanilac Petroglyphs Historic State Park
57. Saugatuck Dunes State Park
58. Seven Lakes State Park
59. Silver Lake State Park
60. Sleeper State Park
61. Sleepy Hollow State Park
62. South Higgins Lake State Park
63. Sterling State Park
64. Straits State Park
65. Sturgeon Point State Park
66. Tahquamenon Falls State Park
67. Tawas Point State Park
68. Thompson's Harbor State Park
69. Twin Lakes State Park
70. Van Buren State Park
71. Van Riper State Park
72. Warren Dunes State Park
73. Warren Woods State Park
74. Watkins Lake State Park and County Preserve
75. Wells State Park
76. Wilderness State Park
77. William G. Milliken State Park and Harbor
78. Wilson State Park
79. Young State Park

ALGONAC STATE PARK

COUNTY	ESTABLISHED	AREA (AC/HA)
ST. CLAIR	1937	1,550 / 627

Algonac State Park is most renowned for its scenic views of cargo ships traveling along the St. Clair River. This 1,550-acre park offers half a mile of riverfront, campgrounds, hiking trails, and a dedicated natural area spanning over 1,200 acres. Within the park, you can find unique ecosystems such as lake plain prairies and oak savannas, which provide a habitat for 22 plant, bird, and butterfly species that are either threatened, endangered, or require special attention. The St. Clair River's shoreline is a popular spot for fishing, particularly for catching walleye. For those who prefer boat fishing, there are two boating access sites, Marine City and Algonac North Channel, both located within a 4-mile radius. Paddling is a favorite activity on the St. Clair River, which connects to Lake St. Clair. There's a small boat launch area suitable for kayaks, canoes, and stand-up paddleboards. Hunting is permitted within the state park, but it's advisable to contact the park directly to learn about any specific rules or concerns. During the summer season, naturalists offer weekly nature-based programs from Memorial Day through Labor Day. You can bring your pets along the entire length of the St. Clair River, but they must be on a 6-foot leash and under your immediate control. Any pet waste should be properly disposed of in designated trash bins. The day-use area features a picnic area with tables and charcoal grills available on a first-come, first-served basis. Additionally, there's a picnic shelter in the day-use area with picnic tables, charcoal grills, a water source, electrical service (reservations required), and vault toilets. You can reserve the shelter up to 12 months in advance at MiDNRReservations.com. A swing set is also available in the day-use area for recreation. The park's sanitation station is situated between the contact office and the Riverfront Campground, providing potable water and two lanes for your convenience. For those interested in shooting sports, the Algonac State Park Shooting Range offers outdoor archery, hand trap, and rifle/handgun ranges. Please note that this range is not staffed. The rustic group-use site is available for gatherings of up to 50 people. It includes amenities such as picnic tables, a fire pit, and a vault toilet. To secure reservations for the group camp area, please contact 810-765-5605. Within the modern campground, there are a total of 220 sites, divided into the north and south loops. This campground is renowned for offering close-up views of international freighters navigating the St. Clair River. In general, the campsites are spacious and level, with a majority of them featuring gravel pads. Additionally, there are two campground sites designed to be accessible to individuals with disabilities. Algonac-Modern Wagon

Wheel Campground is aptly named due to its circular layout, resembling a wagon wheel. Nestled in a wooded area, each site in this campground is equipped with a paved pad. The campground exudes a rustic "up north" ambiance, and the St. Clair River is just a short 10-minute walk away. Three of the campground sites are designed to be ADA accessible. The Blazing Star Trail is a half-mile interpretive pathway adorned with a variety of wildflowers that bloom at different times throughout the warmer seasons. This trail is classified as easy and is suitable for families. You can access the trailhead located across from the shooting range. Algonac-Oak Savanna Trail, a 2.4-mile loop, takes you through an oak savanna teeming with diverse plant and wildlife species. The trail is generally flat and can be easily navigated. You can find the trailhead near the Riverfront Campground. The 54-mile Bridge to Bay Trail traces its route along the St. Clair River, spanning from New Baltimore in Macomb County to Algonac State Park in St. Clair County, and further north to Lakeport State Park in the same county. This extensive trail system links trail users to downtown areas, neighborhoods, parks, museums, beaches, lighthouses, and more. The trail offers a diverse range of environments, including boardwalks, riverfront paths, and rail trails, both in urban and natural settings along waterfront and inland corridors.

PASSPORT STAMPS

ALOHA STATE PARK

COUNTY	ESTABLISHED	AREA (AC/HA)
CHEBOYGAN	1923	107 / 43

Aloha State Park is situated on the northeastern shore of Mullett Lake, near the Straits of Mackinac in the northernmost part of Michigan's Lower Peninsula. The park offers a modern campground, a boating access point, a designated swimming beach, and a protected boat harbor where campers can safely store their boats while staying at the park. Mullett Lake is the fourth-largest inland lake in Michigan and serves as the central hub for the Inland Waterway, a network of rivers and lakes that provides 38 miles of water routes for boating and paddling enthusiasts. You can also relish 200 feet of sandy shoreline along Mullett Lake for a relaxing waterfront experience. The 70-mile-long North Eastern State Trail, stretching from Alpena to Mackinaw City, runs along the border of the park and connects with the North Central and North Western state trails. On the eastern side of the park, the North Eastern State Trail permits biking with its crushed limestone surface. Bike and bike trailer rentals are available at the park's contact station; you can inquire for more information at 231-625-2522. Fishing is a popular activity on Mullett Lake, and there are paddling opportunities both on the lake itself and along the Inland Waterway. A public boating access site in the campground offers access to Mullett Lake from the park's boat harbor. Additionally, a fish-cleaning station is conveniently located in the parking lot of the park's boating access site, near the eastern end of the boat harbor. For those who enjoy picnics, there are charcoal grills and picnic tables available near the park's entrance. A picnic shelter in the day-use area is equipped with picnic tables, charcoal grills, electrical service (reservations required), and modern restrooms. You can make reservations for the shelter up to 12 months in advance at MiDNRReservations.com. The park also provides swings and a volleyball court near the entrance. During the winter months, the eastern side of the park's North Eastern State Trail is open for snowmobiling from December 1 to March 31. In the day-use area and campground, there is a designated swimming area for visitors to enjoy. The park's sanitation station is located at the campground entrance and offers potable water and two lanes for your convenience. The campsite, situated on the picturesque Mullett Lake, offers generously sized and well-lit sites. It is organized into three sections with multiple loops. In the southern section, all campsites are equipped with full-hookup facilities, including water and sewer connections. It's worth noting that the south campground does not have a dedicated bathroom building. This campground is a favored choice for boating enthusiasts, as it encompasses the park's boating access site and a sheltered boat basin. Registered campers have the convenience of leaving their boats securely moored in the protected boat basin for the entirety of their stay.

DATE(S) VISITED .... ☐ SPRING ☐ SUMMER ☐ FALL ☐ WINTER

LODGING .... ☐ ☀ ☐ ☁ ☐ 🌧 ☐ ☁ ☐ ❄

WHO I WENT WITH .... FEE(S) .... PARK HOURS .... TEMP:.........

WILL I RETURN? YES / NO   RATING ☆ ☆ ☆ ☆ ☆

PASSPORT STAMPS

BARAGA STATE PARK

COUNTY	ESTABLISHED	AREA (AC/HA)
LAFAYETTE	1970	968 / 392

Baraga State Park, situated along the picturesque Keweenaw Bay of Lake Superior, is a popular destination for hiking, kayaking, camping, and accommodating off-road vehicle (ORV) enthusiasts. It also serves as an excellent home base for travelers exploring various destinations in the western Upper Peninsula. This park stands out as one of the few state parks that permit the use of ORVs to access nearby ORV trails, allowing campers to conveniently connect to Twin Lakes and Bewabic state parks, as well as the Bond Falls Scenic Site, through several motorized routes. Within the day-use area, you'll find a picnic spot with picnic tables and charcoal grills available on a first-come, first-served basis. The day-use area also features swings for recreational use. Paddling is a favored activity on Keweenaw Bay, and visitors can take advantage of a quarter-mile stretch of rocky shoreline along Lake Superior's Keweenaw Bay. Three concrete walkways provide direct access to the lake. For your convenience, the park's sanitation station is located in the campground area, offering potable water and two lanes for use. Along the entire length of the Lake Superior shoreline, spanning a quarter of a mile, pets are welcome, but they must always be leashed with a 6-foot lead and under the immediate control of their owners. Proper disposal of pet waste in designated trash receptacles is required. In the winter months, the park provides easy access to local snowmobile and ORV trails directly from its premises. It also connects to Twin Lakes and Bewabic state parks, as well as the Bond Falls Scenic Site, through various motorized routes. Additionally, from early May to late October, visitors can enjoy free WiFi access at the park, enhancing connectivity during their stay. The mini cabin is situated within the modern campground of the park and is designed to accommodate four people. Inside, you'll find a bunk bed with a full-size bed on the bottom and a single bed on top, along with a cot for additional sleeping space. The cabin is equipped with amenities like a mini refrigerator, microwave, coffee maker, and an electric wall heater for comfort. Outside the cabin, there are provisions for outdoor dining and cooking, including a picnic table, bench, fire pit, and a waist-high cooking grill. The cabin is wired for electricity, but you are responsible for providing your own bedding and linens. The modern campground is divided into two sections, the north loop and south loop, and offers a variety of camping sites, including back-in, pull-through, and accessible sites. Most of these sites are level, generously sized, and shaded by oak, maple, and pine trees, providing a pleasant camping environment. For those who enjoy nature walks, the Nature

Trail offers a 0.75-mile looped path that meanders through the forest. This trail is considered relatively easy and can be accessed near the north toilet/shower building in the campground.

DATE(S) VISITED .... ☐ SPRING ☐ SUMMER ☐ FALL ☐ WINTER

LODGING .... ☐ ☀ ☐ ☁ ☐ 🌧 ☐ ⛅ ☐ ❄

WHO I WENT WITH .... FEE(S) .... PARK HOURS .... TEMP:.........

WILL I RETURN? YES / NO RATING ☆ ☆ ☆ ☆ ☆

PASSPORT STAMPS

BAY CITY STATE PARK

COUNTY	ESTABLISHED	AREA (AC/HA)
BAY	1923	2,389 / 967

Bay City State Park, located on the shores of Saginaw Bay, is home to one of the largest remaining freshwater coastal wetlands in the Great Lakes, known as Tobico Marsh. This wetland spans over 2,000 acres and comprises a diverse range of habitats, including wetland woods, meadows, cattail marshes, and oak savannah prairies, making it a crucial stopover for migratory birds. The park has gained recognition for its rich birdlife and its role as a sanctuary for wetland wildlife and plants. A brand-new "Play by The Bay" inclusive playground is a prominent feature, offering decorative cattails, mushroom-shaped stepping stones, acorn-shaped seats, and lifelike rock walls and logs. Notably, the playground boasts a large fish-shaped play structure with a springy balance board tail, climbing bars, and ropes. Additionally, the park features a popular spray park for visitors to enjoy. For enhanced accessibility, the park now provides a track chair that visitors can borrow. These chairs are capable of traversing trails, snow, sand, and even up to 4 inches of water, allowing users to explore areas of the park that may be challenging for traditional wheelchairs. The three-mile Andersen Natural Trail follows a former railway corridor and connects to the Bay City Trailway System to the park's south. Bicycles are permitted on designated park roads and specified trails. Fishing enthusiasts can try their luck in Tobico Lagoon, which is home to pike, carp, bass, and panfish. An accessible fishing pier makes shore fishing accessible to all, and there are additional DNR-managed boating access sites just a few miles from the park. In the winter months, ice fishing is an option just off the park's shoreline. Over seven miles of trails within the park offer opportunities for visitors to explore the wetlands. These trails include over three miles of paved pathways, three observation towers, boardwalks, viewing platforms, and shoreline spotting scopes. Bicycles and rollerblades are welcome on these trails. Hunting is permitted during open seasons for deer, waterfowl, and small game within the park. Visitors can enjoy picnicking on the sandy shoreline of the Bay or under the shade of tall cottonwood and ash trees bordering Tobico Lagoon. Picnic facilities include tables and fire pits or grills. The park also offers five shelters available for rent, which can be reserved up to one year in advance by contacting 1-800-447-2757 or visiting their website. The Saginaw Bay Visitor Center, an award-winning facility, is a must-visit for park guests. This center provides valuable information about the unique natural features of the coastal wetland and Saginaw Bay and offers interpretive programs to help visitors discover the richness of the wetlands. Inside the center, visitors can explore the Jennison Exhibit Hall, shop at the Wetland Wonders Gift Shop, observe wildlife from the Wildlife Observation Room and the Marsh Camera, experience the multi-image presentation "The Saginaw Bay Story," and enjoy the changing lobby exhibits. To enhance beach access, the park provides a seasonal accessible beach mat, and a mobile beach chair is available for year-round use.

DATE(S) VISITED .... ☐ SPRING ☐ SUMMER ☐ FALL ☐ WINTER

LODGING .... ☐ ☀ ☐ ☁ ☐ 🌧 ☐ 🌫 ☐ ❄

WHO I WENT WITH .... FEE(S) .... PARK HOURS .... TEMP:.........

WILL I RETURN? YES / NO   RATING ☆ ☆ ☆ ☆ ☆

PASSPORT STAMPS

BELLE ISLE PARK

COUNTY	ESTABLISHED	AREA (AC/HA)
WAYNE	1845	982 / 397

Belle Isle Park, a 982-acre island located in the Detroit River near downtown Detroit, offers stunning views of Detroit to the north and Canada to the south. The park is home to a range of cultural and natural attractions, including the James Scott Memorial Fountain, the Anna Scripps Whitcomb Conservatory, the Belle Isle Aquarium, the Ralph Wilson Gateway (the official starting point of Michigan's Iron Belle Trail), a golf course, and much more. Visitors can enjoy activities such as swimming at the designated beach, cycling, fishing, and paddling. The island also features numerous food trucks, with a popular location at Kids Row near the giant slide. Bicycling is a popular way to explore the park, with dedicated bicycle lanes along the main perimeter road and the new multi-use Eugene and Elaine C. Driker Trail on the east end of the island. Bike rentals are available through Simple Adventures, including MoGo bicycle rentals, with hours dependent on weather conditions. For reservations and rental rates, you can visit simpleadventures.net. Memorial Day through Labor Day, Simple Adventures also offers canoe, kayak, and stand-up paddleboard rentals at the designated swim beach. Two accessible fishing piers are situated off Riverbank Road and Strand Road for fishing enthusiasts. On the north end of the island, you can find the Livingstone Memorial Lighthouse, the oldest marble lighthouse in the United States, which was built in 1929 as a tribute to William Livingstone, the president of the Lakes Carriers Association from 1902 to 1925. While it remains a working lighthouse, public tours are not available. Belle Isle Park provides 13 restrooms, each equipped with an accessible stall. Two of these restrooms, Bus Stop 7 in the aquarium parking lot and Sunset Point, also offer accessible parking, sidewalks, and ramps. Fishing in the Detroit River is a popular pastime, with a variety of fish species like bass, walleye, and catfish. The park offers several picnic areas scattered throughout the island, along with 15 picnic shelters that come with picnic tables and charcoal grills. Shelters #2 and #8 have electrical service and restrooms connected to them. You can reserve these shelters up to 12 months in advance at MiDNRReservations.com. For special events involving 200 or more people, you can contact the events office at 313-821-9851 or DNR BelleIsleParkEvents@Michigan.gov. Belle Isle Park provides numerous paddling opportunities on the Detroit River, inland lakes, canals, and lagoons. There are two accessible kayak launches: one along Woodside Drive and the other across from the Detroit Yacht Club (follow signs for Detroit Jet Ski). Additionally, Kids Row on Central Avenue features an accessible playground with a rubberized surface to improve access for individuals of all mobility levels, as well as the giant slide (open from Memorial Day through Labor Day, Wednesday to Sunday, from noon to 8 p.m.). A designated swimming area is open from Memorial Day through Labor Day, although there are no lifeguards on duty. Belle Isle, the third-largest island in the Detroit River, is home to several bodies of water, including Lake Muskoday, the Blue Heron Lagoon, Lake Okonoka, Lake Tacoma, and a network of canals that connect the lakes and the river. The DNR is also involved in the restoration of 200 acres of globally rare, forested wetland along the river.

DATE(S) VISITED .... □ SPRING □ SUMMER □ FALL □ WINTER

LODGING .... □ ☼ □ ☁ □ ☂ □ 🌫 □ ❄

WHO I WENT WITH .... FEE(S) .... PARK HOURS .... TEMP:.........

WILL I RETURN? YES / NO   RATING ☆ ☆ ☆ ☆ ☆

PASSPORT STAMPS

BEWABIC STATE PARK

COUNTY	ESTABLISHED	AREA (AC/HA)
IRON	1923	315 / 127

Bewabic State Park is located on the shores of Fortune Lake, which is part of the larger Fortune Lakes Chain. This park offers a mix of modern and rustic campsites, a day-use area, a tennis court, hiking trails, a boat launch, and more. Its historical significance is rooted in the Civilian Conservation Corps (CCC) era, as evidenced by the presence of several CCC structures that are still in use. Bewabic is among the select state parks that permit the operation of off-road vehicles (ORVs) between the campground and nearby ORV trails. These trails connect to Twin Lakes and Baraga state parks, as well as the Bond Falls Scenic Site via a network of motorized routes. It's important to note that ORV use is restricted to entering and exiting the park, and not for travel within the park itself. The park serves as site #9 along the Iron County Heritage Trail system, making it a part of the broader trail network. For water enthusiasts, the park offers kayak, stand-up paddleboard, and canoe rentals from Memorial Day through September. Visitors can make rental arrangements by visiting the campground office or calling the park at 906-875-3324. The day-use area of the park, situated on the picturesque Fortune Lake, includes a beach house with restroom facilities. An accessible boat launch on Fortune Lake provides the only public boating access to the Fortune Lakes Chain, making it a popular spot for fishing. The picnic area in the day-use section features picnic tables and charcoal grills available on a first-come, first-served basis. Additionally, there's a picnic shelter in the day-use area equipped with picnic tables, charcoal grills, electrical service (reservations required), and restrooms. Reservations for the shelter can be made up to 12 months in advance at MiDNRReservations.com. A playground with swings and a slide is also located in the day-use area. The park provides direct access to the Heritage Trail and connects to Twin Lakes and Baraga state parks and the Bond Falls Scenic Site via motorized routes. ORV route and trail maps are available for purchase at the park. For campers, Bewabic State Park features a 130-site modern campground with three loops (A, B, and C), including many shaded and wooded sites. These sites are popular for their increased privacy, thanks to trees and vegetation that separate them. Additionally, there are four rustic walk-in campsites (#107-110) that require a short walk (within 125 yards) from the parking area, and these do not have electrical hookups. The Nature Trail, spanning 2 miles, provides visitors with a scenic journey through the park. Along the trail, benches offer opportunities to stop and enjoy the picturesque views. Access points to the trail can be found in both the modern campground and the park's day-use area.

DATE(S) VISITED .... ☐ SPRING ☐ SUMMER ☐ FALL ☐ WINTER

LODGING .... ☐ ☀ ☐ ☁ ☐ 🌧 ☐ 🌫 ☐ ❄

WHO I WENT WITH .... FEE(S) .... PARK HOURS .... TEMP:.........

WILL I RETURN? YES / NO   RATING ☆ ☆ ☆ ☆ ☆

PASSPORT STAMPS

BRIMLEY STATE PARK

COUNTY	ESTABLISHED	AREA (AC/HA)
CHIPPEWA	1923	151 / 61

Brimley State Park, situated on the picturesque shores of Lake Superior's Whitefish Bay, encompasses 100 acres of lakeside recreational space. Established in 1923, it ranks among the oldest state parks in the Upper Peninsula. The land for the park's initial acreage was gifted by the Village of Brimley to the Department of Natural Resources (DNR). The park offers a range of amenities, including a campground, overnight lodging facility, boat launch, sandy swimming beach, picnic area, and a shelter. Visitors can relish the experience of observing passing freighters and gazing across the lake at Canada from the sandy shoreline or the observation area. The nearby bays and rivers are known for their excellent fishing opportunities, with several designated trout streams located within a half-hour drive in the Hiawatha National Forest. Anglers will find a variety of fish, including whitefish, perch, northern pike, bass, and walleye, in the nearby bays and rivers. Popular fishing locations include Brimley Bay to the west of the park, as well as Izaak Walton and Mosquito bays to the east. The park provides a paved boat ramp in the day-use area, although it's important to note that there is no courtesy pier or dock, and the water depth at the launch can be affected by heavy wave action. Seasonal naturalists offer weekly nature-based programs from Memorial Day through Labor Day. Additionally, modern restrooms are linked to the picnic shelter in the day-use area. A viewing area overlooking Lake Superior and the St. Marys River can be found in the day-use area, with a crushed limestone pathway connecting it to the picnic shelter. Here, visitors can delight in the sight of passing freighters and views of Canada across the lake, with a viewing telescope available seasonally. Exploring the Lake Superior shoreline is made easy, with carry-in launching permitted from the day-use area beach, outside the designated swim area. Picnic tables and charcoal grills are scattered throughout the grassy areas in the day-use section, available on a first-come, first-served basis. For larger gatherings, there's an enclosed picnic shelter in the day-use area that can accommodate up to 100 people. It includes picnic tables, two large charcoal grills, and electrical outlets. The shelter can be reserved seasonally, typically from mid-May to mid-October, coinciding with modern restroom availability. Reservations can be made up to 12 months in advance at MIDNRReservations.com or by calling 1-800-447-2757. A playscape structure with a woodchipped surface is located in the day-use area and can be accessed from the shelter via a crushed limestone pathway. Additional playground areas with a swing set and slide are situated in the day-use area, south of the playscape and near the campground. The park's seasonal sanitation station is located just before the campground entrance, offering potable water and two lanes. A designated swim area is available in the day-use area, boasting 2,000 feet of sandy shoreline along Lake Superior. The beach flag warning system is in place to indicate water safety, with red flags signaling unsafe conditions and the prohibition of swimming. It's important to avoid swimming near or jumping off break walls or navigational channel walls and to stay alert to changing conditions. Pets are allowed along the Lake Superior shoreline outside the designated swimming area, provided they are kept on a leash of 6 feet or less and under immediate control. Proper disposal of pet waste in trash receptacles is mandatory. There is a vault toilet in the day-use area near the modern campground. For group camping, the Brimley-Group-Use Area is an open space surrounded by woods, suitable for gatherings of up to 25 people with tents. It connects to the day-use parking area via a narrow, wooded pathway that allows for limited vehicle access. Two vault toilets are available within the group-use area, and there's a water spigot for filling containers in the nearby day-use parking area. Reservations for this area can be made by contacting the park office at 906-248-3422 up to six months in advance. The Brimley-Mini Cabin provides accommodation for up to four people with two sets of single bunk beds. The cabin is equipped with electricity, lighting, a mini refrigerator, microwave, box fan, and an electric space heater. While there is no water source within the cabin, modern restrooms with showers are available seasonally in the campground. Outdoors, a picnic table, fire pit, and charcoal grill are provided. Guests are required to bring their own linens, and please note that pets are not allowed in the cabin. The spacious modern campground offers sites that are open and protected from the Lake Superior shoreline by a windbreak of vegetation. The southern and eastern boundaries of the campground are densely wooded. Most campsites are level and grassy, with some offering unpaved pull-over sites that include 50-amp electrical service. Every site has access to 20/30-amp service, and a seasonal sanitation station is available. Recycling facilities are also provided.

DATE(S) VISITED .... ☐ SPRING   ☐ SUMMER   ☐ FALL   ☐ WINTER

LODGING .... ☐ ☀   ☐ ☁   ☐ 🌧   ☐ ⛈   ☐ ❄

WHO I WENT WITH .... FEE(S) ....   PARK HOURS .... TEMP:.........

WILL I RETURN? YES / NO   RATING ☆ ☆ ☆ ☆ ☆

PASSPORT STAMPS

BURT LAKE STATE PARK

COUNTY	ESTABLISHED	AREA (AC/HA)
CHEBOYGAN	1921	406 / 164

Established in 1921, Burt Lake State Park is located on the southeastern edge of the picturesque Burt Lake. The park boasts 2,000 feet of sandy shoreline, a shallow designated swim area, modern camping facilities, opportunities for boating, fishing, sightseeing, and much more. It is a favored family-friendly destination and serves as a launching point for exploring attractions like Mackinac Island, Tahquamenon Falls, Harbor Springs, Petoskey, Historic Mill Creek Discovery Park, and other regional points of interest. Situated at the heart of the Inland Waterway, the park is part of a network of interconnected rivers and lakes that offer approximately 38 miles of boating enjoyment. Visitors can access the North Central State Trail from the park through a paved pathway. The beach house, located on the shores of Burt Lake, provides restrooms, food concessions, and kayak rentals. Burt Lake is a central component of the Inland Waterway, a navigable system of rivers and lakes spanning 38 miles from Crooked Lake to Lake Huron. The beach house offers food concessions and kayak rentals, with more information available at laketolakerentals.com. Burt Lake, covering 27 square miles, is renowned for its walleye fishing. Seasonal naturalists offer weekly nature-based programs from Memorial Day through Labor Day. Paddling is a popular activity on the Sturgeon River. The day-use area includes a picnic area with tables and charcoal grills available on a first-come, first-served basis. Additionally, there is a picnic shelter in the day-use area equipped with picnic tables, charcoal grills, electrical service (for reservations only), and vault toilets. Reservations for the shelter can be made up to 12 months in advance at MiDNRReservations.com. Swings and slides are located in the day-use area near the water. The park's sanitation station is situated in the modern campground and provides potable water and two lanes. A designated swim area is located in the day-use area. Pets are welcome throughout the park, excluding the designated swim beach. An animal beach designated for pets is situated at the south end of the park. Pets should always be on a leash of 6 feet or less and under the owner's immediate control, with all pet waste properly disposed of in trash receptacles. The rustic group-use campground is available for youth groups with reservations made by contacting the park. The tent-only site can accommodate up to 25 campers. The modern campground is divided into two loops, the east loop and west loop. Campsites with views of Burt Lake are spacious and sunny, while the remaining sites are shaded by oak, maple, and pine trees. The campground is conveniently located near the designated swimming beach, a boat ramp, swings, slides, and a picnic area. Both 20/30-amp and 50-amp electrical service is available throughout the campground, and there is a sanitation station on-site. Recycling facilities are also provided. The mini cabin accommodates four people and includes two sets of single bunk beds. It is equipped with a mini refrigerator, microwave, and electric wall heater. Outdoors, a picnic table and a fire pit are provided. The cabins have electricity, but guests are required to bring their own linens and cookware. The park offers two trails on either side of the entrance road. The trail on the north side of the road runs along the Sturgeon River, while the trail on the south side takes visitors through the forest and into the modern campground. Access to the trail is available by parking near the contact station. Near the park, you can visit the world's largest "Cross in the Woods." Historic Mackinaw City and Mackinac Island are located approximately 30 miles to the north via I-75. There are nearby trails for hiking, cross-country skiing, ORV riding, and snowmobiling, as well as numerous golf courses and restaurants to explore.

DATE(S) VISITED .... □ SPRING □ SUMMER □ FALL □ WINTER

LODGING .... □ ☼ □ ☁ □ 🌧 □ ⛆ □ ☃

WHO I WENT WITH .... FEE(S) .... PARK HOURS .... TEMP:.........

WILL I RETURN? YES / NO RATING ☆ ☆ ☆ ☆ ☆

PASSPORT STAMPS

CAMBRIDGE JUNCTION HISTORIC STATE PARK

COUNTY	ESTABLISHED	AREA (AC/HA)
LENAWEE	1965	80 / 32

Cambridge Junction State Historic Park, which is open from May to October, is nestled in the scenic region of Michigan known as the Irish Hills. This park encompasses several historical attractions, including Walker Tavern, Hewitt House, a reconstructed 1840s barn, an open-air farmers market, vintage baseball games, concerts, and more. During the 1840s, Sylvester Walker's farmhouse tavern served as a popular resting place for travelers journeying westward along the Old Chicago Road. Today, this 80-acre park has become a beloved stopover in the heart of the Irish Hills. The historic sites within the park are managed by the DNR's Michigan History Center. Visitors can explore a permanent exhibit that delves into life along the Chicago Road during the era of the Walkers, as well as an exhibit highlighting early-to-mid-20th century tourist attractions in the Irish Hills. A tour of the park typically takes one to two hours. Modern restrooms are accessible when the Hewitt House is open, with portable toilets available during other times of the year. The park's day-use area features a picnic area equipped with picnic tables and charcoal grills, and these are available on a first-come, first-served basis. Cambridge Junction - Hiking Trail is a 1-mile loop that winds through wetlands and forested areas within the park. This trail is considered easy and offers a pleasant outdoor experience.

DATE(S) VISITED .... ☐ SPRING ☐ SUMMER ☐ FALL ☐ WINTER

LODGING .... ☐ ☀ ☐ ☁ ☐ 🌧 ☐ 🌩 ☐ ❄

WHO I WENT WITH .... FEE(S) .... PARK HOURS .... TEMP:.........

WILL I RETURN? YES / NO RATING ☆ ☆ ☆ ☆ ☆

PASSPORT STAMPS

CHEBOYGAN STATE PARK

COUNTY	ESTABLISHED	AREA (AC/HA)
CHEBOYGAN	1962	1,250 / 510

Cheboygan State Park, open year-round, offers a wide range of recreational activities. The park is located in the picturesque region of Michigan known as the Irish Hills. Elliot Creek flows through the park and is known for its trout, while a carry-in boat launch provides access to Duncan Bay, a great spot for fishing. The beach features shallow and clear water, making it perfect for children to enjoy splashing around. Please note that glass containers are not allowed on the beach. Visitors to Cheboygan State Park can explore a system of well-marked trails that offer access to beautiful vistas of Lake Huron and opportunities to spot rare wildflowers. The park provides various accommodation options, including modern camping, rustic cabins, tepees, and a fully-furnished modern lodge. Fishing is available on Duncan Bay and Elliot Creek, which is renowned for its speckled brown trout. To reach the park, take I-75 to exit 326, proceed east through the town of Cheboygan to US-23, and continue three miles east of town to the park entrance on the north side of the road. For outdoor enthusiasts, the park offers single and tandem kayak rentals available at the campground office from mid-May to mid-September. The campground office, located at the old campground site, provides modern facilities. There is a carry-in boat launch that offers access to Duncan Bay. Fishing in the bay can yield catches of northern pike, small and large mouth bass, and pan fish. Elliot Creek, running through the park, is famous for its speckled brown trout. The park boasts several well-marked trails, offering scenic winter views of Lake Huron's shoreline and the surrounding natural areas. Within the day-use area, you'll find picnic tables and fire pits/grills. Additionally, there's a picnic shelter that overlooks Duncan Bay and can be reserved up to one year in advance. The park is home to nearly seven miles of trails on red, black, blue, yellow, and green trail loops, which are shared with hikers. Along the shoreline trails, you can also discover rare wildflowers. Cheboygan State Park is located on the northern shore of Michigan's Lower Peninsula. The park offers five interconnected trails that can be hiked together or individually. The Black Trail, which is 0.5 miles long, is easily accessible from the Green and Blue trails. It begins at the Cheboygan Point Light and extends to Cheboygan Point, where it connects with the Blue Trail. The Black Trail offers a variety of terrains, with much of the path running through beach and wetland areas. Hiking and cross-country skiing are permitted on the trail, weather permitting. A notable attraction within the park is the Cheboygan Point Light. The park features the foundation remains of this historic lighthouse, which was initially constructed on a pier in Lake Huron in 1851. Later, it was rebuilt on the shore and operated until 1930. In 1930, the lighthouse and its surrounding properties were transferred to the State of Michigan for public park use. Cheboygan State Park is situated along the Huron Shores Heritage Route, offering 200 miles of breathtaking scenic views of Lake Huron along US-23. For those seeking accommodation, the Cheboygan State Park Lodge is a recently renovated 3-bedroom, 1-bath ranch-style house that is ADA accessible. The lodge accommodates eight people comfortably and includes a fully equipped kitchen with a refrigerator, stove, microwave, pots and pans, dishes, linens, and towels. The lodge is open year-round and is approximately 1 mile from Duncan Bay and 3 miles from town. Please note that a minimum stay of 3 days applies to reservations made within 30 days and 4 days for reservations made more than 30 days in advance. If you're interested in rustic cabins, please be aware that these cabins are located on seasonal, unpaved "two-track" roads that may be unplowed under certain weather conditions. If roads are closed, access to the cabins may require a hike. The walking distance from the trailhead parking to the cabins is approximately 0.25 miles for Poe Reef Cabin, 1 mile for 14-Foot Shoals Cabin, and 1.5 miles for Light House Point. Poe Reef Cabin accommodates 8 people, featuring 4 sets of bunk beds, a table and chairs, a wood stove for heat, no linens, and is located 1.5 miles from the park, with modern restrooms 1.5 miles away, a playground 3 miles away, the lake 60 yards away, the day use area 3.5 miles away, the pavilion 3 miles away, and a boat launch 4.5 miles away. There is no electricity or air conditioning/fans provided. Lighthouse Point Cabin accommodates 8 people and has a 24x10 screen porch, 4 sets of bunk beds, a table and chairs, a wood stove for heat, no linens, and is located 2.5 miles from the park office, 3.5 miles from the playground, 60 yards from the lake, 3.5 miles from the day use area, 3.5 miles from the pavilion, and 5 miles from the boat launch. There is no electricity or air conditioning/fans provided. 14-Foot Shoals Cabin accommodates 8 people, featuring 4 sets of bunk beds, a table and chairs, a wood stove for heat, no linens, and is located 3 miles from the playground, 40 yards from the lake, 3 miles from the day use area, 3 miles from the pavilion, and 4 miles from the boat launch. There is no electricity or air conditioning/fans provided.

PASSPORT STAMPS

CLEAR LAKE STATE PARK

COUNTY	ESTABLISHED	AREA (AC/HA)
MONTMORENCY	1966	290 / 120

Clear Lake State Park, true to its name, is celebrated for its crystal-clear waters. Nestled along two-thirds of the lake's shoreline, this serene park offers a modern campground, scenic trails, overnight lodging options, a designated swim beach, and even a disc golf course. It's a peaceful retreat for campers, paddlers, anglers, boaters, and nature enthusiasts. Situated in Michigan's elk country, it's not uncommon to hear the majestic bugling of elk in the area. Clear Lake State Park is situated within the expansive Mackinaw State Forest, which encompasses the northern eight counties of Michigan's Lower Peninsula. This forested region is abundant with wildlife, including deer, elk, turkey, and small game. Elk sightings and their echoing calls are particularly common during the spring and fall, especially in the early morning and evening. One unique feature of this park is that it permits the operation of Off-Road Vehicles (ORVs) between the campground and nearby ORV trails, providing convenient access to the Atlanta ORV route and the Michigan Cross Country Cycle Trail. An ORV trailhead parking lot is located opposite the park's contact station. Clear Lake itself is renowned for its pristine waters. The park offers a designated swim area within the day-use area, making it perfect for a refreshing dip. For those looking to explore the lake further, canoes, kayaks, stand-up paddleboards, and rowboats are available for rent at the park's contact station. An accessible boating access site in the day-use area features 50 parking spots for vehicles and trailers. Clear Lake, covering 133 acres, is spring-fed and boasts a depth of 90 feet. The lake has been stocked with various fish species, making it an excellent destination for trout, splake, and smallmouth bass fishing. For disc golf enthusiasts, the park features a nine-hole course. The course includes a universally accessible gravel walking path connecting each hole. The most challenging hole on the course is a 429-foot-par four. Within the day-use area, visitors will find a picnic area equipped with picnic tables and charcoal grills, available on a first-come, first-served basis. Additionally, there is a picnic shelter offering picnic tables, charcoal grills, electrical service (available through reservations), and vault toilets. Reservations for the shelter can be made up to 12 months in advance on MiDNRReservations.com. For families, there's a slide and swings available in the day-use area. Seasonal naturalists at the park provide weekly nature-based programs from Memorial Day through Labor Day. Families with pets are welcome to enjoy the Clear Lake lakeshore, except for the designated swim beach and boating access site. Pets should be leashed at all times and under the owner's immediate control. Owners are responsible for properly disposing of all pet waste in trash receptacles. The park offers an Elk Tiny House, situated near the boating access site, boasting scenic views of Clear Lake. The tiny house accommodates up to four guests, with a full-size sleeper sofa and a trundle bed on the main floor. Although the tiny house has electricity, it lacks running water. However, guests can access water at the campground's fill station. Inside the tiny house, you'll find a range of amenities, including a digital fireplace and a heater, a small table and two chairs, a mini fridge, a microwave, and a coffee maker. Outdoors, a picnic table, fire pit, and grill are available for guest use. Visitors are required to bring their own bedding and cookware. An accessible mini cabin, accommodating up to four people on two bunk beds, is located in the modern campground at site #196. The cabin features a counter with barstools, a microwave, and a mini fridge. Outdoors, you'll find a picnic table, a fire ring, and a grill. Electric heat and a fan are available in the cabin, but guests must provide their own linens and cookware. The park's rustic group-use area is ideal for groups of up to 30 and offers picnic tables and a fire pit. To reserve the group camp area, you can call 231-347-2311. The modern campground is divided into two loops, the upper and lower loops, with several pull-through sites. The campsites vary in size, with some shaded by oaks and pines, and all offer picturesque views of Clear Lake. The campground boasts its own designated swimming beach and a convenient boating access site. Recycling is available on-site. The park's sanitation station is conveniently located just inside the modern campground. Here, you'll find potable water available and two lanes for your convenience. The Clear Lake/Jackson Lake Pathway spans 7.5 miles and is located 10 miles north of Atlanta. The pathway links Clear Lake State Park with the High Country Pathway Spur to Jackson Lake State Forest Campground. It can be easily accessed at both of these points. A portion of this pathway is part of the larger High Country Pathway, a 70-mile system located in the Pigeon River Country State Forest. Visitors planning on cross-country skiing can only do so on parts 2, 6, and 7 of the trail. Hiking and biking are permitted on all segments of the trail, weather permitting. The Canada Creek Nature Trail, spanning 4.5 miles, consists of several interconnected loops. This trail takes you along the shoreline of Clear Lake, through the park's day-use area, and across wooded hills. Access points for the trail include the day-use area, the tiny house area, and the modern campground.

PASSPORT STAMPS

COLDWATER LAKE STATE PARK

COUNTY	ESTABLISHED	AREA (AC/HA)
BRANCH	1988	400 / 160

Coldwater Lake State Park comprises 400 acres of mostly undeveloped parkland nestled between Copeland Road and the southern shoreline of Coldwater Lake. The park encompasses a diverse landscape, including former farmland, wetlands, hardwood forest, and native grasslands. Coldwater Lake itself is situated toward the rear of the park property and isn't readily accessible from the park. There are various boating access sites outside of the park, such as the Coldwater Lake boating access site located on the west side of the lake. It's worth noting that this park is the sole public land in the county open to hunting. If you plan to hunt in the park, it's advisable to contact the park directly to inquire about any specific rules, concerns, or considerations. For those planning to visit the park, the park recommends purchasing a Recreation Passport in advance. However, there is a fee pipe available in the parking lot where you can obtain one. The park also boasts native grass fields that are part of a pheasant restoration project.

DATE(S) VISITED .... ☐ SPRING ☐ SUMMER ☐ FALL ☐ WINTER

LODGING ....

WHO I WENT WITH .... FEE(S) .... PARK HOURS .... TEMP:.........

WILL I RETURN? YES / NO   RATING ☆ ☆ ☆ ☆ ☆

PASSPORT STAMPS

COLONIAL MICHILIMACKINAC HISTORIC STATE PARK

COUNTY	ESTABLISHED	AREA (AC/HA)
EMMET	1960	37 / 15

Interpreters play a vital role as guides within this reconstructed fur-trading village and military outpost from the 1700s, as well as at the 1892 lighthouse. To reach the park, take I-75 to exit 339, situated at the southern end of the Mackinac Bridge. At Fort Mackinac, visitors can experience history coming to life with cannon blasts, rifle fire, and soldiers marching. The site includes the oldest building in Michigan and 13 other historical structures, each housing exhibits that cover a wide range of topics, from military training and battles to medical treatments and family life within the fort. Beyond its role as a military outpost, Fort Mackinac also served as a home for soldiers and their families. Eventually, it became the headquarters for Mackinac National Park, attracting tourists to the island who visited the grand fortress on the bluff, much like they do today. The Old Mackinac Point Lighthouse, in operation since 1889, has been a point of reference during storms and a guiding beacon for ships navigating the perilous waters of the Straits of Mackinac. The tower offers breathtaking views, and the original buildings feature authentic restoration, including the original lens. An audiovisual program titled "Shipwrecks of the Straits" adds to the lighthouse's appeal, making it a true gem of the Great Lakes, often referred to as the "Castle of the Straits." The Richard and Jane Manoogian Mackinac Art Museum is among the most diverse art museums in the region. Its collection is rich in beauty and history, encompassing a wide range of artifacts. These include hand-beaded Native American garments, 17th and 18th-century maps of the Great Lakes, and unique pieces from the Victorian era on Mackinac Island. The museum also houses original photographs dating from the mid-19th to the mid-20th century, showcasing the natural beauty of Mackinac Island as captured through the lens of a camera. This collection features works by William H. Gardiner, including many of his famous hand-tinted views from the early twentieth century. For visitors looking to enjoy outdoor activities, there are fire pits and grills available within the park.

DATE(S) VISITED .... ☐ SPRING ☐ SUMMER ☐ FALL ☐ WINTER

LODGING .... ☐ ☀ ☐ ☁ ☐ 🌦 ☐ 🌧 ☐ ❄

WHO I WENT WITH .... FEE(S) .... PARK HOURS .... TEMP:.........

WILL I RETURN? YES / NO   RATING ☆ ☆ ☆ ☆ ☆

PASSPORT STAMPS

CRAIG LAKE STATE PARK

COUNTY	ESTABLISHED	AREA (AC/HA)
BARAGA, MARQUETTE	1956	9,700 / 3,925

Craig Lake State Park, encompassing over 9,700 acres in Baraga and Marquette counties, stands as Michigan's most remote state park. Within the park, visitors will discover hike-in backcountry campsites (available by reservation), rustic cabins, yurts, extensive trail networks, including a portion of the North Country Trail, six lakes, and a diverse array of wildlife. The park offers an opportunity to observe moose, particularly during their spring, summer, and fall habitation. Accessing the park can be a challenge due to its rugged and natural terrain. The park's roads are rocky and rough, making it essential for vehicles to have high ground clearance and four-wheel drive for ease of travel. In 2022, the U.P. Land Conservancy donated almost 1,300 acres of pristine highlands wilderness to the park, including three sections that constituted the conservancy's Peshekee Headwaters Nature Preserve, located along the eastern edge of the park. Craig Lake State Park boasts six lakes, with three named after Frederick Miller's children from the renowned Miller Brewing Company. Numerous small ponds and a variety of wildlife, such as deer, black bears, beavers, loons, and moose, can be found throughout the park. Notably, Craig Lake, spanning 374 acres, features six islands and high granite bluffs on its northern shoreline. In line with the Miller beer theme, a nearby lake situated northwest of the park is aptly named High Life Lake. The park's water bodies include Craig Lake, Keewaydin Lake (the only lake permitting motorized boating), and four other inland lakes. An accessible boating access site can be found on Keewaydin Lake. Fishing opportunities abound in the park's six lakes, though it's crucial to be aware of specific fishing regulations for Craig Lake. Paddling is also a favored activity on these lakes, with an undeveloped canoe launch located near the park entrance. Visitors can portage (carry) from Craig Lake to Clair and Crooked lakes. The park accommodates Snowmobile Trail No. 8, allowing for snowmobiling enthusiasts to traverse its grounds. Hunting is permitted within the state park; however, it's advisable to contact the park directly to inquire about specific rules, concerns, or considerations. Craig Lake State Park welcomes pets along its shorelines, except for the designated swim beach area. Pets must be leashed, not exceeding six feet in length, and under the owner's immediate control. Proper disposal of pet waste in trash receptacles is required. For those seeking to immerse themselves in the park's natural beauty, there are 22 designated backcountry campsites, ranging from a short 0.2-mile hike to a 6-7 mile journey. Campsites are numbered and furnished with a metal fire ring. Each site accommodates up to six campers. To obtain your camper pass and check-in for your campsite, please visit Van Riper State Park. Registration takes place at the campground office, not at park headquarters. During the park's snow season, occurring between November 1 and May 15, the roads are not maintained, rendering them impassable to vehicles. All backcountry campsites are now reservation-only sites as of May 2023. Reservations can be made up to six months in advance at MIDNRReservations.com. The Keewaydin Lake Yurt, located in the dense forest surrounding Keewaydin Lake, offers a secluded retreat. The 20-foot-diameter yurt accommodates six people and is equipped with two bunk beds, an armoire, tables and chairs, a woodstove for heating and cooking (with a cooktop), and a small propane grill (guests must provide their own 1-pound propane bottles). The yurt has no running water or electricity, but there is a vault toilet nearby. Guests of the yurt are provided with a canoe for their use. Between mid-May and mid-October, two paddles and two adult-sized life jackets are available. Note that canoes are not available during the winter months. Firewood is supplied from September 15 to June 1 for use in the indoor woodstove. Guests are responsible for bringing their own linens, towels, and cookware. Drinking water can be brought by guests or filtered from the lake. Please be aware that from November to mid-May, park roads are impassable by vehicles. The yurt is situated 4.8 miles (one-way) from the nearest plowed parking lot and is accessible solely by hiking, snowshoeing, skiing, or snowmobiling. Visitors are advised to be prepared for all possible situations, with an understanding that trekking at dusk is not recommended. Additionally, cell phone coverage within the park is limited to nonexistent. The park also offers rustic cabins, including the historic "Old Miller" cabins, which are a two-mile hike along the Main Trail. The large cabin accommodates up to 14 people and features a stone fireplace and woodstove with a cooktop, three bedrooms with four sets of twin bunks, two futon couches, a kitchen and dining table, and chairs. Wood for indoor heating and cooking is provided from September 15 to June 1. Two canoes are available for guest use at the cabin. The cabin lacks electricity and running water, though a hand pump offers potable water. The small cabin accommodates eight people and is pet-friendly. Up to two pets (cats and dogs only) are allowed. The cabin is equipped with a woodstove for heating and cooking, one large bedroom with three log bunk beds and one full-size log bed, a kitchen counter, and table and chairs. Similar to the large cabin, the small cabin has no electricity or running water but provides wood for indoor heating and cooking from September 15 to June 1. Two canoes are available for guest use at the cabin, along with a hand pump for obtaining potable water. The Teddy Lake Yurt, situated in the dense forest surrounding Teddy Lake, accommodates four people within its 16-foot-diameter structure. The yurt comes with bunk beds, mattresses, a wood stove, and essential tools like an axe, bow saw, and cooking and eating utensils. There is no running water or electricity in the yurt, but a vault toilet is located nearby. The yurt is also pet-friendly. Up to two pets (cats and dogs only) are allowed. Guests are provided with a canoe, two paddles, and two adult-sized life jackets, which are available from mid-May to mid-October. However, canoes are not accessible during the winter months. Firewood for the indoor woodstove is provided from September 15 to June 1. Just like in the other accommodations, guests are required to bring their own linens, towels, and cookware. They can either bring their own water or filter it from the lake. The park features the 8-mile Main Trail, which encircles Craig Lake and connects to the North Country National Scenic Trail. The trail offers picturesque views of the lake and its resident wildlife, much of which is set on rocky outcrops with varying terrain difficulties. The main trailhead is located on the southern side of Craig Lake, with a second trailhead situated just beyond the Keewaydin Lake yurt. This trail provides access to routes leading to the Peshekee Headwaters. Self-registration stations can be found at the main trailhead and at the intersection of Nelligan Lake and Keewaydin Lake roads. A 7-mile section of the North Country National Scenic Trail traverses Craig Lake State Park, journeying through northern hardwood stands and evergreen-lined paths. The trail is graced with two newly constructed pedestrian bridges, which cross the Peshekee River as the trail extends westward from the park. Along the trail, three backcountry campsites, available by reservation only, are conveniently located. The main trailhead is located on the south side of Craig Lake, and a second trailhead lies just beyond the Keewaydin Lake yurt, granting access to trails leading to the Peshekee Headwaters. Self-registration stations are present at the main trailhead and at the intersection of Nelligan Lake and Keewaydin Lake roads.

DATE(S) VISITED .... ☐ SPRING ☐ SUMMER ☐ FALL ☐ WINTER

LODGING .... ☐ ☀ ☐ ☁ ☐ 🌦 ☐ 🌧 ☐ ❄

WHO I WENT WITH .... FEE(S) .... PARK HOURS .... TEMP:........

WILL I RETURN? YES / NO   RATING ☆ ☆ ☆ ☆ ☆

- -

- -

PASSPORT STAMPS

DODGE #4 STATE PARK

COUNTY	ESTABLISHED	AREA (AC/HA)
OAKLAND	1922	139 / 56

Dodge #4 State Park, conveniently located only 30 miles from Detroit, is primarily recognized for its beautiful sandy beach and a 1-mile expanse of shoreline bordering Cass Lake. Cass Lake, covering 1,280 acres, stands as the largest inland lake in southeastern Michigan and ranks among the most popular recreational lakes in the region. The park is a sought-after destination for fishing enthusiasts, boaters, kayakers, and those looking to relax on the inviting swim beach. The origin of this state park can be traced back to a generous donation from the Dodge Brothers Corporation in 1922. It's essential to be aware that when Dodge #4 State Park reaches its full capacity, it will temporarily cease to accommodate vehicle traffic. Therefore, if your group is not traveling together in a single vehicle, it's advisable that everyone arrives at the park simultaneously. Notably, the park's popular boating access site often reaches full capacity by 10 a.m. during the period between Memorial Day and Labor Day. Visitors will find a beach house within the park's day-use area, which includes restroom facilities. Adjacent to this area, you'll encounter space designated for rotating food trucks that usually operate on Fridays and Saturdays from Memorial Day through Labor Day. A boating access site is available alongside a carry-in kayak launch, integrated into the accessible pier, both of which are situated near the designated swim beach. It's essential to note that no single vehicles are permitted at the boating access site. Vehicles without trailers should park in the Bay Parking area. The park is positioned on a peninsula along the northern shore of Cass Lake, an expansive inland lake in southeastern Michigan. With its 1,280-acre size, Cass Lake is renowned as one of the busiest recreational lakes in the region. The park features a designated swim area in its day-use section, with an accessible pathway leading to the water from the beach. Fishing enthusiasts can enjoy angling activities along the 150-acre Cass Lake from the shoreline, pier, or boats. There's an accessible fishing pier on Cass Lake, equipped with an accessible carry-in kayak launch. Visitors are encouraged to ensure they clean up all fishing tackle equipment, as wildlife is at risk of becoming entangled in stray fishing lines and hooks. For those interested in watercraft rentals, Cass Lake Boat Rentals provides pontoons, kayaks, and paddleboards, while Surf Our Lakes offers E-jet surfboards. These services are available from Memorial Day through Labor Day. The park provides various locations where kayaks, canoes, and stand-up paddleboards can be launched. Additionally, the pier offers an accessible carry-in kayak launch. It's important to be aware that the boating access site tends to fill up quickly, particularly on weekends and holidays, often reaching capacity by 10 a.m. For safety reasons, no watercraft are allowed within the designated swim beach area. Food concessions are conveniently available through rotating food trucks located outside the beach house in the day-use area, typically open on Fridays and Saturdays from Memorial Day through Labor Day. Additionally, watercraft rentals are offered near the designated swim beach. The park boasts a crushed limestone trail that traverses its grounds, suitable for biking enthusiasts. Throughout the park, multiple areas feature picnic tables and charcoal grills that are available on a first-come, first-served basis. An accessible Bay Picnic Shelter is equipped with picnic tables, charcoal grills, and vault toilets. The Hill Shelter provides access to modern restrooms and electrical service. Reservations for these shelters can be made up to 12 months in advance at MiDNRReservations.com. For pet owners, there's a pet-friendly beach located just outside the designated swim area. However, pets must always be kept on a leash, not exceeding 6 feet in length, and under the immediate control of their owners. It's essential that all pet waste is properly disposed of in provided trash receptacles. Lastly, it's worth noting that alcoholic beverages are prohibited within the park at all times, unless written authorization has been granted by the park manager through an event permit.

DUCK LAKE STATE PARK

COUNTY	ESTABLISHED	AREA (AC/HA)
MUSKEGON	1988	728 / 295

Duck Lake State Park is a well-loved day-use park situated on the shores of Lake Michigan, connected to Duck Lake by a shallow channel. The park offers various amenities, including a boat launch, kayak rentals, a picnic area with a shelter, and opportunities for activities such as paddling, fishing, hiking, hunting, and cross-country skiing on the park's extensive 7 miles of natural surface trails. The park is characterized by its towering dunes along the lakeshore, surrounded by a mix of mature forests, pine plantations, and occasional open meadows further inland. The forested areas in the park play a crucial role as stopover and nesting sites for migratory birds, including the Cerulean and hooded warblers. Visitors will find two separate parking lots within the park, one bordering Lake Michigan and the other adjacent to Duck Lake. A boardwalk beneath Scenic Drive connects these two sides of the park. The park boasts half a mile of Lake Michigan shoreline and the presence of Duck Lake. Kayaks are available for rent at the park's contact station during Fridays, Saturdays, and Sundays. For more detailed information, visitors can call 231-744-3480. Duck Lake features a boating access site and a carry-in launch, although it does not connect to Lake Michigan. Duck Lake is home to various fish species, making it an ideal spot for fishing. Paddling is a favorite activity on Duck Lake, facilitated by the carry-in launch; however, it doesn't provide access to Lake Michigan. The picnic area is situated near the Duck Lake picnic shelter, equipped with picnic tables and charcoal grills available on a first-come, first-served basis. Additionally, an accessible picnic shelter can be found in the day-use area, offering picnic tables, charcoal grills, electrical service (reservations required), and a modern restroom (not accessible). Reservations for this shelter can be made up to 12 months in advance at MiDNRReservations.com. Hunting is permitted within the state park; however, it is advisable to directly contact the park for specific rules, concerns, or considerations. During the winter, the park is closed to motor vehicle traffic, but it remains accessible via skiing and snowmobiles. The trails are open for cross-country skiing, although they are not groomed. Dogs are allowed along the entire length of the Lake Michigan shoreline (0.5 miles) and around Duck Lake. It's essential for pets to be leashed, with a maximum leash length of 6 feet, and under the immediate control of their owners. Responsible disposal of pet waste is required in the provided trash receptacles. Duck Lake Paved Trail - This short paved trail, running along the picturesque Duck Lake, offers an out-and-back route. It can be accessed at the picnic shelter's east end or near the park entrance on Scenic Drive at the west end. Duck Lake Trail #2 (Green/Blue) - This trail follows the scenic shoreline of Duck Lake and passes by the Ford monument. Both the Green and Blue trail segments connect to the Red and White trails, starting near the picnic shelter at the end of the Paved Trail. Duck Lake Trail #3 (Yellow) - This is a brief connector trail linking the Blue and White trail sections. Duck Lake Trail #4 (Red) - This trail guides you through a beautiful red pine plantation and stands as the longest uninterrupted trail within the park. It commences on Scenic Drive and crosses the park from west to east. Duck Lake Trail #5 (White) - This trail offers an easy hike along the abandoned Wabaningo roadbed. It can be accessed from the main road just north of the day-use parking lot.

DATE(S) VISITED .... □ SPRING □ SUMMER □ FALL □ WINTER

LODGING .... □ ☼ □ ☁ □ ☔ □ ☁ □ ❄

WHO I WENT WITH .... FEE(S) .... PARK HOURS .... TEMP:.........

WILL I RETURN? YES / NO   RATING ☆ ☆ ☆ ☆ ☆

PASSPORT STAMPS

FAYETTE HISTORIC STATE PARK

COUNTY	ESTABLISHED	AREA (AC/HA)
DELTA	1959	711 / 288

Experience breathtaking scenery and step back in time at Fayette Historic State Park, a unique fusion of history and nature located along the shores of Big Bay de Noc. This area lies on Lake Michigan, nestled between Snail Shell Harbor and Sand Bay, situated in the southern region of Michigan's Upper Peninsula. Visitors to the park will discover a well-preserved historic townsite, a modern campground, Snail Shell Harbor, a visitor center, a boating access site, a designated swim area, and more. The park's extensive 5-mile trail network offers remarkable vistas from 90-foot limestone cliffs that encircle the harbor. Access points can be found near the campground and the historic townsite. Fayette Historic Townsite is a representation of a once-thriving industrial community that produced charcoal pig iron between 1867 and 1891 at the tip of the Garden Peninsula. Here, visitors can stroll through buildings that have stood for over a century, gaining insights into life during the 19th century. The park offers both self-guided and guided tour options (available during the summer months). Situated along Lake Michigan's Big Bay de Noc in the Upper Peninsula, the park features a designated swim area in the picnic area. Kayaks and an 18-foot canoe can be rented from June through September at the park's contact station, and from October through May at the park headquarters. Rentals include personal floatation devices and paddles, provided on a first-come, first-served basis (no reservations). For additional information, call 906-644-2603. Positioned between the campground and the day-use area, the boating access site provides access to Big Bay de Noc. This location is renowned for its excellent fishing opportunities, including perch, smallmouth bass, northern pike, walleye, and salmon in the Great Lakes. The park also provides plenty of fishing possibilities from the shore, harbor, or open waters via boats. A fishing pier is available on Big Bay de Noc in Snail Shell Harbor. Paddling is a favored activity in Big Bay de Noc. The picnic area is located next to the designated swim beach and offers grills, a picnic shelter, a water fountain/spigot, and vault toilets. Additionally, there is a picnic shelter in the day-use area, furnished with picnic tables, charcoal grills, and vault toilets. Reservations for the shelter can be made up to 12 months in advance at MiDNRReservations.com. The A. Gene Gazlay Visitor Center houses a scale model of the 1880s company town of Fayette, information on the ancient forest and bluffs, a museum store, concessions, and modern restrooms. A sanitation station is positioned between the contact station and the modern campground. Free WiFi is available at the historic townsite, visitor center, and modern campground. The park features 400 acres of land open to hunting. Pets are allowed along the entire length of the Lake Michigan shoreline, except for the designated swim beach. Pets must be leashed at all times with a maximum leash length of 6 feet and under the immediate control of their owners. It is essential to properly dispose of pet waste in the provided trash receptacles. Furnace Hill Lodge - This fully furnished lodge, offering a rustic ambiance, can accommodate up to 10 people. Originally constructed in the early 1970s, the lodge once served as the manager's residence. Nestled at the edge of the woods just off the entrance road, the lodge provides a private setting within walking distance of the park's historic townsite. The lodge is equipped with cedar-framed beds, including full, queen, and a single-over-full bunk. Additionally, a futon and a pull-out (full) sofa bed are available in the living area. The kitchen boasts maple cabinetry and includes a refrigerator, an electric stove, a microwave, a toaster, and a coffeemaker. It is stocked with dishes, pots, cutlery, glassware, mixing bowls, and other essentials. The single bathroom features a tub/shower unit, flush toilet, and sink. Amenities like a fuel-efficient furnace, central air conditioning, bedding, towels, and all kitchen linens are provided. A two-night minimum stay is required for reservations from Memorial Day through Labor Day. Check-in time is 4 p.m. (EST), and check-out time is noon. All reservations must be made via direct phone contact at 906-644-2603 or in person. Wood fires are permitted exclusively in the backyard fire circle. Firewood is not included but can be purchased at the contact station. Prior to departure, visitors are expected to vacuum, wash dishes, strip beds, and clean the residence for the next set of guests. Brooms, mops, and cleaning supplies are provided. The modern campground is divided into three loops, with most sites being of moderate size and shaded by maple and cedar trees. Each loop terminates with a small path leading to Lake Michigan's Big Bay de Noc. All sites provide 20/30-amp service, while pull-through sites offer 20/30/50-amp service. Fayette Historic Townsite is a short walk to the north, and the designated swim beach and picnic area are a short walk to the south. Recycling facilities are available.

DATE(S) VISITED .... □ SPRING □ SUMMER □ FALL □ WINTER

LODGING .... □ ☼ □ ☁ □ 🌦 □ 🌧 □ ❄

WHO I WENT WITH .... FEE(S) .... PARK HOURS .... TEMP:.........

WILL I RETURN? YES / NO   RATING ☆ ☆ ☆ ☆ ☆

PASSPORT STAMPS

FISHERMAN'S ISLAND STATE PARK

COUNTY	ESTABLISHED	AREA (AC/HA)
CHARLEVOIX	1975	2,678 / 1,084

Fisherman's Island State Park, situated just 4 miles from downtown Charlevoix along Lake Michigan's coastline, offers a pristine natural environment. The park features over 6 miles of unspoiled Lake Michigan shoreline, with the southern end designated as primitive. At times of lower water levels, the island the park was named after connects to the shore, forming a peninsula. Spanning 2,678 acres, the park is characterized by rolling dunes covered with maple, birch, and aspen trees, interspersed with cedar and black spruce bogs. It houses a rustic campground, a 2.5-mile hiking trail, and a day-use area. During the fall season, the park is popular among hunters and rock collectors. The park encompasses 6 miles of unspoiled Lake Michigan shoreline, including a half-mile of sandy beach. The remaining forested shoreline is rocky and a favorite spot for Petoskey stone hunters. An attractive paddling route closely follows the Lake Michigan shoreline. The picnic area within the day-use zone offers picnic tables and charcoal grills, available on a first-come, first-serve basis. While hunting is permitted in the state park, it is advisable to contact the park directly to inquire about specific rules and any additional considerations. Park roads are accessible to snowmobilers; however, snowmobiles are prohibited on park trails. Certain sections of the shoreline are pet-friendly. Pets must be kept on a 6-foot leash and under their owner's immediate control, and all pet waste must be properly disposed of in trash receptacles. Fisherman's Island State Park's rustic campground provides a unique and secluded camping experience, unlike typical modern campgrounds. The campground features 80 campsites suitable for tents and compact campers, with most of them distributed among three loops. Additionally, 15 sites are nestled in the dune area along Lake Michigan. Each loop is equipped with vault toilets and hand-pumped water. There are no modern restrooms, showers, or electricity available. The park offers a 2.5-mile foot trail (one way) that winds through the surrounding old dunes and wooded areas. The trail crosses McGeech Creek and passes through maple, birch, and aspen forests. Trailheads are conveniently located on Bells Bay Road and within the day-use area.

DATE(S) VISITED .... ☐ SPRING ☐ SUMMER ☐ FALL ☐ WINTER

LODGING .... ☐ ☀ ☐ ☁ ☐ 🌧 ☐ 🌫 ☐ ❄

WHO I WENT WITH .... FEE(S) .... PARK HOURS .... TEMP:.........

WILL I RETURN? YES / NO   RATING ☆ ☆ ☆ ☆ ☆

PASSPORT STAMPS

FORT WILKINS HISTORIC STATE PARK

COUNTY	ESTABLISHED	AREA (AC/HA)
KEWEENAW	1923	711 / 288

Fort Wilkins Historic State Park is situated at the northern tip of the Keweenaw Peninsula and offers a range of attractions, including a modern campground, hiking trails, a historic fort with a living history program, and two 1860s lighthouses overlooking Lake Superior. Visitors can explore a quarter-mile of rocky Lake Superior shoreline, enjoy the scenic beauty of Lake Fanny Hooe, and relax on a quarter-mile sandy beach at Lake Manganese. The park is known for its well-preserved 1844 army military outpost, featuring 19 historic buildings. The Michigan History Center conducts a living history program, allowing visitors to experience life on the northern frontier during the mid-1800s when soldiers were stationed in Michigan's Upper Peninsula. The famous Brockway Mountain Drive offers picturesque views of Lake Superior, inland lakes, and the panoramic landscapes of the Keewenaw Peninsula. Nearby attractions include waterfalls, Isle Royale, shipwrecks, museums, shops, and restaurants. Paddling is a popular activity in Copper Harbor and Lake Fanny Hooe, with a concrete ramp available on Lake Fanny Hooe. Lake Fanny Hooe is known for its excellent fishing, offering walleye, trout, and splake opportunities. An accessible fishing pier is located by the Lake Fanny Hooe boat launch. Between the east and west campgrounds, Sundae in the Park provides various amenities such as food, souvenirs, camping supplies, clothing, and ice cream. During the summer months, the park's living history program provides insights into the mid-1800s through a restored 1844 military outpost consisting of 19 buildings. Moreover, visitors can explore the Copper Harbor lighthouses built in 1866 and 1868, with two observation decks providing scenic views of Lake Fanny Hooe. The day-use picnic area features 25 picnic tables and six charcoal grills available on a first-come, first-served basis. Additionally, there is a picnic shelter offering picnic tables, charcoal grills, and electrical service (reservations only). A playground equipped with swings, slides, and climbing structures is available in the park's picnic area. During the summer, free WiFi is accessible in both east and west campgrounds as well as at the park store. The park allows hunting, but visitors are encouraged to contact the park directly to inquire about specific rules and considerations. Fort Wilkins offers a Fanny Hooe Camper Cabin, a rustic cabin located on Lake Fanny Hooe that accommodates up to six people. The cabin features two small bedrooms with bunk beds, a living room with a futon, a microwave, a hot plate, lamps, and a ceiling fan. Outdoors, guests will find a picnic table, a deck with chairs, a fire pit, and a cook grill. Guests must bring their own linens, towels, cookware, and utensils. Vault toilets and potable water are available nearby. The group-use area comprises four rustic sites with a capacity of up to 100 people, providing access to drinking water and vault toilets. To make a reservation, visitors can call 906-289-4215. Another accommodation option is the mini cabin, located in the west campground, and it can sleep four people with a bunk bed and a futon. The cabin is equipped with a mini refrigerator, microwave, coffee pot, and electric wall heater. Outdoors, guests can find a picnic table, bench, fire pit, and cook grill. Linens, towels, cookware, and utensils are not provided. The cabin is located near the modern restroom and shower building and potable water. During the off-season, there is no access to running water or the modern restroom, but a vault toilet is available nearby. The park features a modern campground consisting of east and west campgrounds, both offering easy access to Lake Fanny Hooe. A laundry facility is available in the east campground, near the restroom, and recycling facilities are provided. The east campground features multiple loops with sunny sites, a playground west of the campground, and a centrally located modern restroom with showers. The west campground offers two loops with shady sites, and the western end provides nine 50-amp, pull-through sites. A playground is centrally located between the two loops, and a modern restroom with showers is centrally located in the east loop. The Fort Wilkins Foot Trail is a scenic loop that meanders through the historic townsite, the fort cemetery, the woods, and the lighthouse overlook. It provides the opportunity to explore historical landmarks and enjoy beautiful views of Lake Fanny Hooe and Lake Superior. Access points are available at the historic site, the campground, and other marked starting points.

DATE(S) VISITED .... □ SPRING □ SUMMER □ FALL □ WINTER

LODGING .... □ ☼ □ ☁ □ 🌧 □ ☁ □ ❄

WHO I WENT WITH .... FEE(S) .... PARK HOURS .... TEMP:.........

WILL I RETURN? YES / NO   RATING ☆ ☆ ☆ ☆ ☆

PASSPORT STAMPS

GRAND HAVEN STATE PARK

COUNTY	ESTABLISHED	AREA (AC/HA)
OTTAWA	1920	48 / 19

Grand Haven State Park spans 48 acres and is situated along the sandy half-mile shoreline of Lake Michigan on the park's west side. It also extends along the Grand River, encompassing the river's mouth on the park's north side. The park primarily features beach sand and offers captivating vistas of the Grand Haven pier and two lighthouses. The park offers various amenities, including a modern campground, an overnight lodge, a designated swim beach, picnic areas, and a beach pavilion. Along the Grand River's edge, an adjoining boardwalk is a popular spot for fishing enthusiasts. Visitors can enjoy the sandy shoreline on Lake Michigan's west side and the Grand River at its mouth on the park's north side. It's important to pay attention to the beach flag warning system in designated swim areas; red flags signify unsafe water conditions, and swimming or entering the water is not recommended. Swimmers should not be near or jump off the pier, and they must stay vigilant regarding changing conditions. The park provides a designated swim area along its entire shoreline, along with an ADA-accessible walkway to the water's edge. Multiple beach wheelchairs are also available for borrowing from the campground office. Additionally, the park boasts a pier and boardwalk along the Grand River's mouth on the north side, which are popular spots for anglers. The beach house, situated right on the beach, offers modern restroom facilities. Grand Haven State Park boasts two lighthouses that are visible from the park and located along the pier on the park's northern boundary. The Grand Haven Lighthouse Conservancy is actively involved in preservation, restoration efforts, and special projects related to these lighthouses. Picnic facilities in the day-use area feature picnic tables and charcoal grills, available on a first-come, first-served basis. A playground is conveniently located next to the picnic tables, while an accessible playground in the day-use area features a rubberized surface for enhanced mobility. The park's sanitation station is located within the campground, along with potable water and two lanes for your convenience. It's important to note that alcohol consumption is prohibited in the park unless the park manager has granted written authorization through an event permit. The modern campground at Grand Haven State Park offers a unique camping experience, with sites closer in proximity and the feeling of camping right on the beach. The campsites are paved and provide easy access to the designated swim beach and the Grand River, both just a few steps away. While firepits are not provided, campers are allowed to bring their own portable firepits as long as they are at least 6 inches above the sand and completely enclosed with a cover. Ground fires are not allowed, and firepits must not be used on the asphalt or within 15 feet of any camping unit. Old-style washtub fire pits are no longer permitted. Recycling facilities are available within the park to promote environmental sustainability.

DATE(S) VISITED .... ☐ SPRING ☐ SUMMER ☐ FALL ☐ WINTER

LODGING .... ☐☀ ☐☁ ☐🌧 ☐🌬 ☐❄

WHO I WENT WITH .... FEE(S) .... PARK HOURS .... TEMP:.........

WILL I RETURN? YES / NO   RATING ☆ ☆ ☆ ☆ ☆

PASSPORT STAMPS

GRAND MERE STATE PARK

COUNTY	ESTABLISHED	AREA (AC/HA)
BERRIEN	1973	985 / 399

Grand Mere State Park is distinguished by its stunning sand dunes, deep blowouts, and a half-mile of Lake Michigan shoreline, which visitors can access via the park's two trails. In the undeveloped natural area beyond the dunes, you'll find two inland lakes. The park is particularly popular among hikers and runners. Visitors can relish the beauty of a half-mile of sandy shoreline along Lake Michigan, and there are two trails in the park that provide access to this area. Additionally, the park's two inland lakes, South and Middle Lakes, are known for bluegill fishing. A picnic shelter is conveniently located near the main parking lot, equipped with picnic tables, charcoal grills, and vault toilets. You can make reservations for the shelter up to 12 months in advance on MiDNRReservations.com. It's essential to be aware that alcoholic beverages are not allowed in the park from March 1 through September 30, unless written authorization has been granted by the park manager through an event permit. Hunting is permitted in the state park, but it's advisable to contact the park directly to inquire about any specific rules, concerns, or considerations related to hunting. The park designates a pet-friendly area, allowing pets along the Lake Michigan shoreline for half a mile. However, pets must always be on a 6-foot leash and under the immediate control of their owner. It is imperative to properly dispose of all pet waste in the provided trash receptacles. Dune Trail: This is the most direct route to Lake Michigan, taking you through a sandy trail that passes along the north side of the park's large dune. The trail covers a distance of 0.5 miles (one way) and guides you through an open sand dune area, ultimately leading to the Lake Michigan shoreline. Paved Trail: Starting from the parking lot, this 0.7-mile (one way) this trail runs along the west side of the park's large dune. After 0.7 miles, the paved trail transitions into a dune climb as it enters the sand dune area. This section becomes a loop that leads visitors to the Lake Michigan shoreline. An additional flat trail extends from the loop to Wishart Road, which is a private drive. Along this trail, you'll encounter ferns, oaks, sassafras, and various other plant species.

DATE(S) VISITED .... □ SPRING □ SUMMER □ FALL □ WINTER

LODGING .... □ ☀ □ ☁ □ 🌧 □ ⛅ □ ❄

WHO I WENT WITH .... FEE(S) .... PARK HOURS .... TEMP:.........

WILL I RETURN? YES / NO   RATING ☆ ☆ ☆ ☆ ☆

HARRISVILLE STATE PARK

COUNTY	ESTABLISHED	AREA (AC/HA)
ALCONA	1921	107 / 43

Harrisville State Park is situated along the sandy shores of Lake Huron and offers a range of amenities, including a day-use area nestled in a stand of pine and cedar trees, a modern campground, a designated swim beach, various trails, and lodging options. Established in 1921, it holds the distinction of being one of Michigan's oldest state parks. The park extends along 1 mile of Lake Huron shoreline, where visitors can enjoy the beach. Safety at the beach is indicated by a beach flag warning system; red flags are used to signal unsafe water conditions, and swimming or entering the water is not advised. A specific swim area is located within the park's day-use area. Additionally, there is a carry-in boat launch at the southern end of the day-use parking lot. The park is conveniently within walking distance of the resort town of Harrisville, making it easily accessible for park-goers. It is also in proximity to attractions like the Sturgeon Point Lighthouse and Negwegon State Park. The park boasts a 2-mile paved Heritage Trail that runs north and south through the park and connects to Harrisville via Third Street. Seasonal naturalists offer weekly nature-based programs during the summer months, from Memorial Day through Labor Day. Within the park's day-use area, the picnic area features picnic tables and charcoal grills available on a first-come, first-served basis. Two locations within the park offer accessibility features. A picnic shelter in the day-use area provides picnic tables, charcoal grills, electrical service (reservations only), and modern restrooms. Reservations for the shelter can be made up to 12 months in advance on MiDNRReservations.com. The day-use area also includes slides and swings for recreational use. A pet-friendly beach in the modern campground is open to non-campers, although public parking is not available. All pets must be leashed and under an owner's immediate control. Proper disposal of pet waste in designated trash receptacles is essential. Mini Cabins: There are two mini cabins, each accommodating up to four people. These cabins are equipped with electricity, an electric heater, a mini-fridge, a coffee maker (filters not provided), a microwave, a fire circle, and an outdoor grill. While there is no modern toilet and shower facility available from mid-October through late April, a vault toilet is accessible in the campground, and running water is available at the headquarters. Mini cabin #186, located in the campground, follows a saltbox design and is pet-friendly with an additional pet fee. Mini cabin #300, located near the campground entrance, has an A-frame style and features a bunk bed and a full-sized futon. Visitors must bring their own linens and cookware. Sunrise

Rustic Cabin: Accommodating up to six people, this cabin was built in 1952 and offers a perfect spot to watch the sunrise over Lake Huron. It includes three wooden bunk beds, a dining table, benches made of cherry wood from a park tree, propane heat, a propane range/stovetop, an outside picnic table, a grill, and access to a nearby vault toilet. This cabin is available for year-round use but does not have electricity. Visitors must provide their own linens and cookware. The modern campground at Harrisville State Park offers various amenities. Most of the campsite locations provide views of Lake Huron and are shaded by cedar, pine, and some maple trees. Additionally, the campground features a pet-friendly beach in the northeast corner, although the size of the beach is influenced by water levels. Campsites are equipped with electrical service, which includes options for 20-amp, 30-amp, or 20-, 30-, and 50-amp service. Other facilities in the campground include a sanitation station for waste disposal and a dishwashing station for added convenience. Harrisville State Park features two trails. Cedar Run Nature Trail: This 2-mile trail winds through towering pines and cedar trees, and a portion of it overlaps with the Heritage Trail. Various access points are available, including the day-use parking lot. Paved Heritage Trail: Extending for 2 miles in a north-south direction, this paved trail passes through the day-use area and the campground. It connects with Third Street, allowing visitors to follow the road into the town of Harrisville. Multiple access points, including the campground and day-use parking lot, are available.

DATE(S) VISITED .... ☐ SPRING ☐ SUMMER ☐ FALL ☐ WINTER

LODGING .... ☐ ☼ ☐ ☁ ☐ 🌧 ☐ 🌩 ☐ ❄

WHO I WENT WITH .... FEE(S) .... PARK HOURS .... TEMP:.........

WILL I RETURN? YES / NO   RATING ☆ ☆ ☆ ☆ ☆

PASSPORT STAMPS

HARTWICK PINES STATE PARK

COUNTY	ESTABLISHED	AREA (AC/HA)
CRAWFORD	1927	9,672 / 3,914

Hartwick Pines State Park, situated in Grayling and known as one of the largest state parks in Michigan's Lower Peninsula, is celebrated for its 49 acres of ancient pine forest, which represents one of the last remaining old-growth pine stands in the state. The park offers a picturesque landscape of rolling hills that overlook the East Branch of the AuSable River Valley, four small lakes, and distinctive timberland. The park is equipped with various amenities, including a seasonal modern campground, a year-round rustic cabin, a group-use area, boat launches, a picnic area, and an extensive network of year-round trails covering a total of 21 miles. Among these trails, the 1.25-mile accessible paved Old Growth Forest Trail stands adjacent to the visitor center. This park is a fantastic destination for outdoor enthusiasts interested in activities such as hiking, paddling, mountain biking, cross-country skiing, snowshoeing, hunting, fishing, birding, and exploring Michigan's natural beauty. The Hartwick Pines Visitor Center is fully accessible and serves as a gateway to the last remaining old-growth pine forest in Michigan. Visitors can access educational exhibits, obtain park information and merchandise, and seek assistance from the park staff. The center also houses a classroom that can accommodate up to 35 guests, and reservations can be made by contacting the Hartwick Pines Visitor Center. The center typically operates from 9 a.m. to 5 p.m. daily from April to October, and from November through March, it is open on weekends only from 10 a.m. to 4:30 p.m., excluding holidays. It's advisable to verify the center's hours by calling ahead. The park offers nature-based programming led by professional interpretive naturalists based at the Hartwick Pines Visitor Center. The park is also home to the Hartwick Pines Logging Museum, situated along the paved Old Growth Forest Trail, approximately a quarter-mile walk from the visitor center. The Michigan History Center provides live demonstrations and self-guided exhibits focusing on the logging camps of the 1890s during the summer season. The museum's hours vary based on the season, but it's generally open from early May to late October, with varying hours during these periods. Hikers can access the Grayling Bicycle Turnpike, a 10-mile paved nonmotorized trail suitable for bicycling, from the park entrance. This scenic multiuse trail, measuring 10 feet in width, runs parallel to the road, connecting Hartwick Pines State Park to downtown Grayling and extending to Hanson Hills Recreation Area. It's important to note that snowmobiling is generally not allowed in the park, except for the Lewiston Grade, which crosses the park and can be accessed at a trailhead on Wilcox Bridge Road just outside the park. Four small lakes are located within the park's boundaries, including Bright Lake, Glory Lake, Hartwick Lake, and Karen Lake. Both Bright and Glory Lakes are kettle lakes with depths of approximately 40 feet. They feature undeveloped gravel boat launches and accessible fishing piers. Typical fish species found in these lakes include largemouth bass, rainbow trout, smallmouth bass, sucker, sunfish, and yellow perch. The lakes can be accessed by car when traveling east to the park on M-93 from I-75, with signs indicating their locations before reaching the park entrance. Alternatively, visitors can reach the lakes by taking a quarter-mile trail from the campground. Accessible fishing piers are available at both Bright and Glory Lakes. There are undeveloped gravel boat launches at both Bright and Glory Lakes. Kayaks are available for rent on Bright and Glory Lakes from 9 a.m. to 8 p.m. Renters can register at the contact station, where they will receive a life vest, paddle, and a key to lock the kayak. Currently, the park offers four single-person kayaks and two tandem kayaks. Within the park, the Friends of Hartwick Pines State Park operate a bookstore and gift shop located in the visitor center. Proceeds from the store contribute to the group's programs and projects within the park. Restrooms are available in the visitor center and remain open year-round, even when the visitor center is closed. An additional seasonal restroom, closed in winter, can be found in the day-use area. The day-use area is situated on the road from the visitor center, and visitors can follow the signs to reach it, or they can access it via the Old Growth Forest Trail. This area offers charcoal grills and picnic tables on a first-come, first-served basis, along with seasonal modern restrooms, drinking fountains, and a playground. An open shelter located within the day-use area near the Old Growth Trail is equipped with picnic tables, group grilling facilities, lighting, two 15-amp electrical outlets, and a fireplace. The shelter can accommodate 96 people with seating arranged in four rows, each with four tables for six people. Modern restrooms attached to the shelter remain open to the public during rentals. Shelter reservations can be made up to 12 months in advance at MIDNRReservations.com. Hunting is permitted in the state park, excluding the old-growth forest, developed areas, and safety zones. The park provides signs to indicate areas closed to hunting, and printed maps are available at the park entrance contact station during hunting season. The group-use area is an open space surrounded by woods and can accommodate up to 100 people. Facilities in the group-use area include two vault toilets, a hand pump for water, two fire rings, and picnic tables. During the winter, the road leading to the group-use area is not plowed, but groups often park at a nearby trailhead and walk to the site. Visitors can reach the group-use area by traveling east to the park on M-93 from I-75 and continuing past the park entrance for about a mile. They can then turn onto Bob Cat Trail dirt road and proceed south for three-quarters of a mile to reach the group camp sign on the east side of the road. Reservations for the group-use area can be made by calling the park office at 989-348-7068. The modern campground at the park offers various campsites. It consists of 64 electric-only sites and 36 pull-through sites with full hook-ups, all featuring 20/30-amp service. Four ADA sites are available at specific locations within the campground (sites 52, 57, 60, and 86). The campground offers a range of sites, from open pull-through locations to wooded sites in between and behind. Amenities in the campground include a sanitation station, recycling facilities, a playground, a sand volleyball court, and trail connections, including access to Bright and Glory Lakes and a spur from the campground road leading to the park's mountain biking trails. The park's sanitation station is situated along the campground entrance road near the dumpster. Potable water is available, and there are two lanes for campers to use. The park also offers a Rustic Cabin adjacent to Bright Lake, which accommodates up to seven people. This cabin is accessible but does not have electricity. However, it is equipped with propane heating for warmth. The cabin includes a single room with a table and benches, as well as three bunk beds. One of these beds is a full-size bed, with a single bunk above. Outside the cabin, there is a hand pump for water, a vault toilet, a picnic table, a charcoal grill, and a fire ring. Visitors are required to bring their own bedding and cooking supplies. Please note that pets are not allowed in the cabin. The cabin is available year-round and offers beautiful lake views, especially in the winter. Hikers and outdoor enthusiasts will find several trails within the park, each offering a unique experience. The Aspen Trail is a 3-mile loop that begins at the visitor center parking lot. This trail is open for hiking, mountain biking, cross-country skiing, and snowshoeing. The trail is mostly flat with rolling hills and passes through old-growth pines. It is divided into three sections and connects to the Deer Run Trail and Weary Legs Trail, offering different lengths of 3, 5, and 7.5 miles. The Old Growth Forest Trail is a 1.25-mile accessible paved trail loop that takes visitors through the 49 acres of old-growth forest and past various historic buildings. It is open for hiking, snowshoeing, and cross-country skiing. The Weary Legs Trail is a 7.5-mile loop that is open for hiking, mountain biking, cross-country skiing, and snowshoeing. This trail includes rolling hills and some steep climbs towards the end. Additionally, the park features the Mertz Grade Trail, a 2.5-mile trail loop that passes through lowland and mixed forests. This trail is excellent for spotting wildlife and observing wildflowers during spring and summer. It is open for hiking, snowshoeing, and cross-country skiing. The Au Sable River Trail is a 3.9-mile trail loop that passes through old-growth trees along the banks of the Au Sable River. This trail crosses the East Branch of the Au Sable River twice and takes visitors through a grove of old-growth eastern hemlock trees and plantations of red pine. Birding opportunities are abundant along this trail. The terrain is suitable for beginners, making it an ideal hike for visitors of all ages.

The Bright and Glory Lakes Trail is a quarter-mile foot trail that leads hikers from the campground to Bright and Glory Lakes. This trail is suitable for beginners and all ages and winds through aspen, dense northern white cedar stands, and a blowdown area. The Deer Run Trail is a 5-mile loop that begins at the visitor center parking lot and is open for hiking, mountain biking, cross-country skiing, and snowshoeing. The Mertz Grade Trail is a 2.5-mile trail loop that follows an abandoned railroad area and takes visitors through lowland and mixed forests. The trail is filled with abundant plant life and wildlife. The trail offers beautiful wildflowers during the spring and summer months, and it's known for increased wildlife activity during the winter. Please note that biking is not permitted on the Old Growth Forest Trail. Visitors are encouraged to explore these trails and enjoy the natural beauty of Hartwick Pines State Park.

DATE(S) VISITED ....   □ SPRING   □ SUMMER   □ FALL   □ WINTER

LODGING ....   □ ☼   □ ☁   □ 🌧   □ ⛅   □ ❄

WHO I WENT WITH ....   FEE(S) .... PARK HOURS .... TEMP:.........

WILL I RETURN? YES / NO   RATING ☆ ☆ ☆ ☆ ☆

PASSPORT STAMPS

HAYES STATE PARK

COUNTY	ESTABLISHED	AREA (AC/HA)
LENAWEE, JACKSON, WASHTENAW	1920	654 / 265

Hayes State Park is located within the picturesque Irish Hills region, nestled between Wamplers and Round lakes. This area is renowned for its rolling hills and lush natural beauty. Covering 654 acres, the park boasts a modern campground, a spacious swimming area, two boating access sites, a fishing pier, trails, picnic areas, interpretive programs, and more. It offers a wide array of activities, including boating, paddling, fishing, camping, and more. Don't forget to explore the other state parks in the Irish Hills. Within a 5-mile radius, you'll find two additional state parks offering unique experiences. Cambridge Junction Historic State Park houses the Walker Tavern Historic Site, a farmer's market, a reconstructed 1840s barn, vintage baseball games, and more. Watkins Lake State Park and County Preserve is known for its serene atmosphere, wildlife observation opportunities, and a 5-mile trail. Hayes State Park is conveniently close to Michigan International Speedway, Hidden Lake Gardens, distinctive shops, antique stores, wine tasting venues, golf courses, restaurants, and various tourist attractions. The day-use area is situated on Wamplers Lake, which is suitable for all types of water sports, while the modern campground is located on Round Lake, known for its calm, no-wake conditions. A designated swim area can be found on Wamplers Lake. Kayaks and stand-up paddleboards are available for rent at the campground office during Memorial Day through Labor Day weekends. Accessible boating access sites can be found on Wamplers and Round lakes. It's worth noting that Round Lake is a no-wake lake with limited parking. Wamplers Lake, an all-sports lake, is famous for its diverse fish species, including largemouth bass, crappie, and bluegill. On the other hand, Round Lake, a no-wake kettle lake, is popular for pan fishing. An accessible fishing pier is located on Round Lake, near the boating access site. Paddling is a popular activity on the park's two lakes, and accessible restrooms and changing rooms are available in the beach house within the day-use area on Wamplers Lake. JR's Food Concessions operates a general store that sells food, camping supplies, and rents float mats. During the Memorial Day through Labor Day period, seasonal naturalists offer weekly nature-based programs. The park's picnic area, situated within the day-use area, provides picnic tables and charcoal grills available on a first-come, first-served basis. Additionally, there is a picnic shelter in the day-use area with picnic tables, charcoal grills, and electrical service for those with reservations. Reservations for the shelter can be made up to 12 months in advance at MiDNRReservations.com. Modern restrooms are conveniently connected. Two playgrounds are also available within the park's day-use area. While pets are not allowed on the designated swim beach, they are permitted along the shoreline as long as they are on a 6-foot leash and under the immediate control of their owner. Pet waste must be properly disposed of in trash receptacles. The modern campground, situated along Round Lake, is divided into two loops: the west and east loops. It offers a total of 180 campsites, two mini cabins, and two tiny houses. The campground provides a mix of sunny and shady sites, all featuring an asphalt pad and either 20- or 30-amp electrical service. Sites 1-10 are equipped with full water hookups. A designated swimming beach is located across the street in the day-use area, situated on Wamplers Lake. The park's Red and Blue trails are positioned between the two campground loops. Additionally, the park features a sanitation station within the modern campground. Potable water is accessible, and there are three lanes available. The park's two new tiny houses, Superior and Wolverine, can be found in the modern campground. Each tiny house accommodates up to four people, with a full-size bed and two single beds in the loft. The Superior tiny house is designed to be accessible. These tiny houses offer electrical service, including air conditioning, ceiling lights, and a bathroom with a toilet, shower, and sink. Amenities include a couch, a small table with chairs, a mini fridge, a cooktop stove, a kitchen sink, a microwave, and a coffee maker. Each tiny house is equipped with a deck or porch, a picnic table, and a fire pit outdoors. Guests must provide their own bedding and cookware. For those who enjoy hiking, the park offers the Red and Blue Trail, a 2-mile trail featuring two 1-mile loops. This trail is nestled between the east and west campground loops and takes you through the forest while offering glimpses of wetlands and Round Lake. The trail is considered to be easy, making it suitable for various skill levels.

DATE(S) VISITED .... ☐ SPRING ☐ SUMMER ☐ FALL ☐ WINTER

LODGING .... ☐ ☀ ☐ ☁ ☐ 🌧 ☐ ⛆ ☐ ❄

WHO I WENT WITH .... FEE(S) .... PARK HOURS .... TEMP:.........

WILL I RETURN? YES / NO   RATING ☆ ☆ ☆ ☆ ☆

PASSPORT STAMPS

HISTORIC MILL CREEK DISCOVERY PARK

COUNTY	ESTABLISHED	AREA (AC/HA)
CHEBOYGAN	1978	625 / 253

This park provides a glimpse into the way of life during the 1700s, a time when the industrial revolution was just starting to impact sawmills throughout northern Michigan. Park includes approximately 1 mile of the eponymous creek's watercourse as it flows downhill toward Lake Huron, but not the wetland. The creek dam and sawmill (c. 1790) were rebuilt in 1984. The Visitor's Center and Millwright's House have exhibits on the history of the site featuring archaeological artifacts. Park has three miles of trails that contain beautiful forests, wildflowers and scenic views. A variety of wildlife species make their homes here. Visitors can make use of fire pits and grills for cooking.

DATE(S) VISITED .... ☐ SPRING ☐ SUMMER ☐ FALL ☐ WINTER

LODGING .... ☐ ☼ ☐ ☁ ☐ 🌧 ☐ 🌬 ☐ ❄

WHO I WENT WITH .... FEE(S) .... PARK HOURS .... TEMP:.........

WILL I RETURN? YES / NO   RATING ☆ ☆ ☆ ☆ ☆

PASSPORT STAMPS

HOEFT STATE PARK

COUNTY	ESTABLISHED	AREA (AC/HA)
PRESQUE ISLE	1922	340 / 137

Hoeft State Park is a densely forested 340-acre park that boasts a one-mile stretch of sandy Lake Huron shoreline. The influence of Lake Huron helps moderate temperatures, making both summers and winters less extreme compared to areas a few miles inland. This park was one of the original 14 Michigan State Parks, with the initial property being a donation from the lumber baron Paul H. Hoeft on January 2, 1922. In the late 1930s, the Civilian Conservation Corps constructed a still-functional picnic shelter in the day-use area. The park offers 126 campsites and a mini cabin for visitors. It's an ideal rest stop or base camp for those planning activities in the Straits region, with the Mackinac Bridge being 50 miles northwest via US-23. Bicyclists can utilize the bike trail to reach Rogers City, a mere four and a half miles away. The park features a beautiful sandy beach on Lake Huron, which is perfect for sunbathing and swimming and is located within 100 yards of the modern campground. There is a ten-foot wide paved non-motorized trail that starts in the day-use area and connects to the Huron Sunrise Trail at the park entrance. This trail runs alongside the beach of Lake Huron and goes all the way to Calcite Limestone Quarry, which is the world's largest open pit limestone mine. Additionally, the trail connects to the Herman Vogler Conservation Area, which features seven miles of hiking and biking trails. The park offers four and a half miles of trails that meander through gently rolling mixed hardwood and conifer forests as well as along the Lake Huron shoreline. The spring season is especially great for viewing wildflowers. Although the trails are not groomed, they provide a picturesque outdoor experience. The Sears and Roebuck Modern Lodge, which dates back to the 1920s, provides ample space for eight guests. It offers three queen-size beds, a set of bunk beds, and two futon couches in the living room for additional sleeping capacity. The lodge features two bedrooms and a half bath on the second floor, as well as a first-floor master bed and bathroom. Amenities within the lodge include a refrigerator, electric stove, microwave, coffee maker, and toaster. Guests will find linens, towels, dishware, utensils, pots, bakeware, pans, a grill (charcoal not provided), a fire pit (wood available for purchase in the park), and a picnic table. Before departure, guests are expected to clean the lodge. Smoking and pets are prohibited inside the lodge, and it's available year-round. For information or reservations, call 989-734-2543. The Beach Trail in P.H. Hoeft State Park runs along the Lake Huron shoreline and is 1.5 miles long. It offers easy access to the beach for those looking to swim during the summer. The trail is suitable for hiking, cross-country skiing, and biking, weather permitting. Additionally, there are picnic areas along the trail, providing the perfect opportunity for a beach-view picnic during your journey. The park's picnic area is equipped with fire pits and grills, and a stone-and-log picnic shelter, built in 1938 by the Civilian Conservation Corps, offers a stunning view of Lake Huron. This area also includes a group grill, a potable water source, and restrooms equipped with soap and paper towels. Visitors share a 55-vehicle parking lot with other guests. The shelter can be reserved up to a year in advance by calling 1-800-447-2757 or visiting MiDNRReservations.com. Two playgrounds are available within the park, one in the day-use area and one in the campground. There are two horseshoe pits, one in the day-use area and one in the campground, and horseshoes can be obtained at the contact station. Furthermore, there are two volleyball pits in the campground beach area. Hunting is permitted on the west side of US-23, and for hunting information, you can call the park at (989) 734-2543. Seasonal naturalists offer weekly nature-based programs from Memorial Day through Labor Day. The park has a mini cabin that can accommodate four people and is furnished with a bunk bed and futon, along with an electric heater, a small table, and two chairs. There is no plumbing within the cabin, but outside, you will find a grill, fire ring, and picnic table. Guests are required to bring their own linens and cookware. The Hardwoods Trail is 1.5 miles long and stretches through a heavily wooded area along the sandy Lake Huron shoreline. The terrain is relatively easy, traversing rolling mixed hardwood forests near the shoreline. This trail provides an opportunity to experience the beautiful fall colors, spring wildflowers, and towering trees in the winter. Hiking, biking, and cross-country skiing are all allowed on the trail, weather permitting. The Nagel Creek Trail is 0.75 miles long and leads to the shores of Nagel Creek, passing through hardwood forests and sandy beach terrain. You can easily connect the Nagel Creek Trail with the Beach and Pavilion Trails for a longer journey along the coastline. Similar to other trails in the park, hiking, cross-country skiing, and biking are allowed, weather permitting. The Pavilion Trail is 0.25 miles long, offering a short and easy hike. You can conveniently extend your hike by connecting to the Beach or Nagel Creek Trail. The Pavilion Trail connects to the Organization Campground and provides easy beach access, as it is linked to the Beach Trail. This trail is suitable for hiking, cross-country skiing, and biking, weather permitting.

DATE(S) VISITED .... ☐ SPRING ☐ SUMMER ☐ FALL ☐ WINTER

LODGING .... ☐ ☀ ☐ ☁ ☐ 🌧 ☐ 🌫 ☐ ❄

WHO I WENT WITH .... FEE(S) .... PARK HOURS .... TEMP:.........

WILL I RETURN? YES / NO RATING ☆ ☆ ☆ ☆ ☆

PASSPORT STAMPS

HOFFMASTER STATE PARK

COUNTY	ESTABLISHED	AREA (AC/HA)
MUSKEGON, OTTAWA	1963	1,100 / 450

P.J. Hoffmaster State Park, situated in Muskegon, Michigan, boasts a stunning three-mile stretch of Lake Michigan shoreline. The park offers a modern campground, impressive sand dunes, 10 miles of scenic trails, and the Gillette Sand Dune Visitor Center. One of the park's primary attractions is the Dune Overlook Trail, which features a dune climb that spans about half a mile in total. This climb includes approximately 220 steps and benches along the way. For a moderately steep hike, visitors can opt for the 2-mile-long (roundtrip) Homestead Trail, which also provides access to Lake Michigan. To gain a better understanding of the forested dunes' formation, you can visit the Gillette Sand Dune Visitor Center, where you'll find informative exhibits and programs. The park's three-mile sandy shoreline along Lake Michigan is perfect for sunbathing and swimming. It's important to pay attention to the beach flag warning system in designated swim areas; red flags indicate unsafe water conditions, and swimming is prohibited. There are two designated swim areas, one located in the park's day-use area and another a short five-minute walk from the campground. The park also offers two beach wheelchairs that visitors can borrow (by calling the park or checking at the contact station). In the day-use area, two beach houses are available; one provides restrooms and changing rooms, while the other offers restrooms and a vending machine. Picnic areas in the day-use area feature picnic tables and charcoal grills that are available on a first-come, first-served basis. Vault toilets are easily accessible. In addition, there is a picnic shelter in the day-use area, equipped with picnic tables, charcoal grills, and vault toilets. Reservations for the shelter can be made up to 12 months in advance at MIDNRReservations.com. From Memorial Day through Labor Day, seasonal naturalists offer weekly nature-based programs. These programs are led by professional interpretive naturalists and are based out of the Gillette Sand Dunes Visitor Center. Pets are welcome along the entire Lake Michigan shoreline, except within the designated swim area. However, pets must always be on a 6-foot leash and under the owner's immediate control, and pet waste must be properly disposed of in trash receptacles. Alcoholic beverages are prohibited in the campground from April 1 through Labor Day, unless written authorization has been granted by the park manager through an event permit. The park also offers a rustic group campground suitable for youth groups of up to 54 people. There are two sites, each accommodating up to 27 campers. Each site provides a picnic table, fire pit, and easy access to a potable water faucet. Campers can use the modern toilet and shower facilities located in the modern campground. To reserve the group camp area, you can call 231-798-3711. The modern campground is divided into three loops, and most sites are spacious and shaded by oak, maple, beech, and pine trees. The campground is conveniently located just a short five-minute walk from a designated swimming beach and offers access to trails, dune areas, and Little Black Creek. Electrical service, including 20/30-amp (with some sites offering 50-amp service), is available at each site, and there is a sanitation .station for campers. Recycling facilities are also provided. The campground includes four semi-modern sites (B1, B2, C1, and C2) without electrical service, as well as two ADA-accessible sites with crushed limestone surfaces. The Dune Overlook Trail is one of the park's key attractions. It features a roughly half-mile roundtrip dune climb with around 220 steps and benches for resting. At the trail's summit, you'll find two observation platforms that offer breathtaking panoramic views of Lake Michigan and the surrounding sand dunes. The trailhead is located near the visitor center. The Homestead Trail, approximately 3 miles in length, winds through forested dunes and provides access to Lake Michigan. This loop trail, with various optional segments to customize your hike's length, includes moderate climbs, access to a designated natural area, and connects to the Dune Overlook Trail. The trailhead can be found near the visitor center. Although the trail features some climbs, they are typically manageable even for young children. If you visit during the summer, don't forget to bring your swimsuit and enjoy a lakeside picnic on the shores of Lake Michigan. The Walk-a-Mile trail is a 1.6-mile loop that traverses areas with sassafras, oak, maple, and beech trees, along dune ridges and moss-covered paths near a ravine. As you ascend the sandy slopes of the dunes, you'll enjoy stunning views of Lake Michigan, culminating in a hike that leads you to the beach. The trailhead is accessible from the overflow parking lot in the day-use area.

PASSPORT STAMPS

HOLLAND STATE PARK

COUNTY	ESTABLISHED	AREA (AC/HA)
OTTAWA	1926	617 / 250

Holland State Park, renowned for its sugar sand beaches, picturesque sunsets, and the iconic "Big Red" lighthouse, offers a range of attractions. The park comprises two large campgrounds, an accessible playground, opportunities for paddling and fishing, and connections to non-motorized trails. It is divided into the Lake Macatawa and Lake Michigan units, both located on the northern side of the channel that links Lake Macatawa with Lake Michigan. Additionally, there's a boat launch with a fish cleaning station about a mile east of the park. The park now provides two free EV charging stations. Visitors can enjoy a quarter-mile of sandy shoreline along Lake Michigan and nearly a quarter-mile along Lake Macatawa. They should be mindful of the beach flag warning system, with red flags indicating unsafe water conditions, prohibiting swimming or entering the water. It's important not to swim near or jump off the pier or navigational channel walls and to stay alert to changing conditions. Designated swim areas are available in both the Lake Michigan and Lake Macatawa day-use areas. An accessible walkway to the water is provided, and two beach wheelchairs are available for use on Lake Michigan. Paddling is a popular activity on Lake Macatawa and, when conditions permit, on Lake Michigan. The Macatawa Boat House, located across from the Lake Macatawa Campground, offers rentals of stand-up paddle boards, canoes, and kayaks. For more information, you can visit MacBoathouse.com. Although there are no boating access sites in the park, the Lake Macatawa boating access site is just one mile away in the direction of Holland on Ottawa Beach Road. Fishing is a common pastime along the channel walkway on Lake Michigan and along Ottawa County's boardwalk on Lake Macatawa. Additionally, a boat launch with a fish cleaning station can be found one mile east of the park. The Lake Michigan day-use area features a beach house that includes restrooms, food concessions, vending machines, and changing rooms. Beachplace, located in the beach house, offers food, ice cream, beach supplies, and more. A 20-mile paved Lakeshore Trail runs parallel to Lakeshore Drive, providing a continuous route from Grand Haven State Park to Holland State Park, with the iconic "Big Red" lighthouse visible from the park and located just outside the park across the channel. Picnic areas in both the Lake Michigan and Lake Macatawa day-use areas are equipped with picnic tables and charcoal grills available on a first-come, first-served basis. Additionally, there's a picnic shelter in the Lake Michigan day-use area, which includes picnic tables, charcoal grills, and electrical service (reservations required and can be made up to 12 months in advance at MiDNRReservations.com). An accessible playground in the Lake Michigan day-use area offers slides, spinners, and other interactive features set on a rubberized surface that enhances accessibility for individuals of all mobility levels. Alcoholic beverages are not permitted at any time in the park, unless written authorization has been granted by the park manager through an event permit. Seasonal naturalists offer weekly nature-based programs from Memorial Day through Labor Day. Pets are allowed in the designated dog beach along Lake Macatawa, but they must always be on a 6-foot leash and under the owner's immediate control, and all pet waste must be disposed of properly in trash receptacles. The park offers two camper cabins, Whitetail and Beacon, which both offer fantastic views of the "Big Red" lighthouse and the channel. These cabins accommodate up to seven people in bunk beds with twin and full mattresses in two rooms. They are equipped with a coffee maker, microwave, refrigerator, tables and chairs, and a small kitchen counter, and they each have two assigned parking spots. The cabins feature electric heat and electrical service. Guests are required to bring their own linens and cookware. The Lake Macatawa Campground provides a mix of wooded and sunny campsites, with most located on grass or gravel. All campsites offer either 30- or 50-amp electrical service, and there are 12 ADA-accessible campsites available. The campground also features two play structures, a sand volleyball court, and a horseshoe area. A small swimming beach is situated on Lake Macatawa, just across from the campground entrance. There is a sanitation station within the Lake Macatawa Campground, and potable water is accessible with two lanes for convenience. Registration for both campgrounds is handled at the Lake Macatawa Campground located at 2175 Ottawa Beach Road. The modern campground is located just beyond the dune from Lake Michigan. Most of the sites provide 30-amp electrical service, with 31 campsites offering full hook-ups (50-amp electric, water, and sewer). All camping equipment must remain on the pavement, including commercial fire pits. Firepits are not provided, but campers can bring their own portable fire pits. These fire pits must be at least 6 inches above the sand and fully enclosed with a cover. Ground fires are not permitted, and firepits cannot be placed on the asphalt or within 15 feet of any camping unit. Old-style washtub fire pits are also not allowed. Registration for both campgrounds can be completed at the Lake Macatawa Campground at 2175 Ottawa Beach Road. The Dune Trail is a 1-mile, out-and-back trail that leads visitors to the summit of the Mount Pisguah sand dune. Although it offers fantastic views of Lake Michigan, this trail does not provide direct access to the water. The trail begins along Ottawa County's boardwalk and dune climb, which includes stairs, and then continues along the DNR's wooded trail. The trailhead is located along Ottawa Beach Road near the park headquarters, with parking available near the U.S. Coast Guard station.

DATE(S) VISITED .... □ SPRING □ SUMMER □ FALL □ WINTER

LODGING .... □ ☀ □ ☁ □ 🌧 □ 🌬 □ ❄

WHO I WENT WITH .... FEE(S) .... PARK HOURS .... TEMP:........

WILL I RETURN? YES / NO   RATING ☆ ☆ ☆ ☆ ☆

PASSPORT STAMPS

INDIAN LAKE STATE PARK

COUNTY	ESTABLISHED	AREA (AC/HA)
SCHOOLCRAFT	1932	567 / 229

Indian Lake State Park, situated on the shores of Indian Lake in Michigan's Upper Peninsula, is a 567-acre park divided into two units, separated by the lake and located three miles apart. The south unit hosts a modern campground overlooking the lake, while the west unit offers semi-modern campsites in a wooded setting. The park features several amenities, including two picnic shelters built by the Civilian Conservation Corps, a designated swim beach, a quarter-mile paved trail along the lake, and a boat access site. Indian Lake, measuring 6 miles in length and 3 miles in width, stands as the fourth-largest inland lake in the Upper Peninsula. In the 1850s, the lake was originally named M'O'Nistique Lake, and historical records from that era suggest that Native Americans resided in log cabins near the lake's outlet. A nearby attraction is Palms Book State Park, located just 7 miles northwest of Indian Lake State Park. Visitors can explore ancient tree trunks, lime-encrusted branches, and observe lake trout through the emerald waters of the "Big Spring" using a self-guided observation raft. The mouth of Thompson Creek and the Manistique River is well-known for salmon and steelhead fishing during the season. The Thompson State Fish Hatchery, situated 2 miles from the park, supports this popular activity. Additionally, the Hiawatha National Forest and Lake Superior State Forest offer numerous opportunities for forest-based recreational activities, while the Seney National Wildlife Refuge is a favorite destination for birdwatchers and wildlife enthusiasts. The park provides a small, 75-yard sandy beach area on Indian Lake, situated in front of a shelter adjacent to the Beach Shelter. The park's day-use area near the Beach Shelter includes a designated swim area with a clean, sandy beach and shallow water, making it an ideal spot for swimming. Visitors will find a carry-in launch on Indian Lake, located within the semi-modern campground's day-use area. Additionally, there is a paved boat launch in the park's day-use area, suitable for smaller boats. Kayaks are available for rent, with rentals offered on a first-come, first-served basis. Indian Lake, covering 8,400 acres, is the fourth-largest inland lake in the Upper Peninsula and offers fishing opportunities for a variety of species, including perch, walleye, northern pike, muskellunge, rock bass, smallmouth bass, bluegill, sturgeon, and brown trout. The park's picnic area is located within the day-use area and includes picnic tables and charcoal grills available on a first-come, first-served basis. There are also two reservable picnic shelters situated in the day-use area. The accessible Beach Shelter, located in the beach house, boasts a lake overlook, fireplace, water supply, electricity, picnic tables, and a group charcoal grill. Restrooms and changing rooms are available within the building. Another Picnic Shelter offers restrooms, a water supply, electricity (available during reservations only), picnic tables, and a group charcoal grill. Both shelters are conveniently located near the playground, horseshoe pits, and volleyball court. While the Beach Shelter is accessible, the Picnic Shelter is not. Reservations for these shelters can be made up to 12 months in advance at MiDNRReservations.com. There is also a swing set within the west shore unit of the park, located within the semi-modern campground's day-use area. Seasonal naturalists offer weekly nature-based programs during the period from Memorial Day to Labor Day. The park permits hunting, although it's advisable to contact the park directly to inquire about any specific rules, concerns, or considerations. The modern campground is found in the park's south unit on the shores of Indian Lake. It features a range of campsites, including accessible sites, pull-through sites, and tent-only sites. Many of these sites offer scenic waterfront views of the lake. The campground is nestled amid trees, and it's conveniently located near the designated swimming beach, a boat ramp, a picnic area, and picnic shelters. Each site offers 20/30-amp electrical service, and there are several 50-amp sites available. A sanitation station is provided. Within the modern campground, there are two accessible mini cabins. These cabins are designed for one-bedroom occupancy and can sleep up to four people. They are equipped with electricity, lighting, a full-size bed with a single bunk above, a cot, tables and chairs, an electric heater, a microwave, a portable fan, and a mini refrigerator. Outside the cabin, you'll find a charcoal grill, fire ring, and picnic table. Guests are required to bring their own linens, and please note that pets are not allowed inside the cabin. The semi-modern campground is located on Indian Lake, within the park's west shore unit, which is situated 4 miles northwest of the park along County Road 455. It offers a more rustic camping experience compared to the modern campground and is typically open from mid-June through Labor Day. Campsites in the semi-modern campground are available on a first-come, first-served basis, and self-registration can be completed at the west shore unit's contact station when entering the campground or at the modern campground office in the south shore unit. The west shore unit features a small day-use area with a carry-in boat launch on Indian Lake and a swing set. The semi-modern campground offers 20-amp electrical service at each site, but restrooms are limited to vault toilets. Hand pumps are available for obtaining water. Indian Lake State Park has 2 miles of trails open for hiking, cross-country skiing, and snowshoeing. The park features a quarter-mile paved accessible trail that offers scenic lake overlooks and runs along Indian Lake within the day-use area. The Dufour Creek Loop includes bridges crossing the Dufour Creek at two points, and the trail may become quite wet during certain seasons, particularly in spring and fall. The park also manages the nearby Indian Lake Pathway, which is located 6 miles northwest of the park along M-149. The Indian Lake Pathway offers an additional 8.5 miles of hiking and groomed cross-country ski trails.

DATE(S) VISITED .... □ SPRING □ SUMMER □ FALL □ WINTER

LODGING ....

WHO I WENT WITH .... FEE(S) .... PARK HOURS .... TEMP:.........

WILL I RETURN? YES / NO   RATING ☆ ☆ ☆ ☆ ☆

PASSPORT STAMPS

INTERLOCHEN STATE PARK

COUNTY	ESTABLISHED	AREA (AC/HA)
GRAND TRAVERSE	1917	187 / 76

Interlochen State Park, located approximately 15 miles southwest of Traverse City, is nestled between two popular lakes for fishing and swimming: Green Lake and Duck Lake. The park offers a range of outdoor activities, including camping, paddling, fishing, swimming, and more. Michigan's first state park, Interlochen State Park, was established by the Michigan Legislature in 1917 when they purchased the land for $60,000. In 1928, the Interlochen Center for the Arts, a national music camp, was founded on the property adjacent to the park's northern boundary. The park provides boat launches in each loop of the campground, with one located on Duck Lake and another in the rustic campground area on Green Lake. Additionally, an accessible kayak launch is situated on Duck Lake, positioned between the boat launch and the picnic area. Simple Adventures, located in the beach house within the day-use area on Duck Lake, offers kayak and stand-up paddleboard rentals from Memorial Day through Labor Day. Both Green Lake and Duck Lake provide opportunities for fishing, with bass, pike, and bluegill being common catches during the summer months. Ice fishing enthusiasts often target smelt and pike in the lakes during the winter. Paddlers can explore the waters of Green Lake and Duck Lake, and a kayak launch with accessible features is available on Duck Lake, situated between the boat launch and the picnic area. Within the picnic area, fire pits and grills are provided for visitor use. Additionally, there is a picnic shelter available for reservations, which can be made up to one year in advance by calling 1-800-447-2757 or visiting www.midnrreservations.com. Interlochen State Park offers camper cabins in three locations: South A, South B, and North A. The camper cabin in South A features a stairway leading to the lake, electric heating, a refrigerator, a microwave, and a coffee maker. It is ADA accessible, but pets are not permitted. The camper cabin in South B accommodates up to six people and includes an electric fireplace, a refrigerator, a microwave, and a coffee maker. It is also ADA accessible and does not allow pets. The camper cabin in North A sleeps up to six people and provides an electric fireplace, a refrigerator, a microwave, and a coffee maker. However, it is not ADA accessible and does not permit pets. To make reservations for these camper cabins, you can visit midnrreservations.com or call 800-447-2757. Interlochen State Park offers two rent-a-tents for visitors.

DATE(S) VISITED .... ☐ SPRING ☐ SUMMER ☐ FALL ☐ WINTER

LODGING .... ☐ ☀ ☐ ☁ ☐ 🌧 ☐ 🌫 ☐ ❄

WHO I WENT WITH .... FEE(S) .... PARK HOURS .... TEMP:........

WILL I RETURN? YES / NO   RATING ☆ ☆ ☆ ☆ ☆

PASSPORT STAMPS

KEITH J. CHARTERS TRAVERSE CITY STATE PARK

COUNTY	ESTABLISHED	AREA (AC/HA)
GRAND TRAVERSE	1920	75 / 30

Keith J. Charters Traverse City State Park, conveniently located just 2 miles southwest of Traverse City, is a popular urban park situated on the east arm of the Grand Traverse Bay. Covering 75 acres, the park offers a range of amenities, including a modern campground, a well-equipped lodge, mini cabins, and a day-use area. Across the road from the park, the day-use area includes a quarter-mile of sandy beach along the eastern shore of the Grand Traverse Bay, a small beach house, and a picnic area. Established in 1920, the park was founded on approximately 16 acres of land in response to the decline of the logging industry. In 2011, an additional 30 acres of undeveloped woodland were acquired. Visitors can enjoy a quarter-mile stretch of sandy shoreline along the east arm of the Grand Traverse Bay, with an overpass pedestrian bridge providing safe passage across U.S. 31. An accessible walkway to the water is available, and a beach wheelchair can be used when water levels permit. Beach safety is indicated through the beach flag warning system, with red flags signifying unsafe water conditions and no swimming allowed. The park's day-use area offers a designated swim area on Grand Traverse Bay. Paddling is a popular activity on the bay, and kayak, bike, and stand-up paddleboard rentals/tours are offered by Paddle TC. The mouth of Mitchell Creek, located across U.S. 31 in the day-use area, is a favored fishing spot. A beach house located in the day-use area, directly across from the park along Grand Traverse Bay, contains restrooms and changing facilities. The park is adjacent to the 10.5-mile-long TART Trail, a paved urban trail that extends from Acme Township to Traverse City. The Leelanau Trail, connected to the TART Trail, adds 17 miles of paved trail between Traverse City and Suttons Bay, providing opportunities for biking, walking, and other trail-related activities. Within the park's day-use area, a picnic area offers picnic tables, grills, and bathroom facilities. An accessible playground is also available for visitors to enjoy. For pet owners, there is a designated pet walk area between the campground and U.S. 31, accessible via the pedestrian bridge. Pets must always be on a 6-foot leash and under the owner's immediate control, and pet waste should be disposed of properly in designated trash receptacles. The modern campground is divided into three loops: west, central, and east. It is surrounded by a forested landscape, offering shade and tranquility. The central and east loops provide 20- and 30-amp electrical service, while the west loop offers 20-, 30-, and 50-amp service. Recycling facilities are available in the campground. The park also offers several lodging options: Grand Traverse Bay

Mini Cabin: This cabin has been recently renovated and is located in the modern campground near the woods. It accommodates up to four people and includes a kitchenette with a mini refrigerator, microwave, electric heater, flat-screen fireplace, ceiling fan, electrical outlets with USB ports, and a bar area with stools. The cabin features a bunkbed (full mattress on the bottom and a twin on top) and a futon. Outdoors, there is a covered front porch, a picnic table, a fire pit, and a grill. Guests must bring their own linens and cookware. Mitchell Creek Mini Cabin: Situated on the south side of the campground near the campground office, this cabin can accommodate up to five people. It includes two sets of bunkbeds (one double bed and three single beds), a mini refrigerator, a microwave, and an electric wall heater. Outside, there is a picnic table, a fire pit, and a waist-high cook grill. The cabin has electricity, and guests need to provide their own linens and cookware. Lodge: The lodge is a fully equipped three-bedroom facility that sleeps up to 11 people. Located at the park's entrance, the lodge offers a range of bedding, including a queen, three doubles, and one single bed, along with a pull-out couch featuring a double bed. The lodge comprises two bathrooms, a complete kitchen with dishes, stove, refrigerator, microwave, dishwasher, pots and pans, coffee maker, utensils, a living room, a dining room, and washer/dryer. It is equipped with electricity, heating, and air conditioning. Outdoors, guests can find a gas grill, a deck, a fire pit, and picnic tables. Linens are provided. The lodge features accessible elements such as an entrance ramp, and a portion of the lodge is ADA accessible, with a walk-in shower and a pull-out couch in the living room. It's important to note that there are steps leading down to the lower bath and three bedrooms. During the period from Memorial Day through Labor Day, weekly rentals are mandatory. In the off-season, a minimum stay of two nights is required.

DATE(S) VISITED .... □ SPRING □ SUMMER □ FALL □ WINTER

LODGING .... □ ☼ □ ☁ □ ☔ □ ☁ □ ❄

WHO I WENT WITH .... FEE(S) .... PARK HOURS .... TEMP:.........

WILL I RETURN? YES / NO   RATING ☆ ☆ ☆ ☆ ☆

PASSPORT STAMPS

LAKE GOGEBIC STATE PARK

COUNTY	ESTABLISHED	AREA (AC/HA)
GOGEBIC	1930	1,329 / 538

Lake Gogebic State Park is situated on the periphery of a vast upland area within the Ottawa National Forest, making it an excellent base for exploring the western Upper Peninsula. The park offers easy access to numerous points of interest in the region. To the east, you can find Bond Falls and Agate Falls, while the northeast boasts beautiful falls and rapids along the Black River and Presque Isle River. To the north, you'll discover the magnificent Porcupine Mountains and the shores of Lake Superior. The park features a two-mile scenic nature trail that forms a loop back to the campgrounds. You can enjoy swimming and sunbathing on the large, sandy beach. For boating enthusiasts, there is a paved boat launch capable of accommodating watercraft of various sizes. Lake Gogebic offers excellent fishing opportunities, with perch, walleye, smallmouth bass, and northern pike being some of the prized catches. The local chamber of commerce hosts annual fishing tournaments on Lake Gogebic. A picnic area with fire pits and grills is available, and the picnic shelter can be reserved up to a year in advance through a phone call to 1-800-447-2757 or by visiting www.midnrreservations.com. The park comprises both a modern campground with 105 sites and a semi-modern campground with 22 sites. During the early and late parts of the camping season, the semi-modern campground sites become rustic when the modern toilet and shower facilities are closed for the winter months. The tiny house at the park sleeps four people, with two on the main floor and two in the loft. It includes a kitchen equipped with a microwave, mini refrigerator, and coffee pot, as well as a dining table with chairs and additional seating. An accessible ramp is provided for ease of access. The tiny house is equipped with electricity and a propane furnace for heating. Potable water can be obtained from the campground or at the park headquarters. Guests must bring their own bedding. Outdoors, there is a fire pit, a picnic table, and a charcoal grill. The Lake Gogebic Forest Trail is located within the heart of the Ottawa National Forest, situated in Lake Gogebic State Park in the Upper Peninsula. This 2.5-mile trail is an excellent way to explore the natural landscape of the western Upper Peninsula, whether on foot or skis. The trail provides access to the true backcountry of this region, offering opportunities for wildlife viewing, fishing, and access to the shores of the largest inland lake in the Upper Peninsula. It is open year-round and can be used for cross-country skiing as soon as the snow falls.

DATE(S) VISITED ....

☐ SPRING   ☐ SUMMER   ☐ FALL   ☐ WINTER

LODGING ....

☐ ☀   ☐ ☁   ☐ 🌧   ☐ 🌫   ☐ ❄

WHO I WENT WITH ....

FEE(S) ....   PARK HOURS ....   TEMP:........

WILL I RETURN? YES / NO

RATING ☆ ☆ ☆ ☆ ☆

PASSPORT STAMPS

LAKEPORT STATE PARK

COUNTY	ESTABLISHED	AREA (AC/HA)
ST. CLAIR	1946	565 / 229

Situated along the shores of Lake Huron, Lakeport State Park offers residents of southeast Michigan access to the Great Lakes. The park is divided into two distinct units, separated by the village of Lakeport. A total of 250 campsites are distributed between these two campgrounds. Each campsite is equipped with a picnic table, fire circle, electricity, and modern toilet/shower facilities. Additionally, there are several pull-through sites and camp pads to make it easier to level campers. Fishing and boating enthusiasts can utilize the state-managed boat launch located ten miles north of the park in Lexington. For outdoor activities like hiking and hunting, the Port Huron State Game Area is reachable within a 15-minute drive. Shoppers will find Birchwood Mall about five miles south of the park. The southern unit of Lakeport State Park, named the Franklin Delano Roosevelt unit, is a day-use area located a mile south of the camping area, adjacent to Lake Huron. Visitors to this area can enjoy the beach and take advantage of various spots for secluded picnics, bird watching, or simply relaxing. The day-use area provides numerous picnic tables, barbecue grills, horseshoe pits, and volleyball nets. The park is divided by Highway US-25, with a pedestrian overpass providing access to both sides of the day-use area. There is a picnic shelter in the day-use area that can be rented for group activities and family reunions. Reservations for the shelter can be made up to a year in advance by calling 1-800-447-2757 or visiting www.midnrreservations.com. Both campgrounds within the park offer a range of play equipment for children. The larger campground also includes one of the few remaining campground stores, which sells campfire wood in addition to the usual supplies. Seasonal naturalists are available from Memorial Day through Labor Day to offer weekly nature-based programming. Access to the beach is exclusive to registered campers. The beach at the day-use area is open to the general public. Within the campground, there are two mini cabins known as White Pine Cabin and Cedar Cabin. These cabins are designed to accommodate four people and come with bunks and mattresses. Each cabin is equipped with electricity and lights and has recently undergone renovation, featuring new ceramic tile floors, paint, mattresses, and handmade wood furniture. The cabins come with a paved parking area, a picnic table, and a firepit on-site. The Lakeport camper cabin, situated in the northern section of the campground, provides direct access to the beach. It can sleep up to six people, with two bunk beds and a sleeper sofa. The cabin features electricity, baseboard heating, a kitchen cart, and a mini-fridge. Additionally, it provides access to two campground restroom/shower buildings located within 500 feet. The cabin comes with a two-car parking area and is ADA accessible, but pets are not allowed. The 54-mile Bridge to Bay Trail traces the St. Clair River from New Baltimore in Macomb County to Algonac State Park in St. Clair County, extending north to Lakeport State Park in St. Clair County. This trail connects users to downtown areas, neighborhoods, parks, museums, beaches, lighthouses, and more. It offers a diverse range of trail styles, including boardwalks, river walks, and rail trails in both urban and natural settings along waterfront and inland corridors. The St. Clair County Parks and Recreation Commission collaborates with 13 local governmental units to develop and complete the 54-mile trail. While the county plays a role in planning and promoting the trail, local entities are responsible for constructing their portion of the trail.

DATE(S) VISITED .... ☐ SPRING   ☐ SUMMER   ☐ FALL   ☐ WINTER

LODGING .... ☐ ☼   ☐ ☁   ☐ 🌧   ☐ 🌫   ☐ ❄

WHO I WENT WITH .... FEE(S) .... PARK HOURS .... TEMP:.........

WILL I RETURN? YES / NO   RATING ☆ ☆ ☆ ☆ ☆

PASSPORT STAMPS

LAUGHING WHITEFISH FALLS STATE PARK

COUNTY	ESTABLISHED	AREA (AC/HA)
ALGER	1946	960 / 390

Laughing Whitefish Falls stands as one of the many awe-inspiring waterfalls found in the Upper Peninsula. The falls flow gracefully through a scenic gorge adorned with ancient white pine and hemlock trees that soar above. The site features three observation platforms, each offering different vantage points of the falls. Visitors can access these platforms by embarking on a half-mile hike through a beech-maple forest, resulting in a one-mile round-trip journey. The upper observation platform does not have stairs leading to it, while a wooden staircase leads to the middle platform (20 stairs from the top) and the lower platform (137 stairs from the top). Near the parking area, there is a charcoal grill and a hand pump for water. However, it is important to note that visitors should carry out all trash with them, as there are no trash cans on-site. Pets are welcome but must be leashed at all times (with a 6-foot leash) and under the owner's immediate control. All pet waste should be properly disposed of later. The North Country Trail traverses the north end of the park, and a 1.9-mile spur trail connects to the park's main trail leading to the falls. This national scenic trail stretches from North Dakota to New York and encompasses over 1,500 miles in Michigan. Indian Lake State Park manages Laughing Whitefish Falls. During the winter, access to the park is limited to snowshoeing or ungroomed cross-country ski trails. The road leading to the park is seasonal and unplowed, with no available turn-around. Additionally, the dirt road leading to the park can become quite muddy at times. To reach Laughing Whitefish Falls, follow these directions: Turn onto Sundell Road (County Highway) from M-94 and continue north for 2 miles. Proceed straight for an additional quarter mile as the paved road transitions into an unpaved road. Then, turn right onto Laughing Whitefish Falls Road (indicated by park signage) and drive 0.4 miles to reach the parking area. From the parking area, a half-mile natural-surface trail leads to three observation platforms, each offering different perspectives of Laughing Whitefish Falls. The upper-level platform provides a view from above the falls and does not have stairs. A wooden staircase then leads to the middle-level platform (20 stairs from the top) and continues to the lower-level platform (137 stairs from the top). For those interested in backcountry trout fishing, there are hike-in opportunities downstream from the falls along the Laughing Whitefish River. Hunting is permitted in the state park, but it is advisable to contact the park directly for specific rules, concerns, or considerations.

DATE(S) VISITED .... ☐ SPRING ☐ SUMMER ☐ FALL ☐ WINTER

LODGING .... ☐ ☀ ☐ ☁ ☐ 🌧 ☐ 🌬 ☐ ❄

WHO I WENT WITH .... FEE(S) .... PARK HOURS .... TEMP:.........

WILL I RETURN? YES / NO   RATING ☆ ☆ ☆ ☆ ☆

PASSPORT STAMPS

LEELANAU STATE PARK

COUNTY	ESTABLISHED	AREA (AC/HA)
LEELANAU	1964	1,550 / 627

Leelanau State Park, located at the northern tip of Michigan's Leelanau Peninsula, offers visitors over 1,550 acres of natural beauty to explore. The park features the Grand Traverse Lighthouse Museum, a rustic campground, mini cabins, the Cathead Bay trail system, an interactive playground, and a picnic area. The park is divided into two sections located a few miles apart. The northern unit encompasses the day-use area, lighthouse, and rustic campground, while the southern unit hosts the park's trail system (Cathead Bay) and a sandy beach accessible via the Lake Michigan Trail. The iconic Grand Traverse Lighthouse, one of the oldest on the Great Lakes, is a prominent feature of the park. Visitors can tour the lighthouse to learn about its history and enjoy stunning views. The lighthouse is managed by the nonprofit Grand Traverse Lighthouse Museum and operates from April through October. It features a working fog signal horn used for demonstrations, a gift shop, and various exhibits. An observation platform is situated along the Lake Michigan Trail in the Cathead Bay trail system, offering panoramic views. On clear days, visitors may see the Fox Islands or witness the sunset over North Manitou Island from this vantage point. The park's picnic area, located in the day-use section, provides picnic tables and charcoal grills on a first-come, first-serve basis. Additionally, there is a picnic shelter with picnic tables, charcoal grills, electrical hookups (for reservations only), and vault toilets. This shelter can be reserved up to one year in advance via MIDNRReservations.com. An accessible interactive playground with features like slides, a log balance beam, a crow's nest, trapeze rings, and more is located in the day-use area. It is installed on a rubberized surface, making it easily accessible for individuals with varying mobility levels. Leelanau State Park allows hunting in some areas, but specific regulations, concerns, or considerations should be addressed by contacting the park directly. The park permits pets along the Lake Michigan shoreline near the lighthouse and campground. However, pets are not allowed along the shoreline in Cathead Bay due to piping plover habitat. There are also two pet-friendly mini cabins available. Pets must be on a leash that is six feet or shorter and under the immediate control of the owner. All pet waste should be disposed of in provided trash receptacles. Leelanau State Park's rustic campground is located at the very tip of the Leelanau Peninsula. This unique campground offers a cool atmosphere with a rocky beach and rustic campsites. Approximately half of the campsites are located along the waterfront, while the others are nestled in the woods, providing more privacy and lake views. The campground offers access to drinking water and a location to fill trailers with potable water. However, it does not have electricity, modern restrooms, or showers. The campground also includes three mini cabins with covered porches: White Pine Cabin, Cedar Cabin, and Hemlock Cabin. Each cabin accommodates up to five people and features two sets of bunk beds (one double bed and three single beds). Additionally, the cabins are equipped with a mini refrigerator, microwave, electric wall heater, Adirondack chairs, a picnic table, a fire pit, and a waist-high cook grill. These cabins have electricity but require visitors to bring their own linens. Both Hemlock and Cedar cabins are pet-friendly. They permit up to two pets (limited to cats and dogs only). An accessible ramp is available for the Evergreen Mini Cabin. A gravel-packed trail leads to the vault toilet. Leelanau State Park's trail system, also known as Cathead Bay trails, is located four miles south of the lighthouse, rustic campground, and day-use area, on separate parkland at the end of Densmore Road, situated off Lighthouse Point Road just north of Woolsey Airport. These scenic trails guide visitors through rolling hills and mature hardwoods, leading to a beautiful sandy beach at Cathead Bay. The trail system includes the following trails: Lake Michigan Trail (blue markers): This 2.2-mile loop is the park's most popular hike. It takes visitors through hardwood forests and provides access to the Manitou Overlook observation platform and the sandy beach at Cathead Bay through two different trail spurs. Mud Lake Trail (orange markers): A 3-mile looped trail, the Mud Lake Trail offers a hilly trek through the peninsula's interior, running alongside the west side of Mud Lake. Two trail spurs are available to adjust the trail's length: the Maple Ridge Cutoff (0.2 miles) and the Tamarack Cutoff (0.5 miles). The first half-mile of the trail features accessible trail elements, including a hard-packed surface and a rope system. Winter Recreation Trail (open Dec. 1-April 1 only): This 5.3-mile trail begins at the trailhead, following the Mud Lake Trail until it reaches the marked Winter Recreation Trail. The route traverses old logging roads and is open to fat-tire bikers, hikers, cross-country skiers, and snowshoers. Fat-tire bikes are only allowed if they have tires measuring 3.7 inches or larger, and there is at least 6 inches of snow. No mountain bikes are permitted. This trail is open and signed from December 1 to April 1.

DATE(S) VISITED .... ☐ SPRING ☐ SUMMER ☐ FALL ☐ WINTER

LODGING .... ☐ ☀ ☐ ☁ ☐ 🌧 ☐ ⛅ ☐ ❄

WHO I WENT WITH .... FEE(S) .... PARK HOURS .... TEMP:.........

WILL I RETURN? YES / NO   RATING ☆ ☆ ☆ ☆ ☆

PASSPORT STAMPS

LUDINGTON STATE PARK

COUNTY	ESTABLISHED	AREA (AC/HA)
MASON	1927	5,300 / 2,100

Ludington State Park, situated between the expansive 5,000-acre Hamlin Lake and 7 miles of pristine Lake Michigan shoreline, offers a diverse range of attractions. The park is graced with scenic sand dunes, three campgrounds, the iconic Big Sable Point Lighthouse, 21 miles of marked trails, and more. The Big Sable River, stretching one mile through the park, provides fantastic opportunities for fishing, paddling, and tubing. The park is a sanctuary for outdoor enthusiasts, featuring sandy beaches, picturesque sand dunes, a historic lighthouse, wetlands, marshlands, and lush forests. Please note that the primary park entrance is at the end of M-116, rather than along Piney Ridge Road, which cannot accommodate large vehicles. The iconic Big Sable Point Lighthouse is accessible by foot or bicycle (though the pathway may be challenging for road bikes) via a 1.8-mile sand-and-gravel trail. This historic lighthouse, constructed in 1867, is open for tours from May through October. It is managed by the Sable Points Lighthouse Keepers Association and features a gift shop and an entrance fee for tower access. Ludington State Park offers 7 miles of sandy Lake Michigan shoreline and 4 miles of shoreline along Hamlin Lake. Visitors should pay attention to the beach flag warning system in designated swim areas; red flags indicate unsafe water conditions, and swimming is prohibited. Swimming near the Big Sable river mouth is prohibited, and conditions should be monitored for changes. Designated swim areas can be found in the Lake Michigan and Hamlin Lake day-use areas. The Lake Michigan day-use area features an accessible walkway to the water and provides beach wheelchairs for visitors. The Hamlin Lake day-use area also offers a beach wheelchair for use. Dune Grass Concessions offers watercraft rentals (kayaks, canoes, and stand-up paddleboards) at Hamlin Lake from mid-May through early October. For more information, call 231-843-1888. Additionally, there is a boating access site on Hamlin Lake with parking for vehicles and boat trailers. This site includes a double-lane boat ramp with a skid pier for trailered boats. An accessible canoe and kayak launch is available on Hamlin Lake, situated about 50 feet from the drop-off site, with designated ADA parking spots. There are racks where visitors can temporarily leave their boats and gear while moving their vehicles to the parking spots. Hamlin Lake and Lake Michigan offer popular paddling opportunities. The protected coves of Lost Lake are perfect for beginners. For more adventurous paddlers, the park offers a unique 4-mile paddling trail through Hamlin Lake and its surrounding marshlands, providing access to areas of the park that are difficult to reach on foot. Paddlers can utilize the park's accessible canoe and kayak launch located north of the main boat launch to access Hamlin Lake. Hamlin Lake is a haven for boaters and anglers, offering abundant fishing opportunities, including northern pike, perch, largemouth and smallmouth bass, walleye, tiger muskie, and panfish. In the spring and fall, salmon, lake trout, steelhead, and brown trout can be found along the Lake Michigan shoreline and in the Big Sable River below the Hamlin Dam. Special fishing regulations apply to the Big Sable River from August 1 to November 1. In this section, terminal fishing gear is restricted to single-pointed hooks or jigs measuring 0.5 inches or less from point to shank, or treble hooks measuring 3/8 inch or less from point to shank. These hooks are only allowed when attached to a body bait, plug, spinner, or spoon. An artificial lure is not primarily constructed of lead. A small fishing pier is located on Hamlin Lake, just upstream from the Hamlin Dam. The historic Lake Michigan beach house, situated in the day-use area, offers interpretive exhibits and programming. It also houses concessions offering food, ice cream, beach equipment, and restroom facilities. The Hamlin Lake beach house features restrooms, changing facilities, a food concession, and rentals for kayaks, canoes, and stand-up paddleboards. Bicycles are permitted on the paved path connecting the campgrounds, the amphitheater, and the Lake Michigan and Hamlin Lake day-use areas, which runs along the Big Sable River. Bicycles are also allowed on the 1.8-mile sand-and-gravel pathway leading to the lighthouse, although it may be challenging for road bikes. Dune Grass Concessions offers bicycle rentals at the concession store located at the front of the Cedar campground, where you can also find firewood, ice, grocery items, and souvenirs. For more information, call 231-843-1888. The park provides an outdoor amphitheater for rent, suitable for open-air weddings and other events. The rental fee covers reserved parking, exclusive use of the amphitheater facility, and electrical service. The venue offers access to the beach and other scenic areas for photo opportunities. For details and reservations, call 231-843-2423. Please refrain from parking and blocking the gateway entrance to the sand-and-gravel pathway leading to the lighthouse. Parking is available near the warming shelter just north of the park entrance. Directions: Follow the signs to the Pines Campground, and then follow the lighthouse symbols painted on the road, guiding you to the sand-and-gravel pathway situated between campsites 58 and 59. Continue along the pathway for the remaining 1.5 miles (one way) to the lighthouse. Visitors can return along the same route or walk the shoreline back to the Lake Michigan day-use area, though high water levels may complicate this return route. Professional interpretive naturalists host weekly nature-based programming centered around the Great Lakes Visitor Center, which also features interpretive displays. An elevated boardwalk along the Skyline Trail offers views of the dunes. Along the trail, specially adapted EnChroma-enabled viewers provide people with color vision deficiencies the ability to appreciate the full spectrum of colors, courtesy of the Friends of the Ludington State Park. Picnic areas, complete with picnic tables and charcoal grills, can be found at the Hamlin Lake day-use area and along the Big Sable River (across from the Cedar Campground). A picnic shelter is available for reservation in the Hamlin Lake day-use area, or it can be used on a first-come, first-served basis if not previously reserved. This shelter can be reserved up to a year in advance by calling 1-800-447-2757 or visiting MiDNRReservations.com. An accessible playground, located in the Hamlin Lake day-use area, offers slides, climbers, and other interactive features. It is set on a rubberized surface to enhance accessibility for individuals with diverse mobility levels. A second playground is located adjacent to the Cedar Campground. Hunting is allowed within the state park, but visitors should contact the park directly to inquire about specific regulations, concerns, or considerations. The areas open and closed to hunting are clearly marked; refer to the park map for approximate hunting locations. The majority of the park's Lake Michigan shoreline is off-limits to pets in order to protect endangered piping plover habitat. However, a pet-friendly beach on Lake Michigan, located between the beach house and the Big Sable River, allows pets. Keep pets on a leash no longer than six feet and under the owner's immediate control at all times. All pet waste should be properly disposed of in designated trash receptacles. Beechwood Campground is a modern camping facility within the park, divided into three separate loops: the back (north) loop, the middle loop, and the front (south) loop. The campsites are generously sized and offer ample shade from large trees. This campground is located on the park's east side, in close proximity to Hamlin Lake. Each campsite provides 20/30 amp electrical service, with some sites in the front (south) loop offering 50-amp service. There is also a nearby sanitation station for campers' convenience. Recycling facilities are available at the Cedar Campground. Each loop provides access to a park trail, including the highly popular Lost Lake-Island Trail loop. Cedar Campground is divided into two loops, the east and west loops. The campsites are spacious, open, and receive plenty of sunlight. In total, there are 106 sites, including eight tent-only sites (without electrical hookups) situated in the west loop of the campground. Each site offers 20/30-amp electrical service, and there is a nearby sanitation station. Recycling facilities are also available within the campground. Pines Campground, another modern campground, is divided into two loops: the back (north) loop and the front (south) loop. The majority of the campsites are relatively small in size and heavily shaded. This campground is located on the park's west side, close to Lake Michigan. Campers can enjoy 20/30-amp electrical service at each site, with some sites equipped with 50-amp service. Additionally, there is a sanitation station nearby, and recycling facilities can be found at the Cedar Campground. The popular Logging Trail starts at the north end of the Pines

Campground and provides an excellent hiking opportunity. The campground serves as a starting point for the 1.8-mile-long (one way) sand-and-gravel pathway leading to the iconic Big Sable Point Lighthouse. The pathway offers limited shade and is considered moderately challenging, especially during hot weather. It is accessible on foot or by bike (although it may be more difficult for road bikes). Rustic, walk-in tent sites (Jack Pine) consist of 10 sites that require a hike of approximately 1 mile from the designated parking area along the 1.8-mile-long, sand-and-gravel pathway leading to the lighthouse. These unique sites are nestled among the dunes and jack pines, with Lake Michigan just steps away. Each site is equipped with vault toilets nearby and a hand pump for water, along with fire rings and picnic tables. Campers can arrange for Dune Grass Concessions to deliver firewood to the sites in the evenings by calling 231-843-1888. Cutting wood from trees is not allowed. Modern restroom and shower facilities at the Pines Campground are available for campers' use. There is a designated parking area for Jack Pine campers located behind the park headquarters. The park features three mini cabins, each situated in Beechwood, Pines, and Cedar campgrounds. Every cabin accommodates up to five people, with one double bed and three single beds. They include a mini refrigerator, electric wall heater, a table, and chairs. Outdoors, campers can enjoy a picnic table, a fire pit, and a waist-high cook grill. The cabins provide electricity, but guests should bring their own linens and cookware. Canoe Trail: This excursion commences at the Hamlin Lake Concessions and traces the shoreline of Hamlin Lake, encircling Desperation Point. Keep an eye out for signs along the route that will guide you into areas of the park inaccessible by foot. Coast Guard Trail (1.5 miles): Starting at Beechwood Campground, this trail leads hikers to a picturesque vantage point overlooking Lake Michigan. Along the way, you'll traverse wooded dunes and marshes, with glimpses of some of the park's larger trees and dunes. The trail connects to the park's three other campgrounds and is frequently traveled. Most of the trails intersect with other park trails, allowing visitors to create longer or looped routes with ease. Island Trail (approximately 2 miles): This trail meanders along the shores of Lost and Hamlin lakes, showcasing the beautiful marshes and wetlands bordering the lakes. Hikers can relish views of the vast open sand dunes to the north and cross various foot bridges and small islands. Many visitors combine this trail with the Lost Lake or Ridge trails to form looped routes. Lighthouse Trail (3 miles): Spanning 3 miles through the park, this trail leads to the Big Sable Point Lighthouse. You'll traverse rolling terrain through open and wooded dunes, enjoying picturesque views of the lighthouse. Hikers can even stop to tour or climb the lighthouse tower. The trail commences north of Beechwood Campground on the Lost Lake Trail and is considered moderately challenging. Most trails intersect with the park's other trails, facilitating the creation of longer or looped routes. Logging Trail (4 miles, out-and-back): This trail follows an old logging road for 4 miles, passing through wooded secondary dunes, mature forests, and wetlands. It begins at the north end of the Pines Campground and passes by two historic Civilian Conservation Corps buildings. Like other park trails, it offers opportunities for longer or looped routes. Lost Lake Trail (1.5 miles): This trail extends 1.5 miles along Lost Lake, leading hikers through woods and sand dunes to a scenic overlook of the lake. It includes an extensive boardwalk over the lake near Beechwood Campground. The trailhead is located at the north end of the Hamlin Lake day-use area, and it intersects with other park trails for extended or looped hikes. Ridge Trail (2.7 miles): The Ridge Trail follows the top of a series of wooded sand dunes for over a mile. The trailhead is situated along the bike path between the park headquarters and the Cedar Campground. Many visitors combine this trail with the Island Trail to form a looped route, and it is considered moderately challenging. Sable River Trail (approximately 1.5 miles): A paved trail that stretches around 1.5 miles, offering a leisurely stroll along the dam and river. Along the way, interpretive panels narrate the history of the village of Hamlin and the area's logging heritage. This area is a prime location for salmon fishing in the fall and steelhead fishing in the spring. The trail intersects with other park trails for added hiking options. Skyline Trail (0.5 miles): An elevated boardwalk trail that follows a wooded ridge, providing breathtaking views over the open dunes in the park's southern section. The hike offers panoramic vistas of Lake Michigan, the mouth of the Big Sable River, and, on clear days, the sand dunes at Silver Lake State Park. Stairs are part of the route, and the trail connects with other park trails for extended or looped hikes.

DATE(S) VISITED .... ☐ SPRING   ☐ SUMMER   ☐ FALL   ☐ WINTER

LODGING .... ☐ ☀ ☐ ☁ ☐ 🌦 ☐ 🌧 ☐ ❄

WHO I WENT WITH .... FEE(S) .... PARK HOURS .... TEMP:.........

WILL I RETURN? YES / NO   RATING ☆ ☆ ☆ ☆ ☆

PASSPORT STAMPS

MACKINAC ISLAND AND FORT MACKINAC HISTORIC PARK

COUNTY	ESTABLISHED	AREA (AC/HA)
MACKINAC	1895	1,800 / 730

This 1,800-acre island situated in Lake Michigan provides a window into life during the late 1700s and early 1800s. Visitors, including bikers, walkers, and equestrians, can explore the island's natural and historical features without the presence of motor vehicles. Fort Mackinac, constructed in 1780, stands as Michigan's sole fort from the revolutionary war era, offering a unique historical experience. The picnic area is equipped with fire pits and grills for visitors to enjoy. Within Fort Mackinac, the atmosphere is brought to life with cannon blasts, rifle fire, and marching soldiers. It serves as the oldest building in Michigan, alongside 13 other historical structures. These buildings house exhibits that cover various aspects of military training, battles, medical practices, and family life within the fort. Beyond its military function, Fort Mackinac also served as a residence for soldiers and their families. Eventually, it became the headquarters for Mackinac National Park, attracting tourists to the island who visited the grand fortress on the bluff, much as they do today. The Old Mackinac Point Lighthouse, in operation since 1889, has been a critical point for ships navigating the perilous waters of the Straits of Mackinac. The lighthouse offers impressive views from its tower and features authentically restored living quarters and exhibits. Among these exhibits, visitors can view the original lens and an audiovisual program titled "Shipwrecks of the Straits," making this structure, often referred to as the "Castle of the Straits," a valuable gem of the Great Lakes. The Richard and Jane Manoogian Mackinac Art Museum, boasting one of the most diverse art collections in the region, provides an array of beauty and history. Its collection includes hand-beaded Native American garments, 17th and 18th-century maps of the Great Lakes, and unique pieces from the Victorian era of Mackinac Island. Original photographs from the mid-19th to the mid-20th century capture the island's beauty through the lens of the camera. The museum showcases the works of William H. Gardiner, including numerous hand-tinted views from the early 20th century.

PASSPORT STAMPS

MAYBURY STATE PARK

COUNTY	ESTABLISHED	AREA (AC/HA)
WAYNE	1971	944 / 382

Maybury State Park, a bustling day-use park, provides a 1,000-acre sanctuary of lush, verdant forest amidst urban development. This park features gently rolling terrain, open meadows, mature forests, and offers various outdoor recreational activities. These include an extensive trail system for activities like hiking, biking, horseback riding, and cross-country skiing. Additionally, the park accommodates youth organizational camping, fishing, educational programs, and even houses a working farm. The state acquired the land in 1971, taking it over from the City of Detroit after the closure of the Maybury Sanatorium, which formerly occupied the area. The park boasts historical significance, featuring the former Maybury Sanitorium. The Friends of Maybury State Park offer an annual history hike, shedding light on this historical aspect. Picnic areas are scattered throughout the park's open spaces and offer some charcoal grills on a first-come, first-served basis. These picnic spots can be found near parking areas and along the extensive trail system. Four picnic shelters (Hickory, Maple, Oak, and Walnut shelters) are available for rent and can be accessed from the Eight Mile Road park entrance parking areas. Reservations for these shelters can be made up to 12 months in advance at MIDNRReservations.com. The park features an inclusive playground near the trailhead building, made possible through various community donations. Seasonal modern restrooms can be found at the trailhead building and next to the Oak Shelter, both located near the Eight Mile Road park entrance parking areas. Additionally, nine vault toilets are situated throughout the park, open year-round. An 8-acre spring-fed fishing pond, located a short walk from the Beck Road park entrance parking area, offers a typical bass and bluegill fish community. It also features a fishing pier. The park encourages snowshoeing on the wooded hiking trails during the winter months, and snowshoers should be cautious when sharing multi-use trails with bikers and cross-country skiers and should avoid groomed ski tracks. The park's regulations prohibit the possession or consumption of alcoholic beverages at any time unless written authorization is granted by the park manager through an event permit. Maybury State Park offers a group-use campground for youth or scout group gatherings, accommodating up to 75 people. It's situated in the northwest part of the park and is accessible with permission through a seasonal road off Napier Road. Facilities are rustic, including a vault toilet and a potable well hand pump. Reservations can be made by calling the park office at 248-349-8390. For horse enthusiasts, the park provides 8 miles of looped horseback riding trails that are open year-round. These trails traverse gently rolling terrain, open meadows, mature forests, and offer a chance to experience abundant wildlife and wildflowers. Horses are only allowed on marked trails, which are indicated in red on the trail map and guide and marked with red confidence markers along the trail. Hunting is not permitted within the park. Riders can transport their horses to a staging area off the Beck Road park entrance, south of Eight Mile Road. This staging area includes various amenities, like a pavilion, vault toilets, picnic tables, picket posts, and a community fire ring. Mounting blocks and hitch posts are also available along the trail, but overnight camping is not allowed. Maybury State Park features 6 miles of hiking trails dedicated to hiking, marked in green on the trail map and guide. Parts of the trail are indicated as an interpretive and history trail. The hiking trail consists of interconnecting loops that lead from the parking areas through the wooded park interior and the grassland area northeast of the ballfield, extending to the pond. In the spring, the area is adorned with trilliums. Hikers can access the trail from the parking areas at either the Eight Mile Road or Beck Road park entrances. A portion of the hiking trail is track-set groomed for cross-country skiing in winter, allowing snowshoeing when conditions are suitable. The park's mountain biking trail encompasses 7 miles of forested, single-track trails that are open to mountain biking throughout the year. The mountain biking trail is shown in yellow on the Maybury trail map and guide and is marked with yellow confidence markers along the trail. While primarily used by mountain bikers, this trail presents a challenging terrain, including steep climbs, rocky and root obstacles, and engineered features. The trail is well maintained and is considered suitable for intermediate riders. Hiking is also allowed on this trail, with hikers advised to walk in the opposite direction of bikers for safety reasons. Access to the mountain biking trail is via the mixed-use paved trail, which is shared by hikers, bikers, and other users. Parking is available in the parking areas at the Eight Mile Road park entrance. The park's 4-mile paved trail, indicated in blue on the Maybury trail map and guide, caters to bicyclists. However, it is also popular for other recreational activities like hiking, rollerblading, and skate skiing. This accessible, multi-use trail can be accessed from the Eight Mile Road park entrance.

DATE(S) VISITED ....   ☐ SPRING   ☐ SUMMER   ☐ FALL   ☐ WINTER

LODGING ....   ☐ ☀   ☐ ☁   ☐ 🌧   ☐ ⛅   ☐ ❄

WHO I WENT WITH ....   FEE(S) .... PARK HOURS .... TEMP:.........

WILL I RETURN? YES / NO   RATING ☆ ☆ ☆ ☆ ☆

PASSPORT STAMPS

MCLAIN STATE PARK

COUNTY	ESTABLISHED	AREA (AC/HA)
HOUGHTON	1930	443 / 179

McLain State Park is positioned at the center of the Keweenaw Peninsula, nestled on the picturesque shores of Lake Superior. It conveniently sits between the cities of Calumet and Hancock. The park boasts a stunning two-mile stretch of sandy beach along Lake Superior, creating a perfect spot for a variety of outdoor activities. Visitors can partake in fishing, windsurfing, berry picking, beachcombing, rock collecting, sightseeing, and hunting. The park is renowned for its breathtaking sunsets, and the view of the lighthouse is truly magnificent. The park's strategic location between Calumet and Hancock serves as an excellent base for visitors to explore the region's attractions, including abandoned shafthouses, tram cars, "poor rock" piles, and ghost towns. Those who venture into the Keweenaw area are encouraged to discover the newly established "Keweenaw National Historic Park," which has preserved remnants from the era when "Copper was King!" Near the park, you can find the Keweenaw Waterway Lighthouse, a notable attraction in the area. Seasonal naturalists offer weekly nature-based programs from Memorial Day through Labor Day. The park's store stocks a wide range of campground supplies and groceries. Visitors can also shop for local crafts and souvenirs. For a delightful treat, you can savor one of their handcrafted waffle ice cream cones, available every day of the week during the camping season. Additionally, the park provides firewood and ice for your convenience. The park offers groomed trails for cross-country skiing, making it an ideal winter activity. Snowshoeing is also popular among visitors at McLain State Park. If you're into horseshoes, you'll find horseshoe pits at both picnic areas within the park. The park offers fire pits and grills for cooking at the picnic areas. Two of the park's picnic shelters are equipped with fireplaces, while all three have large grills available for your cooking needs. You can reserve these shelters up to a year in advance by calling 1-800-447-2757 or visiting www.midnrreservations.com. Moreover, there are two playgrounds for children to enjoy. A portion of the shoreline along Lake Superior at F.J. McLain State Park is designated as pet-friendly. However, there are rules in place: pets must be leashed with a six-foot lead and remain under the owner's direct control at all times. Proper disposal of pet waste in trash receptacles is mandatory. The modern campground at the park provides 117 campsites for visitors to enjoy. For those who seek a more rustic experience, there's a camper cabin available at the park. This cabin accommodates up to 8 people and features propane gas heating and a cook stove. It offers a picturesque view of the lake with screened windows and doors. Outside, there's a fire pit equipped with a grill. F.J. McLain State Park is renowned for its 4-mile hiking and cross-country ski trail, a draw for hikers and skiers alike. The trail provides stunning views of ice formations along Lake Superior during the winter months. The terrain varies from flat, open spaces to wooded hills, offering scenic vistas of Lake Superior. This trail is open year-round for hiking and cross-country skiing, weather permitting.

DATE(S) VISITED .... ☐ SPRING ☐ SUMMER ☐ FALL ☐ WINTER

LODGING .... ☐ ☀ ☐ ☁ ☐ 🌧 ☐ 🌫 ☐ ❄

WHO I WENT WITH .... FEE(S) .... PARK HOURS .... TEMP:.........

WILL I RETURN? YES / NO   RATING ☆ ☆ ☆ ☆ ☆

PASSPORT STAMPS

MEARS STATE PARK

COUNTY	ESTABLISHED	AREA (AC/HA)
OCEANA	1923	50 / 20

Mears State Park, located on the sandy shores of Lake Michigan, offers a designated swimming beach, a fishing pier, a modern campground, an overnight lodge, and a quarter-mile interpretive trail. The park is famous for its breathtaking sunsets. Covering 50 acres, this state park is situated on the northern side of the channel that connects Lake Michigan and Pentwater Lake, just a short walk from the charming and relaxed beach town of Pentwater. This town boasts a diverse array of shops, restaurants, and a Village Green. On beautiful summer days, it's advisable to arrive early as the parking lot can fill up in the afternoon. It's important to note that there is no lighthouse within the park, nor is one visible from it. The land that the park now occupies was once owned by Charles Mears, one of the early settlers of Pentwater. In 1923, Carrie Mears, the daughter of Charles Mears, generously donated the land to the State of Michigan. Visitors can enjoy a quarter-mile stretch of sandy shoreline along Lake Michigan. Safety flags along the beach indicate swimming conditions; red flags warn of unsafe waters, advising against swimming or entering. It is important to avoid swimming near or jumping off break walls or navigational channel walls and to stay alert to changing conditions. There is a designated swim beach on the Lake Michigan side, and two accessible walkways lead to the water. A beach wheelchair is available for borrowing on a first-come, first-served basis. The park's beach house in the day-use area provides restrooms, changing facilities, a park store offering food, concessions, firewood, ice, and more, as well as stand-up paddleboard rentals. Fishing enthusiasts can make use of the accessible pier located at the park's south end. For nature enthusiasts, the park offers a popular, self-guided nature trail that spans a quarter-mile. Throughout the day-use area, near the Lake Michigan shoreline, you'll find picnic tables and charcoal grills available on a first-come, first-served basis. An accessible playground with slides, bars, and swings is located within the day-use area, complete with a rubberized surface that facilitates access for individuals of all mobility levels. Free WiFi is accessible throughout the modern campground. A pet-friendly beach can be found at the park's south end, allowing pets that are always on a 6-foot leash and under their owner's immediate control. Proper disposal of pet waste in trash receptacles is required. The park's modern campground is divided into two loops, known as the east and west loops. All sites feature a concrete pad and are surrounded by sand, providing a short walk to Lake Michigan and the laid-back beach town of Pentwater. The campground is conveniently located near the day-use area, which includes a designated swim beach, fishing pier, playground, and picnic tables. For those seeking a unique camping experience, an expandable hybrid camper is available, which accommodates up to six people. This camper offers two beds and a convertible bed that transforms from a table to a bed. It is equipped with air conditioning, a mini-fridge, microwave, and convection hot plate. While there is no running water, potable water is available at water spigots in the campground. The toilet and shower facility is just steps away from the camper. Guests are required to bring their own bedding, plates, cutlery, and cooking utensils. For larger groups, the Dune Grass Villa modern lodge is situated against the "Old Baldy" dune, behind the campground, and can sleep up to eight guests. The lodge features two sets of bunk beds, a queen-sized bed, and a full-sized bed, in addition to a modern kitchen, two bathrooms with showers, and a family room. The kitchen is fully equipped with a stove, microwave, toaster, refrigerator, pots, pans, and dinnerware. The lodge includes linens (bedding and towels), a washer and dryer, a television, a DVD player, games, and a collection of books. Outdoors, guests will find a picnic table, lawn chairs, grills, and a fire ring. The lively beach town of Pentwater is just a short walk away. It's important to note that a daily cleaning service is not provided, and guests are expected to clean and leave the building ready for the next guests, including washing linens. The park also features the quarter-mile Old Baldy Interpretive Trail, which starts at a set of stairs and winds to the top of Old Baldy, a famous sand-blown dune. It offers an excellent view of Lake Michigan, Pentwater, and the harbor.

DATE(S) VISITED .... ☐ SPRING ☐ SUMMER ☐ FALL ☐ WINTER

LODGING .... ☐ ☀ ☐ ☁ ☐ 🌧 ☐ ⛅ ☐ ❄

WHO I WENT WITH .... FEE(S) .... PARK HOURS .... TEMP:.........

WILL I RETURN? YES / NO   RATING ☆ ☆ ☆ ☆ ☆

PASSPORT STAMPS

MERIDIAN-BASELINE STATE PARK

COUNTY	ESTABLISHED	AREA (AC/HA)
INGHAM, JACKSON	1967	188 / 76

This distinctive and picturesque park is preserved for its historical significance, as it marks the point from which all township, range, and section measurements originate for the entire state. All property descriptions are based on references from these specific points. Within the park, there is a 1.4-mile trail, which is an out-and-back route. Along this trail, visitors can observe two monuments or markers that serve as the foundation for all land surveys conducted in Michigan and certain parts of Ohio. The north-south principal meridian of Michigan was established during the summer of 1815 by a surveyor named Benjamin Hough. The western boundary of the 1807 Treaty of Detroit was chosen as the line for Michigan's principal meridian. Starting from the existing baseline running westward from Youngstown through Defiance, Ohio, Hough extended this line directly north into southern Michigan. Surveying efforts to create Michigan's bisecting baseline commenced in 1824. The eastern baseline was originally intended to be, and indeed is, located 8 miles north of downtown Detroit. However, due to a misinterpretation of instructions in the survey contract by a deputy surveyor, Michigan ended up with a 935.88-foot offset in the east-west baseline. This unique feature sets Michigan apart as the only state in the United States with such an anomaly.

DATE(S) VISITED .... □ SPRING   □ SUMMER   □ FALL   □ WINTER

LODGING ....

WHO I WENT WITH .... FEE(S) .... PARK HOURS .... TEMP:.........

WILL I RETURN? YES / NO   RATING ☆ ☆ ☆ ☆ ☆

PASSPORT STAMPS

MITCHELL STATE PARK

COUNTY	ESTABLISHED	AREA (AC/HA)
WEXFORD	1919	660 / 267

William Mitchell State Park is a well-liked destination for camping, fishing, and boating. Spanning 660 acres, this park is nestled between Lake Mitchell and Lake Cadillac, offering fantastic opportunities to observe diverse wildlife. These two lakes are connected by the quarter-mile Clam Lake Canal. On the eastern side of Lake Cadillac, you can access the Fred Meijer White Pine Trail State Park, which is linked through a network of trails, sidewalks, and road shoulders along the Lake Cadillac shoreline. Within the park, the Carl T. Johnson Hunting and Fishing Center features informative exhibits about Michigan's hunting and fishing history. This center also provides archery and pellet gun ranges, schedules shooting programs during the summer, and offers group tours and guided hikes. For swimmers, there is a designated swim area at Lake Mitchell. Kayak and stand-up paddleboard rentals are offered at the campground contact station by the Friends of Mitchell State Park, with all proceeds benefiting park projects and programs. Both Lake Cadillac and Lake Mitchell are popular fishing spots, and anglers can expect to reel in perch, walleye, northern pike, panfish, and bass. Shore fishing is a common activity at Clam Lake Canal, which links the two lakes. The beach house, located in the Lake Mitchell day-use area, is equipped with restrooms, changing facilities, and a reservable picnic shelter. Paddling is a favorite pastime on Lake Cadillac, Lake Mitchell, and the quarter-mile Clam Lake Canal. A paved trail encircles Lake Cadillac and offers a connection to the Fred Meijer White Pine Trail State Park near the lake's eastern section. The Lake Mitchell day-use area's picnic zone includes picnic tables and charcoal grills available on a first-come, first-served basis. Additionally, there is a picnic shelter in the beach house with picnic tables, charcoal grills, and electrical service (reservation required). While hunting is permitted within the state park, it's advisable to contact the park directly for information on specific rules, concerns, or considerations. Snowmobiles are allowed to operate between the campground and nearby snowmobile trails. With the exception of the designated swim beach, pets are permitted along the entire length of Lake Cadillac and Lake Mitchell, provided they are kept on a 6-foot leash and under the owner's immediate control. All pet waste should be properly disposed of in trash receptacles. The modern campground is located on the banks of the historic Clam Lake Canal and Lake Cadillac. It comprises several loops, a playground, and easy access to Lake Cadillac. The campground boasts numerous mature trees, and several campsites are positioned along the canal. In the modern campground, you'll find the Eagle mini cabin situated on the shores of Lake Cadillac, accommodating up to four people. The cabin features bunk beds, a mini fridge, a small kitchen counter, and two chairs. A deck overlooking the lake, a fire pit, and a picnic table are located outside. Electricity and electric heating are provided, and guests are required to bring their own linens and cookware. Potable water is available within the campground. The accessible Loon camper cabin is also located in the modern campground, right on the shore of Lake Cadillac. This cabin accommodates up to six people in two bedrooms with bunk beds and a pull-out futon in the main room. The cabin is equipped with electricity, electric heating, a mini fridge, a microwave, a small kitchen counter, a futon, a folding table, and chairs. Guests can enjoy a beautiful sunrise over the lake from the two-level deck just outside the front door or relax by the fire pit while listening to the waves lapping on the shore. Like the Eagle cabin, guests must provide their own linens and cookware, and potable water is accessible in the campground. The Heritage Nature Trail is a 2.5-mile looped trail that passes by a lookout tower, a fishing pier, and several boardwalks alongside Lake Cadillac. This trail commences at the Carl T. Johnson Hunting and Fishing Center.

DATE(S) VISITED .... ☐ SPRING ☐ SUMMER ☐ FALL ☐ WINTER

LODGING .... ☐ ☼ ☐ ☁ ☐ 🌧 ☐ 🌫 ☐ ❄

WHO I WENT WITH .... FEE(S) .... PARK HOURS .... TEMP:.........

WILL I RETURN? YES / NO   RATING ☆ ☆ ☆ ☆ ☆

PASSPORT STAMPS

MUSKALLONGE LAKE STATE PARK

COUNTY	ESTABLISHED	AREA (AC/HA)
LUCE	1956	217 / 88

Muskallonge Lake State Park is positioned 28 miles northwest of Newberry in Luce County. This 217-acre park is nestled between Lake Superior and Muskallonge Lake and is renowned for its rich forests, lakes, and streams. Historically, it was the location of Deer Park, a lumbering town in the late 1880s and, before that, an Indian encampment. Muskallonge Lake served as a mill pond for transporting millions of white pine logs brought in by railroad lines. However, by 1900, the virgin pine stands had been exhausted, the mill ceased operations, and the lumbering activities moved elsewhere. Today, the only remnants of this lumbering community are piles of sawdust and a few partially submerged pine logs in the lake. Additionally, the park once housed a Coast Guard Life Saving Station. In the vicinity of the park, there are approximately 70 lakes and five rivers within a 20-mile radius, making it a prime location for outdoor enthusiasts. Visitors can explore historic forts, the Father Marquette National Memorial and Museum, and take day trips to Tahquamenon Falls State Park, offering breathtaking landscapes that include Whitefish Point and multiple waterfalls. In Newberry, you can visit the Logging Museum or embark on a riverboat journey to the falls. To the west of Grand Marais lies the Pictured Rocks National Lakeshore, while southwest of the park, you'll find the Kingston Plains and the Seney National Wildlife Refuge. For those interested in duck and goose hunting, it's permitted on both lakes, although not within the park boundaries. Charter boat fishing is accessible at Grand Marais. The modern campground at Muskallonge Lake State Park provides 159 camp sites for visitors. Within the campground, there's a designated swimming beach, and a boat launch provides easy access to Muskallonge Lake. Anglers can try their luck at catching various fish species, including northern pike, muskallonge, smallmouth bass, walleye, and perch in Muskallonge Lake. Lake Superior is teeming with trout, salmon, and menominee, particularly near the river mouths. The park is traversed by the North Country Trail, with short feeder trails connecting the campground to this national scenic trail, which stretches from North Dakota to New York and covers over 1,500 miles in Michigan. While the park is closed during the winter season, many people still utilize the area for activities like cross-country skiing, snowshoeing, and snowmobiling. Muskallonge Lake is a favorite destination for ice fishermen. Throughout the summer season, seasonal naturalists offer weekly nature-based programs from Memorial Day through Labor Day. The day-use area is located on a small bay of Muskallonge Lake and features a pleasant picnic area. Rock collectors, especially those seeking agate, flock to the Lake Superior shoreline for rock picking.

DATE(S) VISITED .... ☐ SPRING ☐ SUMMER ☐ FALL ☐ WINTER

LODGING .... ☐ ☀ ☐ ☁ ☐ 🌧 ☐ 🌫 ☐ ❄

WHO I WENT WITH .... FEE(S) .... PARK HOURS .... TEMP:.........

WILL I RETURN? YES / NO   RATING ☆ ☆ ☆ ☆ ☆

PASSPORT STAMPS

MUSKEGON STATE PARK

COUNTY	ESTABLISHED	AREA (AC/HA)
MUSKEGON	1923	1,233 / 499

Muskegon State Park boasts a stunning 3 miles of shoreline, with 2 miles along Lake Michigan and an additional mile on Muskegon Lake. The park features Snug Harbor, forested dunes, two campgrounds, picnic areas, various trails, and more. One notable attraction is the blockhouse, originally constructed by the Civilian Conservation Corps (CCC) in the 1930s. This structure, situated at the highest point in Muskegon County, offers panoramic views in all directions. For year-round outdoor adventure, the Muskegon Luge Adventure Sports Park provides an array of activities, including an Olympian-designed luge track, an ice-skating trail, a sledding hill, cross-country ski trails, a 1,300-foot dual zip line, a unique summer luge track, an archery range, and more. Entry requires a ticket, and reservations are available. A designated swim area can be found in the day-use area on Lake Michigan, with an accessible walkway leading to the water, and a beach wheelchair is available for use. Visitors should be aware of the beach flag warning system for designated swim areas; red flags indicate unsafe water conditions, and swimming is not recommended. Additionally, a boat launch located in the Snug Harbor day-use area provides access to Muskegon Lake. The beach house, situated in the Lake Michigan day-use area, offers restroom facilities. Muskegon Lake, accessible via the navigation channel walkway, is home to a variety of fish species, and a fish-cleaning station is available in the Snug Harbor day-use area. An accessible fishing pier can be found in Snug Harbor, along with two popular fishing decks on the navigation channel walkway. Paddling is also a popular activity on Muskegon Lake. The Muskegon Luge Adventure Sports Park offers a range of amenities for visitors, including snacks, slushies, hammocks, frisbees, camping essentials, and merchandise. Cross-country skiing is a favorite winter activity at the Muskegon Luge Adventure Sports Park, which features an Olympian-designed luge track, although an additional fee is required. Seasonal naturalists provide weekly nature-based programs from Memorial Day through Labor Day. The park's blockhouse, built by the CCC in the 1930s, is a prominent feature that allows visitors to enjoy panoramic views in all directions, including those of Lake Michigan. The blockhouse is perched atop the highest point in Muskegon County. Day-use areas on Lake Michigan and in Snug Harbor offer picnic tables and grills. The picnic area in Snug Harbor is accessible. Snug Harbor has two picnic shelters equipped with picnic tables, charcoal grills, and electrical service (Pines Shelter location only). Shelter reservations can be made up to 12 months in advance at

MiDNRReservations.com. It's important to note that alcoholic beverages are prohibited in the park's day-use areas from April 1 through Labor Day, unless the park manager has granted written authorization through an event permit. Pets are permitted along the Lake Michigan shoreline outside the designated swimming area, with the exception of marked piping plover nest habitat. All pets must be on a 6-foot leash and under the immediate control of their owners, and pet waste must be properly disposed of in trash receptacles. Channel Campground: This campground is divided into two loops and is positioned near the navigation channel walkway. The first loop, consisting of sites #1-92, is situated adjacent to the navigation channel, while the second loop, offering sites #101-147, is located near the large dune and Muskegon Lake. The second loop features larger campsites. Lake Michigan Campground: The modern campground, also divided into two loops, is open for year-round camping. It is located on the opposite side of a significant dune from Lake Michigan. Access to Lake Michigan is available via a stairway. Most of the campsites in this area are surrounded by woodlands. Group Use Area Campground: This rustic group campground is intended for civic organizations and is conveniently located between the park's two modern campgrounds on Scenic Drive. There are eight sites that can accommodate groups of up to 130 people. Each site is equipped with a picnic table, fire pit, and easy access to a potable water faucet. A community shelter is also available. To reserve the group camp area, please call 231-744-3480. Two Mini Cabins in Lake Michigan Campground: These cabins are open year-round and offer accommodations for four people. Each cabin features two bunk beds, a mini fridge, microwave, high-top table, bar stools, heat, and lighting. Guests must provide their own linens and cooking equipment. The cabins are equipped with a fire ring for outdoor use, but no cooking equipment is provided. Yurt at Muskegon Luge Adventure Sports Park: The park's yurt is situated in the woods at the far eastern end of the Muskegon Luge Adventure Sports Park. This 20-foot-diameter yurt can accommodate up to seven people and includes two log bunk beds and stacking cots. The yurt is furnished with a table, chairs, a solar lantern, and a woodstove for heating (firewood is provided). While there is a modern toilet and shower building available at the Lake Michigan Campground across the road during the warmer months, there is no electricity or running water provided. Guests must bring their own linens and cooking equipment. A fire ring is located outside the yurt, but no cooking equipment is included. Devil's Kitchen Trail: This 1-mile trail traces the shoreline of Muskegon Lake and derives its unique name from the fog that resembles smoke under specific atmospheric conditions. The trail offers views of wildflowers, marshlands, and a scenic vantage point of Muskegon Lake from the dune ridge. It connects Snug Harbor with the Channel Campground boat launch, with the trailhead located in the Snug Harbor day-use area parking lot. Dune

Ridge Trail: This 1.75-mile hike is designed for more experienced hikers, featuring several steep climbs. The trail passes through open and wooded dunes and provides views of Muskegon Lake, Lake Michigan, and the channel, including glimpses of lighthouses. It connects to the Channel Campground and can be extended via the Hearty Hiker Trail. The trailhead can be found in the Snug Harbor day-use area parking lot or the channel walkway. Hearty Hiker Trail: Comprising numerous hills with diverse terrain, this trail passes tree-covered dunes, wild blueberries, and the Group-Use Area Campground. It also offers connections to the Scenic Ridge Trail and the Dune Ridge Trail for those looking to extend their hike. The trailhead is located in the Snug Harbor day-use area parking lot. Loop to Loop Trail: This relatively flat trail, with a few steeper hills, provides an easier hiking experience. The trailhead is situated in the north parking lot of the blockhouse off Scenic Drive. Lost Lake Trail: This trail winds through a lowland area to Lost Lake, known for its rich variety of wildflowers and native plants. It also connects to two other park trails, the Loop to Loop Trail and the Scenic Ridge Trail for those interested in longer hikes. Along the trail, there is a small observation platform resembling an eagle's nest. The trailhead can be found in the north parking lot of Snug Harbor. Scenic Ridge Trail: Featuring various elevation changes along the dune ridges, this trail offers scenic vistas of the city of Muskegon and includes an open area on the dune ridge known as a blowout, resulting from vegetation disturbance. For those looking to extend their journey, this trail connects to the Lost Lake Trail and the Hearty Hiker Trail. The trailhead is located in the north parking lot of the blockhouse.

DATE(S) VISITED .... ☐ SPRING ☐ SUMMER ☐ FALL ☐ WINTER

LODGING .... ☐ ☀ ☐ ☁ ☐ 🌧 ☐ ⛅ ☐ ☁

WHO I WENT WITH .... FEE(S) .... PARK HOURS .... TEMP:.........

WILL I RETURN? YES / NO RATING ☆ ☆ ☆ ☆ ☆

PASSPORT STAMPS

NEGWEGON STATE PARK

COUNTY	ESTABLISHED	AREA (AC/HA)
ALCONA, ALPENA	1962	4,000 / 1,618

Negwegon State Park is an unspoiled, rustic area that attracts birdwatchers, hikers, backcountry campers, hunters, and beach enthusiasts. Covering 4,000 acres, the park offers 7 miles of Lake Huron shoreline, which includes a beautiful sandy beach stretching for 1 mile. The park's landscape is a mix of lowland regions, small ridges, and pockets of open meadows, adorned with mature pine, hardwood, and aspen forests. This diverse environment is home to unique plant species and wildlife, such as bald eagles, Pitcher's thistle, and Blanding's turtles, among others. Negwegon State Park is also designated as a dark sky preserve, offering excellent opportunities for stargazing. The park receives generous support from the Friends of Negwegon, a non-profit volunteer group that collaborates with the Department of Natural Resources to conserve, safeguard, and promote the park through stewardship, education, and research. Paddlers can explore the Lake Huron shoreline, with carry-in access positioned about 200 feet from the campground's parking area. The park features four rustic hike-in campsites accessible to paddlers or very small, motorized boats capable of anchoring. Hunting is permitted within the state park, and specific rules and considerations can be inquired about by contacting the park directly. Most of the Lake Huron shoreline welcomes pets, provided they are kept on a 6-foot leash and under immediate control by their owners. It's essential to dispose of all pet waste properly in the designated trash receptacles. The park offers four hike-in campsites available from April through November, located approximately 1.1 to 2.2 miles from the main parking lot along the Sand Hill Trail. Each campsite is equipped with a fire ring featuring a cooking grate, a picnic table, a bear pole (campers need to provide their rope), a bear box, and a backcountry composting privy. Potable water is available from a well situated between the parking lot and the beach. Reservations are required and can be made via phone by calling Harrisville State Park at 989-724-5126 or in person at the headquarters building of Harrisville State Park. Self-registration is not available. The park offers three distinct trails for hikers. Algonquin Trail (3.7 miles): This trail meanders along the Lake Huron coast and through the surrounding wilderness, featuring towering white birch trees and young firs. Access to the Chippewa Trail is available via the Algonquin Trail. The trailhead is located in the main parking lot. Chippewa Trail (3.1 miles): This trail guides hikers through hardwood forests of aspen, maple, and paper birch to the rocky South Point, providing scenic views of Lake Huron. The trail can be accessed along the Algonquin Trail or at the north end of the parking area. Potawatomi Trail (3.6 miles): This trail forms a loop along the Lake Huron coastline, offering access to the lakeshore. It traverses areas with towering white pine and cedar trees, allowing visitors to appreciate the sounds of Lake Huron amidst the forest and beach landscapes. The trail can be accessed at the southeast end of the parking area.

DATE(S) VISITED .... ☐ SPRING ☐ SUMMER ☐ FALL ☐ WINTER

LODGING .... ☐ ☀ ☐ ☁ ☐ 🌧 ☐ 🌬 ☐ ❄

WHO I WENT WITH .... FEE(S) .... PARK HOURS .... TEMP:........

WILL I RETURN? YES / NO RATING ☆ ☆ ☆ ☆ ☆

PASSPORT STAMPS

NEWAYGO STATE PARK

COUNTY	ESTABLISHED	AREA (AC/HA)
NEWAYGO	1966	257 / 104

Newaygo State Park is located atop 20-foot embankments, offering stunning views of the Hardy Dam Pond, a 6-mile stretch created by the flooding of the Muskegon River. The park comprises two rustic campgrounds, an 18-hole disc golf course, and a boating access site. It is adjacent to the Manistee National Forest, providing convenient access to trails, hunting opportunities, and various outdoor recreational activities. A 2-mile section of the Dragon Trail (segment 2), managed jointly by the Newaygo and Mecosta county park commissions, runs along the embankment, providing panoramic vistas of the Hardy Dam Pond. The boating access site parking lot is the primary entry point to this trail. Additionally, the Fred Meijer White Pine Trail State Park is just 7 miles east of Newaygo State Park, offering hiking and biking options, with a trailhead staging area in Morley. Visitors should be cautious of the endangered blue Karner butterfly habitat situated on the west side of the powerline and be mindful of their surroundings. The park is situated along the shores of the Hardy Dam Pond, featuring a designated swim area within the Poplar Rustic Campground, a short walk from the boating access site. Parking is available at the boating access site. Kayak rentals are accessible at the campground office from early June through mid-September, and for inquiries, you can call 231-856-4452. There's a boat launch located on Hardy Dam Pond between the two campgrounds, and a limited number of mooring spots are available for registered campers. While most anglers launch their boats from the park's boating access site, there's also a small shoreline section near the channel that's suitable for shore fishing. During the ice fishing season, ORVs and snowmobiles can access the lake, with parking available in the disc golf parking area and a few campsites plowed for additional parking. Paddling is a popular activity on Hardy Dam Pond. The park features a picnic shelter near the disc golf course, complete with picnic tables, charcoal grills, and electrical service for those who make reservations in advance. Shelter reservations can be made up to 12 months in advance at MiDNRReservations.com. Hunting is permitted within the state park, and visitors should reach out to the park directly for specific rules, concerns, or considerations. Poplar and Oak Rustic Campgrounds are well-known for their spacious, private sites and scenic beauty, with 20- to 30-foot wooded buffers between sites. Visitors can access drinking water and fill trailers with potable water at the park's sanitation station. However, there are no electrical hookups, modern restrooms, or showers in these campgrounds. Michigan's Dragon Trail, located along the Hardy Dam in Newaygo and Mecosta Counties, is a collaborative effort between the Newaygo and Mecosta county park commissions. It is a popular destination for mountain biking but is also open for various nonmotorized activities, including hiking, running, and dog sledding. A 2-mile segment (segment 2) traverses Newaygo State Park, offering scenic views of the Hardy Dam Pond. The boating access site parking lot is the most convenient access point in the park. The completed trail system will eventually span 47 miles, with segments open, partially complete, and planned for the future. Poplar Trail, a 2-mile loop trail commencing in the Poplar Campground, is relatively flat and suitable for all visitors, including families. It meanders through forested areas and provides vistas of the Hardy Dam Pond, intersecting with the Dragon Trail. The route is well-marked, and parking is available at the park's boating access site.

DATE(S) VISITED .... □ SPRING □ SUMMER □ FALL □ WINTER

LODGING .... □ ☼ □ ☁ □ 🌧 □ ☁ □ ❄

WHO I WENT WITH .... FEE(S) .... PARK HOURS .... TEMP:.........

WILL I RETURN? YES / NO   RATING ☆ ☆ ☆ ☆ ☆

PASSPORT STAMPS

NORTH HIGGINS LAKE STATE PARK

COUNTY	ESTABLISHED	AREA (AC/HA)
CRAWFORD	1965	449 / 181

North Higgins Lake State Park, situated on the northern shore of Higgins Lake, offers 449 acres of lakeside recreation within a natural wooded setting. The park's location was once home to one of the world's largest seedling nurseries and features a museum dedicated to preserving the history of the nursery, Michigan's forestry, and the Civilian Conservation Corps' contributions to Michigan during the Great Depression. Within a 15-minute drive in either direction, visitors can explore the charming Village of Roscommon and downtown Grayling. The Grayling Chamber of Commerce also provides information on local events. The park boasts two campgrounds, overnight lodging options, a boat launch, a popular swimming beach, a picnic area, and over 8 miles of trails situated adjacent to the CCC Museum. The campgrounds are open year-round. The Higgins Lake Nursery and CCC Museum serves as a historical testament to the Civilian Conservation Corps and their efforts in providing employment to young men during the Great Depression. The Michigan History Center offers historical interpretation. The park's beach is located on Higgins Lake, the 11th largest inland lake in Michigan. The swimming area is demarcated by swim markers to ensure safety. The crystal clear waters create a tropical-like swimming experience. Visitors can rent kayaks and stand-up paddle boards from Load 'N Go in the day-use area. For more information, contact 989-821-1717. 989 BBQ provides float rentals in the day-use area; you can inquire at 800-589-1692 or via email at info@989bbq.com. The boat launch on the north shore of Higgins Lake features two skid piers (docks) and is marked by red and green channel markers for safe boat ingress and egress. There are 11 miles of trails suitable for hiking, biking, and cross-country skiing. These trails are groomed, and seasonal naturalists offer weekly nature-based programs from Memorial Day through Labor Day. The picnic area is equipped with grills for visitors, although firepits are not provided. Shelters can be reserved up to a year in advance by calling 1-800-447-2757 or visiting www.midnrreservations.com. ADA-accessible restrooms and showers can be found in the West Campground. The East Campground offers 82 campsites, while the West Campground offers 92 campsites. The park also provides mini cabins, each containing two bunk beds and electric heating. Additionally, there are grills and picnic tables outside. The Beaver Creek Trail is a part of a trail system comprising three separate loops within North Higgins Lake State Park. The Beaver Creek Trail is the northernmost and longest loop, extending for 6.5 miles. As you traverse this trail, you'll find yourself surrounded by tall pine trees, ferns, and deep forested areas within the state park, often walking alongside the serene Beaver Creek. The trail allows hiking and cross-country skiing, weather permitting. The Bosom Pines Trail is another component of the three-loop trail system within North Higgins Lake State Park. As the middle loop connecting the Upland Nature Trail and the Beaver Creek Trail, it spans 3.8 miles. This trail takes you through tall pine forests, ferns, and the park's lush forested regions. It is open for hiking and cross-country skiing, weather permitting. The Upland Nature Trail, the southernmost of the three loops, extends for 1.6 miles. This trail is accessible right across the street from North Higgins Lake Campground and takes visitors through a winding path in the woods, featuring a dirt and gravel surface. It is open for hiking and cross-country skiing, depending on weather conditions.

DATE(S) VISITED .... ☐ SPRING ☐ SUMMER ☐ FALL ☐ WINTER

LODGING .... ☐ ☀ ☐ ☁ ☐ 🌧 ☐ ⛈ ☐ ❄

WHO I WENT WITH .... FEE(S) .... PARK HOURS .... TEMP:.........

WILL I RETURN? YES / NO RATING ☆ ☆ ☆ ☆ ☆

PASSPORT STAMPS

OLD MISSION STATE PARK

COUNTY	ESTABLISHED	AREA (AC/HA)
GRAND TRAVERSE	1989	520 / 210

Old Mission State Park is situated at the northern tip of the Old Mission Peninsula, precisely on the 45th parallel. This park offers visitors several miles of trails and encompasses 40 acres of woodlands and former orchards that are perfect for exploration. The park shares its southern boundary with Mission Point Lighthouse Park. Peninsula Township is responsible for managing this park under a lease agreement with the Michigan Department of Natural Resources. The funding for the park's development was supplied by the Michigan Natural Resources Trust Fund. The park's trail, which partially runs alongside Grand Traverse Bay, features a flat terrain and is categorized as an easy hike, suitable for most visitors.

DATE(S) VISITED .... ☐ SPRING ☐ SUMMER ☐ FALL ☐ WINTER

LODGING .... ☐ ☀ ☐ ☁ ☐ 🌧 ☐ 🌫 ☐ ❄

WHO I WENT WITH .... FEE(S) .... PARK HOURS .... TEMP:.........

WILL I RETURN? YES / NO   RATING ☆ ☆ ☆ ☆ ☆

PASSPORT STAMPS

ONAWAY STATE PARK

COUNTY	ESTABLISHED	AREA (AC/HA)
PRESQUE ISLE	1921	158 / 64

Onaway State Park is situated on the southeastern shoreline of the stunning Black Lake in Presque Isle County. Covering 158 acres of rugged and picturesque terrain, the park boasts a cobblestone shoreline, unique large rock outcroppings, and wooded areas. It offers a modern campground, overnight lodging options, a designated swim beach, a 3-mile trail encircling the park, and two notable structures, the historic Overlook Shelter and the recently constructed Onaway Pavilion. The newly constructed and accessible Onaway Pavilion, located in the east day-use area, includes a covered porch, modern restrooms, a countertop with a sink, round tables and chairs, a wood-burning fireplace, and a large outdoor grill with a side table. Reservations for this facility can be made up to 12 months in advance through MiDNRReservations.com. The park is positioned on the southeastern shore of Black Lake and features a designated swim area within its west day-use area. Visitors can rent canoes and kayaks at the park contact station during the period between Memorial Day and Labor Day. For more information, inquiries can be directed to 989-733-8279. There is a boating access site on the west side of the park, with parking shared with day-use visitors. Black Lake, covering 10,130 acres, ranks as the seventh-largest lake in Michigan, offering a rich variety of fish, including walleye, muskellunge, northern pike, yellow perch, and smallmouth bass. Paddling is a popular activity on Black Lake, though the lake can become choppy. The vicinity near the historic Overlook Shelter in the west day-use area provides outstanding views of Black Lake. Picnic areas can be found in both the west and east day-use areas, offering picnic tables and charcoal grills available on a first-come, first-served basis. Additionally, a swing and slide are located in the west day-use area, and vault toilets are available in the west day-use area. The park's sanitation station is situated in the campground, and there are two potable water lanes. Pets are permitted along the Black Lake shoreline, except within the designated swim area, provided they are kept on a 6-foot leash and under the immediate control of their owner. All pet waste must be properly disposed of in trash receptacles. The park's modern campground comprises the lower and upper campgrounds. The upper campground is nestled among towering white pines, while the lower campground is surrounded by cedar trees. The lower campground offers lakeside sites, and the east side of the upper campground provides views of the lake. Please note that the modern restrooms and showers require a short walk from the lower campground. The Shoreview Camper Cabin accommodates up to six people and includes two sets of bunk beds and a futon. It comes equipped with a mini refrigerator, a microwave, and an electric wall heater. Outdoors, you'll find Adirondack chairs, a picnic table, a fire pit, and a waist-high cook grill. The cabins have electricity, but guests must bring their own linens. The 3-mile trail encircles the park's perimeter. If you begin at the trailhead near the boating access site on Black Lake, you'll ascend the Civilian Conservation Corps stairs to a bluff with a picturesque view of the lake. The trail takes you through various natural areas, including an oak stand and cedar swamp, offering a diverse hiking experience. Access points to the trail are available at various locations throughout the park. Just 10 miles east of the park is the scenic Ocqueoc Falls, which happens to be the largest waterfall in Michigan's Lower Peninsula. The area is also renowned for its sinkholes, formed by the erosion of soft bedrock by springs, now home to trees, flowers, and wildlife. The nearby city of Onaway holds the title of the "Sturgeon Capital of Michigan." For more historical and cultural exploration, Old Mill Creek Historic State Park and Fort Michilimackinac, a restored 1700s community, are approximately 45 miles away.

DATE(S) VISITED ....   ☐ SPRING   ☐ SUMMER   ☐ FALL   ☐ WINTER

LODGING ....   ☐ ☀ ☐ ☁ ☐ ☔ ☐ 🌫 ☐ ❄

WHO I WENT WITH ....   FEE(S) .... PARK HOURS .... TEMP:.........

WILL I RETURN? YES / NO   RATING ☆ ☆ ☆ ☆ ☆

PASSPORT STAMPS

ORCHARD BEACH STATE PARK

COUNTY	ESTABLISHED	AREA (AC/HA)
MANISTEE	1921	201 / 81

Orchard Beach State Park is positioned on a 100-foot bluff that offers breathtaking views of Lake Michigan, located just 3 miles north of Manistee. The park is renowned for its stunning vistas of Lake Michigan and spectacular sunsets. Please be aware that due to high water levels and erosion, access to the beach, which is only accessible via stairs, is currently closed. The park derives its name from an ancient apple orchard that once thrived here more than a century ago. The park's main attraction is the recently restored and relocated historic structure weighing 850 tons. Although there is no direct fishing access from the park, many campers utilize the nearby boating access site for fishing, targeting coho and king salmon in the fall and steelhead in the spring. A fish-cleaning station is conveniently located adjacent to the campground. The day-use area features a picnic area equipped with picnic tables and charcoal grills available on a first-come, first-served basis. Additionally, there is an accessible picnic and event facility situated within the recently restored 850-ton historic building. This facility includes picnic tables, two substantial stone fireplaces, charcoal grills, electrical service (available by reservation), and modern restroom facilities. Shelter reservations can be made up to 12 months in advance through MiDNRReservations.com. The park's sanitation station is located within the campground, providing potable water and two lanes for your convenience. The modern campground is nestled along the 100-foot bluff overlooking Lake Michigan. Most campsites are generously sized and shaded by oak and maple trees. Campers can choose from 30- or 50-amp service. Recycling services are provided as well. As with beach access, direct fishing access from the park is not available; however, many campers utilize the nearby boating access site for fishing expeditions targeting coho and Chinook salmon in the fall and steelhead in the spring. For those seeking a rustic yet comfortable experience, the camper cabin in the modern campground offers an excellent view of Lake Michigan. The cabin accommodates up to six individuals and includes bunk beds and a pull-out couch, electricity, refrigerator, microwave, table and chairs, and a fire circle. There is no running water within the cabin, but potable water is conveniently located nearby. Guests must provide their own cookware, linens, and towels. Similarly, the mini cabin, also located in the modern campground, boasts the most spectacular view of Lake Michigan in the park. This cabin is designed for up to four occupants and comes equipped with bunk beds, electricity, refrigerator, microwave, a table with chairs, and a fire circle. Running water is not available within the cabin, but a potable water source is situated nearby. As with the camper cabin, guests must supply their own cookware, linens, and towels. The park features an extensive network of trails spanning 3.5 miles that meander through an old-growth forest and areas of former farmland. Along the old-growth section of the Beech Hemlock Trail, visitors can find informative panels providing insight into the environment. The trailhead can be accessed east of the campground office.

DATE(S) VISITED .... ☐ SPRING   ☐ SUMMER   ☐ FALL   ☐ WINTER

LODGING .... ☐ ☀ ☐ ☁ ☐ 🌧 ☐ 🌬 ☐ ❄

WHO I WENT WITH .... FEE(S) .... PARK HOURS .... TEMP:........

WILL I RETURN? YES / NO   RATING ☆ ☆ ☆ ☆ ☆

PASSPORT STAMPS

OTSEGO LAKE STATE PARK

COUNTY	ESTABLISHED	AREA (AC/HA)
OTSEGO	1920	62 / 25

Otsego Lake State Park, conveniently situated near Gaylord with easy access from I-75, spans across 62 acres of lakeside recreational space. The park is renowned for its exquisite half-mile sandy beach, designated swim beach, fishing pier, a quarter-mile pathway, and a picnic area. The park is graced by the presence of the Iron Belle Trail, a trail system that passes the park entrance and offers opportunities for biking, hiking, and snowmobiling. Following an enjoyable day on the lake, many visitors head to the seasonal park store, a popular destination for savoring ice cream while relishing the sunset over the lake. You can delight in a half-mile of sandy shoreline along Otsego Lake. An accessible pathway provides access to both swimming areas within the park, and a beach wheelchair (available on a first-come, first-served basis) can be requested for use. The day-use area features a designated, universally accessible beach and swim area. There is also an additional accessible swim area situated to the north of the day-use area. Lake to Lake Rentals offers kayak, canoe, and stand-up paddleboard rentals at the day-use area beach on a first-come, first-served basis, available from Memorial Day weekend through Labor Day. Furthermore, there's a well-frequented two-lane, paved boating access site on Otsego Lake in the day-use area. Please be aware that parking is offered on a first-come, first-served basis and tends to fill up quickly. This boating access site is one of only two public access points on Otsego Lake, a 1,971-acre lake known for its fishing opportunities, including species like bluegill, perch, crappie, largemouth and smallmouth bass, walleye, northern pike, and sturgeon. The park provides a well-developed boating access site and an accessible fishing pier, available seasonally. An additional universally accessible fishing pier, also open seasonally, can be found near the boating access site in the day-use area. Paddling is a highly favored way to explore Otsego Lake, and you can launch from the boat launch within the day-use area. The beach building in the day-use area incorporates restrooms, a park store, and an attached picnic shelter dating back to the Civilian Conservation Corps era. From the park, visitors can seamlessly access the bicycle-friendly Iron Belle Trail, which traverses the park along Old Highway 27. The park itself does not have groomed trails; however, snowshoeing is a common winter activity within the campground. The park's day-use area on Otsego Lake is home to a picnic area, offering picnic tables and charcoal grills that are available on a first-come, first-served basis. Additionally, there is a Beach Picnic Shelter situated next to the beach in the day-use area on Otsego

Lake. This shelter can comfortably accommodate 50-75 people and boasts a picturesque view of the lake. It comes equipped with picnic tables, a large charcoal grill, electrical outlets, and is accessible by vehicle via reservation. Restrooms are conveniently located adjacent to the shelter within the beach building. A Point Picnic Shelter is also available within the day-use picnic area, accommodating up to 40 people. This shelter includes picnic tables and a small grill. While there is no electricity available, vehicle access is limited to the nearby parking lot located 150 feet away via an accessible pathway. Shelter reservations can be made up to 12 months in advance through MIDNRReservations.com or by calling 1-800-447-2757. Additional amenities found within the day-use area include a swing set, slide on a woodchipped surface, volleyball area, basketball court, and horseshoe pit. Modern restrooms are open seasonally from Memorial Day weekend through Labor Day and are located within the beach building on Otsego Lake. Vault toilets can be found within the day-use area near the boat launch. The park's sanitation station, open seasonally from mid-May to mid-October, depending on weather conditions, is located near the campground office. This station offers potable water and two lanes for added convenience. The modern campground is divided into two sections: the north loop and south loop. Most campsites are generously sized, shaded by oaks, maples, and pines, and afford views of Otsego Lake. Each campsite offers either 20- or 30-amp electrical service, with recycling services provided throughout the campground. Modern restrooms with showers and a sanitation station are open seasonally, typically from mid-May to mid-October. Once these facilities close for the season, the campground remains semi-modern, with vault toilets available and a water spigot located near the park headquarters for filling water containers. Nestled within the south campground loop, an accessible mini cabin overlooks Otsego Lake and is situated near the stairs leading to the lake. The cabin can accommodate up to five guests and features two sets of bunk beds (a single bunk and a full-size bed with a single bunk above). Amenities include a mini refrigerator, microwave, a table with bench, a picnic table, and a fire pit. The cabin is equipped with electricity and lighting but lacks running water and heating. Guests must provide their own linens, and pets are not allowed in the cabin.

PASSPORT STAMPS

PALMS BOOK STATE PARK

COUNTY	ESTABLISHED	AREA (AC/HA)
SCHOOLCRAFT	1926	388 / 157

Palms Book State Park, situated at the northern tip of Indian Lake in Michigan's Upper Peninsula, is famous for Kitch-iti-kipi, also known as "The Big Spring." This natural wonder is Michigan's largest freshwater spring, with an astonishing flow of over 10,000 gallons of water per minute emerging from crevices in the underlying limestone at a constant temperature of 45 degrees Fahrenheit. Visitors can take a self-guided tour on an accessible observation raft to witness the crystal-clear pool with its emerald green bottom. The park provides a seasonal store where you can purchase concessions and souvenirs. Additionally, there's a boating access site that offers access to Indian Lake, which is the fourth-largest inland lake in the Upper Peninsula. The observation raft is open from 8 a.m. until dusk, but it is strictly prohibited to swim, bathe, skin or scuba dive, fish, boat, enter the spring, or place/launch any objects (including underwater cameras) in "The Big Spring." The raft should only be used for observation purposes. The self-guided observation raft provides an opportunity for visitors to behold Kitch-iti-kipi, or the "Big Spring." The crystal-clear water reveals ancient tree trunks, branches encrusted with lime, and lake trout swimming far beneath the surface. The ever-moving sands create a dynamic and ever-changing display of shapes and forms. The observation raft is accessible for all visitors. If you're interested in hiking, the Indian Lake Pathway is located just a short drive away from the park. Kitch-iti-kipi, or the "Big Spring," is Michigan's largest natural freshwater spring, located within the park. Indian Lake, situated in the park's northeast section, can be accessed via Fishing Site Road, not within the park's main entrance. The park's boating access site, located off Fishing Site Road, allows visitors to access Indian Lake, known for fishing opportunities that include perch, walleye, northern pike, muskellunge, rock bass, smallmouth bass, bluegill, sturgeon, and brown trout. The boating access site is located within the park's boundaries but must be reached from Fishing Site Road, not through the main entrance, as it's situated in the northeast part of the park. Hunting is permitted within the state park, but you should contact the park directly to inquire about any specific rules, concerns, or considerations. The picnic area within the park offers picnic tables and charcoal grills, available on a first-come, first-served basis. Additionally, there is a swing set located near the parking lot for visitors to enjoy.

DATE(S) VISITED .... ☐ SPRING ☐ SUMMER ☐ FALL ☐ WINTER

LODGING .... ☐ ☀ ☐ ☁ ☐ 🌧 ☐ 🌫 ☐ ❄

WHO I WENT WITH .... FEE(S) .... PARK HOURS .... TEMP:........

WILL I RETURN? YES / NO   RATING ☆ ☆ ☆ ☆ ☆

PASSPORT STAMPS

PETOSKEY STATE PARK

COUNTY	ESTABLISHED	AREA (AC/HA)
EMMET	1969	203 / 82

Petoskey State Park, nestled along the shores of Little Traverse Bay on Lake Michigan, offers a beautiful 1-mile stretch of sandy beach, two modern campgrounds, and scenic trails. Located just 3 miles northeast of Petoskey and 6 miles south of Harbor Springs, the park is a renowned spot for those seeking Petoskey stones. The Old Baldy Trail, a short half-mile loop leading to the summit of Old Baldy Dune, is a favorite for its picturesque views. For a slightly longer hike, the Portage Trail is a 1-mile out-and-back trail through a wooded dune area. If you wish to explore beyond the park, the Little Traverse Wheelway, a 26-mile paved trail that passes by the park entrance, connects Charlevoix and Harbor Springs. Additionally, the North Western State Trail, just south of the park, links Petoskey and Mackinac City. It's important to note that pets are not permitted along the lakeshore due to piping plover habitat, but they are welcome in other areas of the park. Pets should always be on a leash of six feet or less and under the immediate control of their owner. Properly disposing of pet waste in designated trash receptacles is mandatory. The park's history dates back to Pay-Me-Gwau, who received the land under an Ottawa Indian treaty in July 1855. Later, the W.W. Rice Company occupied much of the land. In 1934, the City of Petoskey acquired the land and named it the Petoskey Bathing Beach. In April 1968, the beach was sold to the State of Michigan, and on May 21, 1969, the state took full ownership. Enjoy a mile of sandy shoreline along Lake Michigan, complete with a designated swim area in the day-use section. An accessible walkway leads to the water, and a beach wheelchair is available upon request at the concession store located in the beach house. Visitors should pay attention to the beach flag warning system, with red flags indicating unsafe water conditions, and swimming or water entry should be avoided. Kayaks and stand-up paddleboards are available for rent from Lake to Lake Rentals, located in the beach house of the day-use area, from Memorial Day through Labor Day. Little Traverse Bay is a popular spot for paddling enthusiasts. The beach house in the day-use area provides restrooms, food concessions, and rentals for bicycles, kayaks, and stand-up paddleboards. An observation deck is available at the top of Mount Baldy, offering spectacular views. The picnic area within the day-use zone provides picnic tables and charcoal grills on a first-come, first-served basis. A picnic shelter is available at the end of the beach house and is also first come, first served. There's a swing set and slide within the day-use area for added enjoyment. The park's sanitation station, with potable water and two lanes, is located near the park entrance. Dunes Modern Campground is known for its family-friendly environment and smaller sites suitable for tents, vans, and compact campers. Many sites are shaded by cedar trees, and there's a short trail leading to the day-use area along Lake Michigan. Electrical service of 20- and 30-amp is available at each site, and recycling facilities are provided. Tannery Creek Modern Campground is located just steps from Little Traverse Bay on Lake Michigan. Paved pads are available at each site, with 20- and 30-amp electrical service, and some sites offer 50-amp service. An overflow parking area is accessible for additional vehicles and guests, and recycling facilities are provided. The campground features two mini cabins, Trillium and Orchid, within the Tannery Creek Campground. Each cabin accommodates up to four people and includes a mini refrigerator and electric wall heater, along with four single beds and a counter with stools. The outdoor area includes a picnic table, a fire pit, and a waist-high cook grill. The cabins are equipped with electricity but do not have running water, and guests should bring their own linens. Group Use Sites are available for groups of up to 24 individuals. Each of the four sites accommodates up to six campers and provides a picnic table, fire pit, a pavilion with a charcoal grill, and a hand pump for water. To reserve the group camp area, contact 231-347-2311. The Campground Trail is a relatively flat half-mile trail that connects the two campgrounds, providing views of the water and access to the dunes along Lake Michigan. The Old Baldy Trail is a short, half-mile loop through a wooded dune area that leads to the summit of Old Baldy, offering stunning vistas of Lake Michigan. The trail can be accessed from the trailhead opposite the campground office near the entrance to the Dunes Campground. The Portage Trail is also available, starting at the same trailhead and leading to the backside of Old Baldy. Visitors will find a sign directing them to the dune.

DATE(S) VISITED .... □ SPRING □ SUMMER □ FALL □ WINTER

LODGING .... □☀ □☁ □🌧 □⛅ □☁

WHO I WENT WITH .... FEE(S) .... PARK HOURS .... TEMP:.........

WILL I RETURN? YES / NO   RATING ☆ ☆ ☆ ☆ ☆

PASSPORT STAMPS

PORCUPINE MOUNTAINS WILDERNESS STATE PARK

COUNTY	ESTABLISHED	AREA (AC/HA)
GOGEBIC, ONTONAGON	1944	60,000 / 24,281

Porcupine Mountains Wilderness State Park, affectionately known as "the Porkies," spans 60,000 acres of pristine old-growth forests, rushing waterfalls, Lake Superior coastline, rivers, trails, and ridges. With its unparalleled natural beauty, this park, Michigan's largest, is a sought-after destination for camping, hiking, snowmobiling, fishing, and more. Visitors can explore a range of natural attractions, including Lake of the Clouds, the picturesque Presque Isle River corridor, the Summit Peak observation tower, Porcupine Mountains Winter Sports Complex, autumn chairlift rides, an 18-hole disc golf course, and many other features. The popular Porcupine Mountains Visitor Center offers interpretive programs, an exhibit hall, information on trail conditions, Wi-Fi, a gift shop, and various other amenities. Visitors can relish 1.6 miles of Lake Superior's Union Bay shoreline along M-107, the scenic Presque Isle River, and numerous other rivers and streams. There is a sandy beach within walking distance, and two boat launches provide access to Lake Superior. The Union Bay Campground boasts the first launch, and the second is located at the mouth of the Big Iron River in Silver City. Additionally, the Porcupine Mountain Outpost near the Union Bay Campground offers canoe and kayak rentals from late May through mid-October, and bicycle rentals are also available. The park offers numerous fishing opportunities, with natural brook trout habitat found throughout the Porkies watershed. Special fishing regulations apply at Lake of the Clouds. An accessible fishing pier is situated at the Union Bay boating access site, adjacent to the campground. Paddling is a popular activity in Union Bay on Lake Superior, with parking available at the Union Bay boating access site. The park boasts 90 miles of hiking trails, including sections of the North Country Trail and Michigan's Iron Belle Trail. For those interested in biking, the Porcupine Mountain Outpost near the Union Bay Campground provides bicycle and tandem bike rentals from late May through mid-October. The park maintains 42 km of groomed cross-country ski trails, with trail grooming supported by donations to the park. Additionally, the Porkies Ski Chalet offers adaptive sit skis in child, teen, and adult sizes, which can be borrowed for use on the park's cross-country and lantern-lit trails. To inquire about availability or assistance, visitors can call 906-885-5270. Some trails are open to snowmobiling during the winter season, with County Road 107 and South Boundary Road transitioning into designated snowmobile trails during that time. During this period, these roads are closed to vehicular traffic until they are deemed safe for travel by the Ontonagon County

Road Commission. Hunting is permitted in the state park, but it is advisable to contact the park directly for specific rules, concerns, or considerations. An 18-hole disc golf course is located in the Porcupine Mountains Winter Sports Complex, and the course is free to use. Discs are available for rent at the park's campground store, located near the entrance to the Union Bay Campground on M-107. The course is open from late May through mid-October. There are multiple observation platforms at various scenic sites throughout the park, including Lake the Clouds (featuring an accessible walkway and observation platform), Summit Peak, Presque Isle River (with an accessible observation platform overlooking Nawadaha on the West River Trail), and East Vista (which offers chairlift rides in the fall). Several picnic areas are situated along M-107, equipped with picnic tables and some charcoal grills, available on a first-come, first-serve basis. In the Presque Isle day-use area, a picnic shelter is provided, including picnic tables, charcoal grills, and vault toilets. Shelter reservations can be made up to 12 months in advance at MIDNRReservations.com. Additionally, the Porcupine Mountains shooting range, managed by the Lake Superior Sportsman Club, includes a rifle and shotgun range. To access the range, an annual membership fee is required, in addition to the Recreation Passport. The park's sanitation station is located at Union Bay modern campground and offers potable water and two lanes. Visitors can enjoy free Wi-Fi at the visitor center from late May through mid-October. The Union Bay campground is the sole modern campground in the park, offering electrical hookups, a contemporary restroom facility, a sanitation station, boat launch, camp store, and various amenities. Many campsites provide the serene sounds of waves crashing along the rocky shoreline of Union Bay, nestled on the shores of Lake Superior. Several of these campsites are positioned along the bay's edge. Additionally, a sandy beach is just a short walk away along M-107. The campground offers a variety of campsite sizes to cater to different preferences, some suited for tents or smaller campers, while others can accommodate larger RVs. The Porcupine Mountains Presque Isle rustic campground hosts 50 campsites adjacent to the scenic and untamed Presque Isle River. Facilities include vault toilets and hand pumps for water. In addition to drive-up sites, there are six walk-in sites situated along the elevated bank of Lake Superior, approximately 50 yards from the parking area. The campground is divided into two loops: the east loop is generator-friendly, while the west loop prohibits generators. Trail access is available to the nearby Presque Isle River and Lake Superior shoreline. Firewood is available for purchase at the campground office.The Union River Outpost is a small, three-site rustic campground located along the Union River, offering solitude and a camping experience different from a typical modern campground. Union River is a classic U.P. trout stream. These sites are well-suited for tent camping, vans, or compact campers. A vault toilet is provided, but there is no running water at any of the outpost campgrounds. Water can be accessed at the park headquarters or visitor center. The Lost Creek Rustic Outpost Campground is another small, three-site rustic campground located on Lost Creek, close to the Lost Lake trailhead. This campground offers solitude and a camping experience that differs from a typical modern campground. The sites are suitable for tent camping, vans, or compact campers. Each site features a vault toilet, but there is no running water available at these outpost campgrounds. To access water, you can visit the park headquarters or visitor center. There are 65 backcountry (primitive) campsites within the park, each designated with a specific number, meaning you must camp at your registered site. These sites come with a metal fire ring. Campers are required to dig a 6-inch hole to bury waste at least a quarter of a mile away from any campsite, trail, or body of water. Some sites have composting privies available. Bear bags must be suspended at least 12 feet above the ground and away from trees to prevent animals from reaching or jumping on them. It is strongly recommended to make reservations between May 15 and October 15 (available up to six months in advance and as late as 72 hours before your arrival) at MiDNRReservations or by calling 1-800-44PARKS. The backcountry rustic cabins offer unique lodging options, with each cabin accommodating between two to eight people. These cabins are equipped with bunk beds, mattresses, a wood-burning stove, table and chairs, a fire circle, an axe, bow saw, and cooking and eating utensils. There is no running water or electricity, although a vault toilet is located nearby (bring your toilet paper). Other amenities include a water boiling pot, washbasin, cooking pot, can opener, and a percolator coffee pot. You must provide your own sheets and towels. These cabins are pet-friendly, except for two, and can require hiking in from a designated trailhead, with distances ranging from 100 yards to 9 miles. Snowshoes or cross-country skis are typically needed between mid-November and May for access. All cabins are located near a body of water, and those on inland lakes come with a boat and personal flotation devices. It is advisable to boil drinking water for a minute or filter it through a 0.5-micron filter, as no hand pumps are available. Additionally, all wood for heating must be taken from dead and downed trees. A designated fire circle is provided alongside the wood-heating stove. Firewood is supplied for heating during the winter months. Backcountry Wilderness Yurts offer lodging for four people and come equipped with bunk beds, mattresses, a wood-burning stove, table and chairs, a fire circle, an axe, bow saw, a water boiling pot, washbasin, cooking pot, can opener, and percolator coffee pot. There is no running water or electricity, but a vault toilet is located nearby (bring your toilet paper). Guests are required to provide their own sheets and towels. Several yurts are pet-friendly. They require hiking in from a designated trailhead, with distances ranging from 100 yards to 2.5 miles. Snowshoes or cross-country skis are typically needed between mid-November and May for access. Potable drinking water is not provided, so it is advisable to boil water for one minute or filter it through a 0.5-micron filter, as no hand pumps are available. Similar to the cabins, all wood for heating must be sourced from dead and downed trees, and a designated fire circle is provided. Firewood is supplied for heating in the winter months. The Union Bay Tiny Quill House is located along the shores of Lake Superior within the Union Bay Campground. Constructed in 2020, this tiny house can accommodate up to four people (two on the main floor and two in the loft). It features a small electric stove, microwave, mini refrigerator, coffee pot, table and chairs, and seating. The facility has electricity and a propane heater, with potable water available in the campground. Guests must provide their own sheets and towels. Outdoor amenities include a fire pit, picnic table, and charcoal grill. The park offers two adjacent rustic group sites intended for youth and civic groups, situated close to the sandy Union Bay beach on Lake Superior. Each site can accommodate up to 24 people and comes equipped with fire pits, trash receptacles, and vault toilets. The Beaver Creek Trail is an ideal choice for a half-day scenic hike and combines perfectly with the Lily Pond Trail. Together, these trails, along with a section of the Little Carp River Trail, create a short, picturesque route through the heart of Porcupine Mountain Wilderness State Park. The trail begins at the start of Beaver Creek Trail and continues for 2 miles until it connects with Lily Pond. This trailhead is located at the parking area at the end of Summit Peak Road. The Correction Line Trail and Cross Trail, located within Porcupine Mountains Wilderness State Park, traverse the park's old-growth forest, connecting the Big Carp River Trail to Mirror Lake. These trails are popular for their scenic beauty, with many hikers combining sections of the Lake Superior Trail and the Big Carp River Trail and returning via the Correction Line and Mirror Lake Trail. The Correction Line Trail is a challenging 2.8-mile loop with steep climbs toward Mirror Lake. The Cross Trail, on the other hand, spans 4.5 miles. The Deer Yard Trail, found in the Porcupine Mountains Wilderness State Park in the Upper Peninsula, is one of several trails in the park's mountain biking and cross-country ski trail system. This trail is situated north of M-107 and passes near the Whitetail Cabin and the White Birch warming shelter. It offers picturesque views of Lake Superior and the surrounding wilderness. The trail can be accessed just north of the downhill ski area. The Double Trail, located within the Porcupine Mountains Wilderness State Park, is part of the mountain biking and cross-country skiing trail system. Stretching for three miles, the Double Trail meanders through the rolling hills of the Porcupine Mountains. This trail connects to the Union Spring Trail and provides easy access to the Triple and Log Camp Trails. Mountain biking and cross-country skiing are permitted on this trail, weather permitting.

DATE(S) VISITED .... ☐ SPRING ☐ SUMMER ☐ FALL ☐ WINTER

LODGING .... ☐ ☀ ☐ ☁ ☐ 🌧 ☐ 🌫 ☐ ❄

WHO I WENT WITH .... FEE(S) .... PARK HOURS .... TEMP:.........

WILL I RETURN? YES / NO   RATING ☆ ☆ ☆ ☆ ☆

PASSPORT STAMPS

PORT CRESCENT STATE PARK

COUNTY	ESTABLISHED	AREA (AC/HA)
HURON	1955	600 / 240

Port Crescent State Park, situated just outside the town of Port Austin at the tip of Michigan's "thumb," spans along 3 miles of sandy Lake Huron shoreline. The park offers a dark sky preserve and features a modern campground with waterfront views, along with ten overnight lodging options such as geodesic domes, camper cabins, and cottages. It also encompasses the scenic Pinnebog River, hiking trails, captivating sunsets, and opportunities for fishing, canoeing, bird-watching, cross-country skiing, hunting, and more. During the nighttime when the sun sets and the stars emerge, visitors can partake in exceptional stargazing in the park's dark sky preserve. The prime location for stargazing can be found near Parking Lot D, where a viewing platform is available. Port Crescent State Park is conveniently located near Turnip Rock, a popular natural attraction that rises from the water and can be accessed via a 7-mile round-trip canoe or kayak journey. Local outfitters offer rentals for this adventure. The park offers opportunities to enjoy the Pinnebog River and 3 miles of undulating sand dunes along Lake Huron. There's a carry-in-only boat launch on the Pinnebog River, with parking available in Parking Lot A. Shore fishing is a favored activity along the Pinnebog River, and paddling is also popular. The park's day-use area features a beach house with restrooms. Hunting is permitted within the state park; however, it's advisable to contact the park directly for any specific rules, concerns, or considerations. Throughout the summer season, seasonal naturalists offer weekly nature-based programs at the park, running from Memorial Day through Labor Day. The day-use area includes charcoal grills and picnic tables adjacent to the beach house. Additionally, there's a picnic shelter available on a first-come, first-served basis within the day-use area, equipped with picnic tables, charcoal grills, and a modern bathroom. The park provides a sanitation station near the campground office in the modern campground, offering potable water and two lanes. Pets are permitted along the entire 3-mile length of the Lake Huron shoreline, with the exception of the designated swim beach in the modern campground. Pets must be kept on a 6-foot leash and under the owner's immediate control at all times. Any pet waste should be properly disposed of in the provided trash receptacles. The park's modern campground is renowned for its scenic views of Lake Huron's Saginaw Bay and sites surrounded by hardwoods. Each site offers either 20- or 30-amp service, along with a sanitation station and a dishwashing station. There are three ADA-accessible campsites located near the accessible modern toilet and shower building. Hammock-Only Sites, found in the modern campground along Lake Huron's lakefront, offer a unique camping experience. These hammock-only sites (sites #H66 and #H67) include four posts and hooks to accommodate up to four hammocks, a picnic table, electric service, and a fire ring. The ground is relatively flat and sandy. Hammock rentals are available (not included in the reservation fee) on a first-come, first-served basis by contacting the park. Mini Cabin A, located at the western end of the modern campground, accommodates up to four individuals in two bunk beds. The cabin features a microwave, mini fridge, and coffee maker. There is a fire pit, grill, table, and cement patio outdoors. The cabin is pet-friendly. It permits up to two pets, limited to cats and dogs. While there is no running water within the cabin, a modern toilet and shower building is situated approximately 300 feet away, and a vault toilet is around 100 feet away. Guests are responsible for providing their own linens and cookware. The cabin has a minimum two-night stay requirement, and check-out time is 11 a.m. The park offers five cottage cabins located in the modern campground, providing views of Lake Huron's Saginaw Bay. These two-room cabins can sleep up to six people and are furnished with a set of bunk beds, a queen bed in the bedroom, and a futon in the living room that accommodates two more individuals. Additionally, each cabin includes a dining table, mini fridge, microwave, and coffee maker. Outdoors, you'll find a fire pit, charcoal grill, table, and screened-in front porch. Cottage C is ADA-accessible. While running water isn't available inside the cabins, a modern toilet and shower building is located roughly 300 feet away, and a vault toilet is situated about 100 feet away. Guests should bring their own linens and cookware. A two-night minimum stay is required, and check-out time is 11 a.m. Camper Cabin E, located at the far eastern end of the modern campground, offers a view of Lake Huron's Saginaw Bay. The cabin accommodates up to six individuals and features two separate bedrooms, each equipped with bunk beds for two, while a futon in the common room can sleep an additional two people. The cabin includes heating, a microwave, a mini fridge, and a small table with two stools. Outdoors, you'll find a fire pit, grill, table, cement patio, covered porch, and deck. While the cabin does not have running water, a modern toilet and shower building is located about 300 feet away, and a vault toilet is situated about 100 feet away. Guests should provide their own linens and cookware. There's a minimum two-night stay requirement, and check-out time is 11 a.m. Cottage H, located at the eastern end of the modern campground, provides scenic views of Lake Huron's Saginaw Bay. This cottage can accommodate up to six individuals and features two separate bedrooms, including one with a queen bed and another with a set of bunk beds (single top, double bottom). The cabin offers amenities like heating, air conditioning, a full bathroom, a kitchen, dining space, and a common area with a futon and a dining room table. The kitchen comes stocked with dishes, cookware, an induction stovetop, a sink, a microwave, and a full-size refrigerator. Outdoors, there's a fire pit, charcoal grill, table, cement patio, and a screened-in front porch. Guests are required to provide their own linens. Two accessible geodesic domes, located in the center of the campground, offer an intimate setting with spruce paneling, skylights, and views of Lake Huron. Each dome can accommodate up to four individuals and provides amenities like air conditioning and heating. There's a queen bed, and up to two individuals can sleep in cot-style bunks. Additional features include a sitting area, coffee maker, microwave, and mini fridge. The grey dome (The Voyager) boasts modern furnishings, while the gold dome (The Nomad) features traditional furnishings. While there's no running water inside the domes, a modern toilet and shower building is located about 300 feet away, and a vault toilet is around 100 feet away. Guests are responsible for providing their own linens and cookware. The 2.3-mile Day-Use Trail takes visitors through wooded areas of pine and oak and rolling sand dunes. Wildlife sightings may include deer, geese, and occasionally an eagle. In the summer, the trailhead is located at Parking Lot C, while in the winter, it can be found near the contact station in the park's day-use area. The Dunes Nature Trail offers visitors the chance to explore the dunes ecosystem along a relatively flat and easy-to-walk 0.75-mile trail. The trailhead is situated on the west side of Parking Lot C. The Organization Area Trail, covering 2.5 miles, offers three scenic overlooks providing stunning views of Lake Huron's Saginaw Bay. The terrain primarily consists of sand dunes. The trailhead is located near the designated swim beach in the modern campground (for campers only) or the old steel bridge on M-25 (for day-use visitors).

DATE(S) VISITED .... □ SPRING □ SUMMER □ FALL □ WINTER

LODGING .... □ ☀ □ ☁ □ 🌧 □ 🌦 □ ❄

WHO I WENT WITH .... FEE(S) .... PARK HOURS .... TEMP:.........

WILL I RETURN? YES / NO   RATING ☆ ☆ ☆ ☆ ☆

PASSPORT STAMPS

SANILAC PETROGLYPHS HISTORIC STATE PARK

COUNTY	ESTABLISHED	AREA (AC/HA)
SANILAC	1971	240 / 97

Sanilac Petroglyphs Historic State Park, situated near Cass City in Michigan's Thumb region, is home to the largest known collection of early Native American teachings etched in stone in the state of Michigan. These carvings, known as "ezhibiigaadek asin" in the Anishinabe language, hold deep cultural significance for the Anishinabek people. To view the petroglyphs, visitors can take a quarter-mile accessible trail made of hard-packed limestone leading to a sheltered enclosure that stands above the petroglyphs viewing area. Visitors can find the seasonal dates and operating hours for viewing the petroglyphs. The park is located along a branch of the Little Cass River. This 240-acre park is jointly managed with the Saginaw Chippewa Indian Tribe of Michigan and is one of the 12 museums and historic sites preserved and interpreted by the DNR's Michigan History Center. Additionally, the park offers a one-mile self-guided interpretive hiking trail loop, which includes crossings over a tributary of the Little Cass River. It's worth noting that this trail has roots and an uneven surface, and it can be prone to flooding, making it muddy or occasionally impassable. The one-mile self-guided interpretive hiking trail loop crosses the branch of the Little Cass River twice, leading visitors through serene forests, past the remnants of a 19th-century logging camp, and beside a 110-year-old white pine. An accessible vault toilet is located in the parking lot at the trailhead. During the summer months, guided tours are provided by the Michigan History Center, with specific dates and hours of operation for viewing the petroglyphs available seasonally. An enclosed viewing area over the petroglyphs provides shelter in inclement weather. There's a picnic table near the parking lot and four additional picnic tables near the petroglyphs area, all available on a first-come, first-served basis.

DATE(S) VISITED .... □ SPRING □ SUMMER □ FALL □ WINTER

LODGING .... □ ☼ □ ☁ □ 🌧 □ 🌦 □ ❄

WHO I WENT WITH .... FEE(S) .... PARK HOURS .... TEMP:.........

WILL I RETURN? YES / NO RATING ☆ ☆ ☆ ☆ ☆

SAUGATUCK DUNES STATE PARK

COUNTY	ESTABLISHED	AREA (AC/HA)
ALLEGAN	1978	1,000 / 400

Saugatuck Dunes State Park offers 2.5 miles of sandy Lake Michigan shoreline, along with coastal dunes, wooded areas, 13 miles of trails, and the 300-acre Patty Birkholz Natural Area. The park features four trails, each providing access to Lake Michigan over a combination of rolling terrain and sandy pathways. The shortest route is the Beach Trail, marked with yellow posts, and it covers a distance of 0.75 miles one way. The Patty Birkholz Natural Area hosts a coastal dune system and is home to three endangered plant species. This area serves as a tribute to the environmental advocate and former state Senator Birkholz, who dedicated herself to the preservation of the coastal dune system. In close proximity to the park, visitors can explore the Felt Estate and the Shore Acres Township Park, which offer a 2-mile mountain bike trail, a disc golf course, and various other outdoor recreational opportunities. Enjoy 2.5 miles of sandy shoreline along Lake Michigan. It's important to exercise caution due to recent high water levels and shoreline erosion. Avoid digging into vertical sand dunes, as they may unexpectedly collapse. Pay attention to the beach flag warning system in designated swim areas: red flags signify unsafe water conditions, and swimming or entering the water is prohibited. Do not swim near or jump off break walls or navigational channel walls and stay alert to changing conditions. The park provides a picnic shelter equipped with picnic tables, a charcoal grill, and a vault toilet. Reservations for the shelter can be made up to 12 months in advance by contacting the park directly at 269-637-2788. Pets are allowed along the entire length of the Lake Michigan shoreline, provided they are kept on a leash that is no longer than six feet and are under the immediate control of their owners. All pet waste must be properly disposed of in designated trash receptacles. The Beach Trail is the shortest path to reach the Lake Michigan shoreline. Covering a distance of 0.75 miles one way, this trail leads you across rolling terrain and offers scenic views of the forest floor. It is commonly considered the easiest route and is marked with yellow post markers. The Livingston Trail is a 1.25-mile trail that takes you through dunes and wooded areas to the Lake Michigan shoreline. Marked by red post markers, it connects to the South Trail (blue) and the Beach Trail (yellow), providing a diverse combination of sand dunes, Lake Michigan vistas, scenic overlooks, and wooded sections. The North Trail (white) spans 1.25 miles one way and guides you through a pine forest to the Lake Michigan shoreline. To reach the shoreline, visitors must navigate loose sand and grassy dunes. The trail is marked by white post markers. The South Trail (blue) is a 2.75-mile trail leading to the Lake Michigan shoreline. The terrain varies from steep slopes to rolling dune hills, offering a moderately challenging route. Along the way, visitors will pass through the 300-acre Patty Birkholz Natural Area, traverse deep dune forests, and enjoy picturesque views of Lake Michigan. The trail is marked with blue post markers.

DATE(S) VISITED .... ☐ SPRING ☐ SUMMER ☐ FALL ☐ WINTER

LODGING .... ☐ ☀ ☐ ☁ ☐ 🌧 ☐ 🌦 ☐ ❄

WHO I WENT WITH .... FEE(S) .... PARK HOURS .... TEMP:.........

WILL I RETURN? YES / NO   RATING ☆ ☆ ☆ ☆ ☆

PASSPORT STAMPS

SEVEN LAKES STATE PARK

COUNTY	ESTABLISHED	AREA (AC/HA)
OAKLAND	1992	1,434 / 580

Seven Lakes State Park encompasses a diverse landscape, featuring a blend of farmland, rolling hills, forests, and around 230 acres of water with several miles of shoreline. This park's unique character stems from its history; it was originally acquired by a development group with grand plans but was later sold to the state in 1969. A dam, built by the developers, merged seven small lakes into one large lake, historically known as DeCoup Lake, hence the park's name, Seven Lakes State Park. The park offers access to a beautiful beach, which is wheelchair accessible via a stab-mat, allowing those in wheelchairs to reach the lake. Boats, including rowboats, canoes, paddle boats, and motorized boats, are available for rent from mid-May to mid-September. You can contact the concession at 810-750-1977 or the park at 248-634-7271 for more information. The park contains two major lakes: the 170-acre Big Seven Lake and the 44-acre Dickinson Lake, both accessible via boat launch sites, allowing motors at no-wake speeds. Anglers of all ages can enjoy fishing for bluegill, bass, pike, tiger muskie, and catfish in these lakes. A fishing pier is also available for shoreline fishing. Seven Lakes State Park boasts diverse topography and ecosystems, and it is crisscrossed by over six and a half miles of well-marked trails. These trails offer scenic views of two lakes, a stream, swamps, and low swales. The park's wetland areas are home to a variety of wildlife, including songbirds, muskrats, beavers, turtles, squirrels, deer, waterfowl, herons, and more. The trail system caters to hikers, cross-country skiers, snowmobilers (when there is at least four inches of snow), and mountain bikers. The park has a designated beach, which includes restrooms, changing facilities, a picnic area with horseshoes, volleyball courts, and playground equipment available on a first-come, first-served basis. Dickinson Lake, the second-largest lake within the park, provides additional recreational opportunities, featuring a boat launch, a floating pier for fishing, a rustic picnic shelter with large grills, playground equipment, horseshoe pits, volleyball, and basketball courts. Seven Lakes State Park has five rentable picnic shelters, one of which is ADA accessible. You can reserve these shelters up to a year in advance by calling 1-800-447-2757 or visiting www.midnrreservations.com. The park is open to hunting in most areas, and you can find a variety of game species, including deer, turkey, waterfowl, rabbit, and squirrel. Seasonal naturalists offer weekly nature-based programming during the summer months. Please note that the Seven Lakes and Pontiac Lake sanitation stations are closed to non-campers due to concerns about the septic system's capacity. The nearest sanitation stations are located at Metamora-Hadley (although expect long lines on Sundays), Holly, and Proud Lake recreation areas. Campers must present a camping permit that expired within the last 24 hours; otherwise, a sanitation station use fee will be applied. The modern campground at the park features 70 campsites, providing a comfortable and convenient place to stay. Additionally, there are several trails within the park. The Dickinson Trail is a 0.3-mile trail connecting the Green Trail to the Nature Trail, offering scenic views of Dickinson Lake. It is designated for hiking and cross-country skiing. The Nature Trail Loop, spanning 0.7 miles, allows you to immerse yourself in the surrounding wilderness and can be accessed from the Dickinson Trail or the campground. In the winter, this trail is groomed for cross-country skiing. The Red Trail Loop, 1.8 miles long, can be combined with the Green Loop for a more extended journey, covering approximately 3.8 miles and passing by the park's three largest lakes. This trail begins at Meadow Ridge Shelter on Big Seven Lake and is open for both hiking and mountain biking.

PASSPORT STAMPS

SILVER LAKE STATE PARK

COUNTY	ESTABLISHED	AREA (AC/HA)
OCEANA	1920	2,936 / 1,188

Silver Lake State Park is a remarkable natural area that features 3 miles of breathtaking Lake Michigan shoreline, a well-equipped modern campground, expansive sand dunes spanning nearly 2,000 acres, a day-use area bordering Silver Lake, and the exceptional 500-acre Silver Lake ORV Area, which is the sole sand dune riding destination east of the Mississippi River. The Silver Lake ORV Area is particularly popular, especially on weekends, and it's advisable to familiarize yourself with the entry procedures, the voucher system, and the special rules and regulations in advance. Visitors have the option to bring their own Off-Road Vehicles (ORVs) or rent them from authorized local businesses. The park provides various ways to explore its beautiful dunes. It now offers a season for shoreline horseback riding from November 1st to November 30th and a fat-tire bike season from December 15th to March 15th. Visitors can relish 3 miles of sandy shoreline along Lake Michigan, with the added bonus of Silver Lake, located southeast of the dunes and adjacent to the campground. A designated swim area is available at the day-use area on Silver Lake, and two beach wheelchairs can be borrowed, with one stationed at the park's entrance booth near the lighthouse parking lot and the second at the campground office. Silver Lake is ideal for paddling, but it's important to note that paddling equipment is not permitted in the designated swim area. Several local businesses offer paddle equipment rentals. In the day-use area on Silver Lake, there is a boat launch, though it doesn't provide access to Lake Michigan. Nearby businesses rent various types of watercraft. The park also stocks Silver Lake with walleye, with fishing being more popular during the non-summer months due to the heavy boat traffic. An accessible beach house, located in the day-use area on Silver Lake, includes restrooms and family restrooms. During Memorial Day weekend through Labor Day, you can find the Lighthouse Grill food trailer near the Lake Michigan shoreline in the ORV area. Additionally, the park is home to the iconic Little Sable Point Lighthouse, situated in the southern part of the park, which can be reached by vehicle or bike. This lighthouse, constructed in 1874, stands at a towering height of over 100 feet and still houses its original third-order Fresnel lens. To access the lighthouse, there's a 10-foot-wide, paved, accessible walkway leading to its base, and vault toilets are available for visitors. The lighthouse is open for tours from mid-May to October and is maintained by the Sable Points Lighthouse Keepers Association. It includes a gift shop, and there's an entrance fee to climb the tower, which involves ascending 130 steps.

While the park doesn't have designated trails, two-thirds of the dunes are reserved for pedestrians only. Many visitors enjoy hiking and walking the dunes, although it's considered a more challenging activity. Parking is available at the pedestrian dune access parking lot at the end of North Shore Drive. Hunting is allowed in most parts of the state park, although it's advisable to contact the park directly for specific rules, concerns, or considerations. In the day-use area on Silver Lake, you'll discover a picnic area featuring picnic tables and charcoal grills, available on a first-come, first-served basis. Furthermore, there are three picnic shelters in the day-use area on Silver Lake that include picnic tables, charcoal grills, electrical access, and modern bathroom facilities, all available on a first-come, first-served basis. For those looking for accessible recreation, a playground with climbers, slides, and other play equipment is situated in the day-use area on Silver Lake. It features a rubberized surface to facilitate access for individuals with different mobility levels. The park's sanitation station is located on the south side of the modern campground and offers potable water and two lanes for campers. Silver Lake State Park's policy allows pets along the entire length of the Lake Michigan shoreline (3 miles) and the park's inland lake, Silver Lake, except for the designated swim beach. Pets must be leashed at all times, with a leash length of 6 feet, and must remain under the owner's immediate control. Proper disposal of all pet waste in designated trash receptacles is required. It's important to note that alcohol is prohibited in the ORV scramble area and within 0.25 miles of its boundaries. The park's modern campground is equipped with 200 campsites, offering either 20- or 30-amp electrical service. A majority of the campground is shaded, and the first 13 sites are situated on Silver Lake, offering convenient access to the park's inland lake. For visitors looking for some added excitement, a designated swim area is within walking distance in the day-use area, allowing registered campers to moor boats in the shallow section of the lake next to the campground. Additionally, there are various stores selling ice and camping supplies, as well as restaurants and local shops that can be reached on foot from the campground.

DATE(S) VISITED .... □ SPRING □ SUMMER □ FALL □ WINTER

LODGING .... □ ☼ □ ☁ □ ☔ □ ⛅ □ ❄

WHO I WENT WITH .... FEE(S) .... PARK HOURS .... TEMP:.........

WILL I RETURN? YES / NO   RATING ☆ ☆ ☆ ☆ ☆

PASSPORT STAMPS

SLEEPER STATE PARK

COUNTY	ESTABLISHED	AREA (AC/HA)
HURON	1924	723 / 293

Sleeper State Park encompasses 723 acres of diverse landscapes, including forests, wetlands, forested dunes, and boasts half a mile of pristine sandy shoreline along Lake Huron's Saginaw Bay. Visitors to this park can revel in the beauty of both sunrise and sunset views, explore the forested trails, unwind on the beach, and enjoy the shaded comforts of the modern campground. An interesting accommodation option offered here is the opportunity to rent safari-style, canvas-walled tents through Tentrr. The park's day-use area is conveniently situated on the other side of M-25/Port Austin Road and features a half-mile of sandy beach, a beach house, and a picnic area. A pedestrian overpass bridge facilitates easy access. Furthermore, there's a fully enclosed kitchen and dining hall equipped with a commercial kitchen, walk-in refrigerator, dining space, outdoor picnic area, and parking. To make reservations and obtain more details, you can contact the park at 989-856-4411. The park was renamed in tribute to Albert E. Sleeper, who was the governor of Michigan from 1917 to 1920 and a resident of Huron County. Sleeper is notable for signing into law the statute that created the state park system. Visitors can savor half a mile of sandy shoreline along Lake Huron's Saginaw Bay, with a designated swim area located in the park's day-use zone. Visitors should be attentive to the beach flag warning system in designated swim areas; red flags signify that the water is unsafe, and swimming is prohibited. For anglers, many access Lake Huron via boats from nearby boating access sites. It's important to note that most of the shoreline is sandy. Anglers frequently utilize the fish-cleaning station located near the campground office after returning from boat launches at nearby sites. Paddlers have the opportunity to explore Lake Huron's Saginaw Bay by launching from outside the designated swim beach. Additionally, the beach house in the day-use area, near the beach parking, provides restrooms and a changing area. Hunting is permitted in the state park; however, it's advisable to contact the park directly for specific rules, concerns, or considerations. Near the campground entrance, visitors can find the Chuck Wagon, which offers coffee, shakes, smoothies, breakfast sandwiches, and nachos. Picnic tables and charcoal grills are distributed throughout the day-use area and are available on a first-come, first-served basis. The day-use area also has a picnic shelter, complete with picnic tables, charcoal grills, electrical service (for reservations only), and modern restrooms. Reservations for the shelter can be made up to 12 months in advance at MiDNRReservations.com. Pets are permitted along the entire length of the

Lake Huron shoreline, except in the designated swim beach area. Pets must be leashed at all times, with a leash length of 6 feet, and they must remain under the immediate control of their owner. Proper disposal of all pet waste in designated trash receptacles is required. The modern campground offers campsites that are quite spacious and shaded by oak and pine trees. Each site provides either 30- or 50-amp electrical service and features a sanitation station. The west end of the campground offers four ADA-accessible sites located near a modern toilet and shower building. Visitors will find that the day-use area is located directly across M-25/Port Austin Road and boasts a half-mile of sandy shoreline along Lake Huron's Saginaw Bay, a beach house, and a picnic area. A pedestrian overpass bridge provides easy access. Additionally, the park offers a mini cabin and Tentrr safari tents to provide unique overnight experiences. The park's mini cabin is situated at the eastern end of the modern campground and can accommodate up to five people. It includes two sets of bunk beds, with one double bed and three single beds. The cabin is equipped with a mini refrigerator, microwave, heater, ceiling fan, and lighting. Outdoor amenities include a picnic table, fire pit, and waist-high cook grill. The cabins have electricity, and water is available in the campground. Please note that you must bring your own linens. The Tentrr safari tents accommodate up to six people. Each site consists of a primary safari-style tent with two occupants and a pop-up tent provided by Tentrr, allowing for an additional four occupants. Bedding is not provided. These spacious safari-style tents are set on raised wooden platforms and come with a comfortable bed for a restful night's sleep, along with Adirondack chairs for relaxation and a fire pit ideal for gatherings and stargazing. Remember to bring marshmallows! The walk-in tent sites are situated in rustic areas outside the park's campground, with some located in wooded areas and others on forested dunes overlooking Lake Huron, just a few steps from the shoreline. Access to these sites requires a short hike from the parking area, and there is one accessible site with a parking spot. Each site includes a queen-size memory foam mattress on a sturdy bed frame, Adirondack chairs, a fire pit with grill, and a picnic table with a pantry storage cabinet. There is no electrical service, so it's essential to bring your own lanterns or flashlights. Bathrooms (with toilets and sinks) and vault toilets are available within walking distance. A shared water spigot is located near both the wooded and beach locations. Campers also have access to a shower building in the modern campground, just a short drive away. The park provides six Tentrr sites: Dodge Brothers Getaway (site E), Red Dawn (site F), Deer Trail (site G), Ford Hilltop Chalet (site J), Eleanor's Tea Tent (site K), and Lower's Lodge (site L). To make a reservation, you can visit MiDNRReservations.com and select the campsite tab, then click on the Tentrr Safari Tent radio button. For hikers, the Candlestick Trail, a short 0.63-mile trail, winds through a variety of terrain, including forested dunes, an oak and pine savanna, and wetlands. This trail connects to the park's three other trails and has trailheads located at either end of the modern campground. There is day-use parking available at the park headquarters, 6573 State Park Road in Caseville. The Deer Run Trail is a 2-mile loop that links to the park's other trails via the Huron Trail. This trail takes visitors through diverse landscapes, including forested dunes, an oak and pine savanna, and wetlands. You can access the trail from either end of the campground via the Candlestick Trail and Huron Trail. Day-use parking with direct access to the Candlestick Trail is available at the park headquarters, 6573 State Park Road in Caseville. The Huron Trail is a quick 0.2-mile trail that connects the Candlestick Trail to the Deer Run Trail. It guides visitors through a variety of terrain, including forested dunes, an oak and pine savanna, and wetlands. Parking with direct access to the Candlestick Trail is available at the park headquarters, 6573 State Park Road in Caseville. The Old Dunes Nature Trail is a looped interpretive trail featuring educational signage about the park's natural features. This trail takes visitors through a variety of terrain, including forested dunes, an oak and pine savanna, and wetlands. Access points to the trail can be found at the west end of the campground or via the Candlestick Trail. Day-use parking with direct access to the Candlestick Trail is available at the park headquarters, 6573 State Park Road in Caseville.

DATE(S) VISITED ....

□ SPRING   □ SUMMER   □ FALL   □ WINTER

LODGING ....

□ ☼   □ ☁   □ ☔   □ ☁   □ ❄

WHO I WENT WITH ....

FEE(S) .... PARK HOURS .... TEMP:.........

WILL I RETURN? YES / NO

RATING ☆ ☆ ☆ ☆ ☆

PASSPORT STAMPS

SLEEPY HOLLOW STATE PARK

COUNTY	ESTABLISHED	AREA (AC/HA)
CLINTON	1965	2,678 / 1,084

Sleepy Hollow State Park, located just 20 minutes north of Lansing in Clinton County, spans over 2,600 acres and is situated off Price Road near St. Johns and Laingsburg, accessible from US-27. The park is characterized by a river meandering through its woodlands and fields, with Lake Ovid nestled at its heart. Lake Ovid, covering 410 acres, was created by damming the Little Maple River. Sleepy Hollow State Park offers recreational opportunities year-round. The park is home to a diverse range of bird species, with more than 228 varieties having been observed in Sleepy Hollow, from common birds like the Blue Jay to the Eastern Bluebird. During migration periods, you can spot waterfowl in Lake Ovid, and rare sightings include the Bonaparte's Gull or Bald Eagle. Besides the activities mentioned above, snowshoeing is a popular pastime at Sleepy Hollow State Park. Canoeing and kayaking are favored activities at Sleepy Hollow State Park. The campground office offers rentals of canoes, kayaks, and stand-up paddleboards from Memorial Day weekend through Labor Day weekend, between 8 a.m. and 8 p.m. For more details, you can reach out to them at 517-651-6217. Lake Ovid is renowned as a great fishing lake, home to various fish species such as muskie, largemouth and smallmouth bass, bluegill, sunfish, crappie, rock bass, perch, catfish, and bullheads. Two fishing piers are available, along with access to multiple shoreline fishing spots. The boat launch and parking area are paved. Lake Ovid is a "no wake" lake within Sleepy Hollow State Park. The park also maintains two boating access sites in Clinton County, namely Muskrat Lake and Looking Glass River. Beach House: Located on Lake Ovid, the beach area features a Mobi-chair floating beach wheelchair and an Amigo mobility scooter for park guests to use, without any rental fees. More than 11 miles of trails are open for biking, mountain biking, and hiking. The hiking trails lead you through prairie grasses, hardwood forests, and pine tree groves. There are 12.9 miles of horse trails, available to visitors who trailer their horses in for the day. Horses are allowed only on designated bridle trails, maintained and managed by the Sleepy Hollow Trail Riders Association. Cross-country skiing is permitted on all park trails. Snowmobiling is allowed in the west end of the park when there's a minimum of four inches of snow on the ground, with snowmobiles prohibited on cross-country ski trails and required to have current registration. The disc golf course is accessible year-round. Park lands are open to hunting and trapping during the appropriate seasons. The park is home to excellent hunting opportunities for ducks, deer, rabbit, and squirrel, with turkey, woodcock, pheasant, quail, and grouse also found in the park. For day visitors, there's a beach located northwest of the campground, equipped with picnic tables, a beach house, and phones. Seasonal naturalists offer weekly nature-based programs during Memorial Day through Labor Day. A section of pet-friendly shoreline, known as 'Dog Beach,' is available 100 yards north of the Lake Ovid swimming beach, as indicated by the signs. Additionally, both the modern cabin and rustic cabin (for reservations beginning Nov. 1, 2021) are pet-friendly. Up to two pets, cats and dogs only, are allowed. Pets must be kept on a six-foot leash, both in and out of the water, and under the immediate control of their owner/handler at all times. Pet waste bags are provided for your use, and pet waste should be disposed of in nearby trash receptacles. The modern campground provides 181 camp sites. Modern Cabin - Constructed in 2014, this family-friendly cabin offers two bedrooms and can accommodate six guests. The cabin is accessible and includes a full bathroom with a shower, a kitchenette, a living/dining area, and a private outdoor grill, fire circle, and picnic table overlooking Lake Ovid. Each bedroom features a full-size bed with a single bunk above. Visitors must bring their own bedding and cooking supplies. The kitchenette includes a sink/faucet, microwave, coffee maker, and toaster oven. In addition to swimming, boating, and fishing opportunities within walking distance, guests also have easy access to over 28 miles of hiking, biking, and horseback riding trails. Rustic Cabin - This one-bedroom cabin sleeps five people and is accessible. It features solar-powered lighting and a propane wall heater for warmth during cold months. Near the cabin, you'll find drinking water and a vault toilet. The bedroom includes a full-size bed with a single bunk above, and there's a full-size futon in the adjoining room. As with the modern cabin, guests should bring their own bedding and cooking supplies. The cabin offers a private outdoor grill, fire ring, and picnic table overlooking Lake Ovid. Similar to the modern cabin, guests have convenient access to swimming, boating, and fishing opportunities, along with access to more than 28 miles of hiking, biking, and horseback riding trails. The park provides four equine picket poles and a manure bunker for equestrian campers, with trailer parking located nearby. The Sleepy Hollow Hiking Trail is a 16-mile trail located in Sleepy Hollow State Park in Laingsburg. The trail winds through picturesque forests, offering frequent views of Lake Ovid, and also passes by the Little Maple river. Hikers can frequently walk alongside the horse trail and enjoy opportunities to stop and picnic during their journey. The trail is open to hiking, biking, snowshoeing, and cross-country skiing, weather permitting. Sleepy Hollow State Park surrounds the beautiful Lake Ovid and features 12.5 miles of trails available for horseback riding. These looped trails provide easy riding through grasslands, pine stands, and scenic forests. Riders can begin their journey at the equestrian staging area at the north end of the park. The trails are well-marked and maintained, featuring four loops including the East and West loops (which can be ridden separately or as one large loop), the West loop (connecting back to the staging area), and the South loop (an old roadbed that is cart-accessible and travels along Lake Ovid). A notable feature is the arched 100-foot bridge along the South loop, leading to the multi-use Island Trail. Horses are not permitted in the lake or creek, as the glacial outwash soils can become soft and slippery when wet. The equestrian staging area is equipped with a pavilion, mounting blocks, picket poles, picnic tables, pit toilets, a manure pit, and water from a hand pump. A seasonal portable toilet is also located near letter O/Site F on the trail map. Visitors should check the trail kiosk for updates before embarking on their ride. Some sections of the trail are multi-use and may be shared with hikers or cyclists. During designated hunting seasons, hunting is allowed, and visitors are advised to wear orange. The park also allows dog sledding on the trails. The park doesn't have an equestrian campground, but the Sleepy Hollow Trail Rider Association hosts two campouts each year. Additionally, there is a two-bedroom modern cabin and a one-bedroom rustic cabin available for rent, both of which are equestrian-friendly.

DATE(S) VISITED .... ☐ SPRING ☐ SUMMER ☐ FALL ☐ WINTER

LODGING .... ☐ ☀ ☐ ☁ ☐ 🌧 ☐ 🌬 ☐ ❄

WHO I WENT WITH .... FEE(S) .... PARK HOURS .... TEMP:.........

WILL I RETURN? YES / NO   RATING ☆ ☆ ☆ ☆ ☆

PASSPORT STAMPS

SOUTH HIGGINS LAKE STATE PARK

COUNTY	ESTABLISHED	AREA (AC/HA)
ROSCOMMON	1924	1,346 / 544

South Higgins Lake State Park is located along a 1-mile stretch of Higgins Lake shoreline and is home to one of Michigan's largest state park campgrounds. It also features a popular boat launch and day-use area. Additionally, the park includes Marl Lake, a smaller, shallower, and less developed lake, which can be found on the southern side of the park across County Road 100, surrounded by 5.5 miles of wooded trails. The 1,364-acre park is renowned for its wide range of water-based recreational activities. Higgins Lake, a large spring-fed lake known for its clear waters, fishing opportunities, and boating, offers a significant boating access site with a boat basin, nine launch ramps, and a boat-washing station. In contrast, Marl Lake offers a more tranquil and natural setting suitable for non-motorized boats and electric motorboats. The park also provides boat rentals. Both Higgins Lake and Marl Lake offer ample opportunities for paddling, with Marl Lake specifically allowing non-motorized boats and electric motors only. The park's primary attraction is its 1-mile sandy shoreline along the 9,900-acre Higgins Lake, a crystal-clear lake renowned for boating, fishing, and swimming. The park also includes 700-acre Marl Lake, which offers a quieter environment for fishing. There are two designated swimming areas within the park's day-use areas. Additionally, the park provides an accessible walkway to the water's edge near the park store and another accessible walkway near the east loop of the modern campground. For those in need, two beach wheelchairs are available to borrow by calling the park or visiting the campground office. The South Higgins Lake State Park Store, located in the day-use area, offers kayak, stand-up paddleboard, and float rentals from mid-May through September. For more information, you can contact them at 989-821-1049. The park boasts a spacious boat access site on Higgins Lake, which includes a protected boat basin with nine launch ramps, day-mooring facilities, a large parking area for vehicles and boats, a two-lane boat wash, and a boat-cleaning station. There is a second boat access site on Marl Lake, located across County Road 100, which is designed for non-motorized or electric motorboats. Higgins Lake, which spans 7 miles and reaches depths of up to 135 feet, is renowned for perch and lake trout fishing. Marl Lake is known for its perch, smallmouth bass, and northern pike. Most anglers prefer to use a canoe or small boat and fish in the center of the lake. Hunting is permitted on the Marl Lake side of County Road 100. However, it is advisable to contact the park directly to inquire about any special rules, concerns, or considerations. The picnic area is situated in the day-use area and includes picnic tables and charcoal grills, available on a first-come, first-served basis. There are also two picnic shelters in the day-use area, which include picnic tables, charcoal grills, electrical service, and modern restroom facilities. Reservations for the shelters can be made up to 12 months in advance at MiDNRReservations.com. The park also features play equipment located throughout the day-use area. The park's sanitation station is located near the campground entrance, and potable water is readily available with four lanes. The park offers seasonal naturalists who provide weekly nature-based programs from Memorial Day through Labor Day. There are three pet-friendly beach areas in the park: one in the day-use area (along the east boundary of the park), one in the campground (west side of the boat access site), and a campers-only area (along the west boundary of the campground). Pets should always be on a 6-foot leash and under the immediate control of their owner. Additionally, pet waste must be properly disposed of in trash receptacles. The park's modern campground is the second-largest in the state park system and offers traditional sites, full hook-up sites, and a mini cabin. Most of the sites are shaded by hardwoods, and many are located closer to each other, making them suitable for reunions and family gatherings. The modern cabin, located in the modern campground, sleeps up to five people and includes two bunk beds (a double bed and two single beds), a mini refrigerator, a microwave, an electric wall heater, a counter with stools, and electricity. Visitors must bring their own linens. The cabin also provides a picnic table, a fire pit, and a waist-high cook grill. Marl Lake Trails - The park features 5.5 miles of looped trails that wind through small wetlands, hardwood forests (including birch, hemlock, and oak), and the peaceful Marl Lake. These trails offer spur trails for hikers to choose from, including 2 miles (Green Loop A), 3.5 miles (Red Loop B), or the full 5.5-mile trail (Blue Loop C). The trail also connects to Markey Township Park, which features a fitness trail, a dog park, and a large playground area, via Green Loop A. Hunting is permitted in this area throughout the seasons, and visitors are advised to wear high-visibility clothing.

STERLING STATE PARK

COUNTY	ESTABLISHED	AREA (AC/HA)
MONROE	1935	1,300 / 530

William C. Sterling State Park, the only Michigan state park on Lake Erie, is located just a short distance from the Ohio border and approximately an hour's drive from Detroit. The park boasts a mile of sandy shoreline and offers a modern campground, fully equipped cottages, a boat launch site, various trails, and numerous fishing opportunities. This park covers over 500 acres of Great Lakes marsh and restored lakeplain prairie habitat, making it a popular spot for walleye and perch fishing. The River Raisin Heritage Trail provides a connection between the park and downtown Monroe, local parks, trails, and the River Raisin National Battlefield Park. Visitors can enjoy a mile of sandy shoreline along Lake Erie, with a designated swim area available in the park's day-use section. The park employs a beach flag warning system, with red flags indicating unsafe water conditions. Swimming near the break wall is discouraged due to changing conditions. Additionally, there's a barrier-free boat launch at the north end of the park, offering access to Lake Erie, with ample parking spaces for vehicles and trailers, as well as five skid piers. Modern restrooms and a fish-cleaning station are also provided. The park offers kayak rentals at the campground office during Memorial Day through Labor Day. Paddling is a popular activity on Lake Erie, and the park provides opportunities for both shoreline and off-shore fishing, particularly for walleye and perch. You'll find a fish-cleaning station at the boating access site's north end, and the day-use area includes a beach house with restrooms and changing stalls. If you're feeling hungry, JR's Food Concessions operates a food truck near the beach house in the day-use area, serving items like corn dogs, French fries, shaved ice, and more. Hunting is permitted within the state park, but it's advisable to contact the park directly to inquire about specific rules, concerns, or considerations. The park features an observation platform and viewing tower along the Marsh Trail, offering excellent wildlife viewing opportunities. In the day-use area, you'll find a picnic area with picnic tables and charcoal grills available on a first-come, first-served basis. Two picnic shelters equipped with picnic tables, charcoal grills, and modern restrooms can be reserved up to 12 months in advance through MiDNRReservations.com. A playground in the day-use area features various equipment, including a multi-access swing, slide, slide ball, bars, and more. Note that alcoholic beverages are prohibited in the park from April 1 through Labor Day, unless authorized by the park manager through an event permit. A vault toilet is located at the boating access site, and the park's sanitation station is located at the modern campground, offering potable water and three lanes. The modern campground offers paved, generously sized sites, with many providing views of Lake Erie and quick access to the sandy shoreline. Site options include 20- or 30-amp service, with 50-amp service available on 76 of the sites. A sanitation station and recycling facilities are available. Vista Recreation, a private operator and DNR partner, manages ten fully equipped cottages along Lake Erie. Each cottage accommodates seven guests and requires a two-night minimum stay. They include one bedroom with a queen bed, a second room with a bunk bed (single top, double base), a bathroom, kitchen, dining space, and a common area with a futon. Kitchen amenities include essential cookware, a cooktop, microwave, and refrigerator. Bedding linens and towels are not provided and must be brought by guests. Note that only one vehicle is permitted per cottage, with overflow parking available in the campground for additional vehicles. The 1-mile River Raisin Heritage (connector) Trail, often referred to as the Wetlands Trail, links Sterling State Park to the River Raisin Heritage Trail, providing access to downtown Monroe, local parks, trails, and the River Raisin National Battlefield Park. The Marsh Trail, a 2.7-mile paved loop, offers scenic views of the marsh and lotus beds and includes an observation platform and viewing tower. The Marsh Trail connects to the 1-mile River Raisin Heritage (connector) Trail, which links Sterling State Park to the River Raisin Heritage Trail. The trailhead, located across from the day-use area, can accommodate 60 vehicles, with an additional 20-vehicle parking area available along the main entrance road, just after the contact station.

DATE(S) VISITED .... ☐ SPRING ☐ SUMMER ☐ FALL ☐ WINTER

LODGING .... ☐ ☀ ☐ ☁ ☐ 🌧 ☐ ⛅ ☐ ❄

WHO I WENT WITH .... FEE(S) .... PARK HOURS .... TEMP:.........

WILL I RETURN? YES / NO   RATING ☆ ☆ ☆ ☆ ☆

PASSPORT STAMPS

STRAITS STATE PARK

COUNTY	ESTABLISHED	AREA (AC/HA)
MACKINAC	1924	181 / 73

Straits State Park encompasses 181 acres of recreational space offering breathtaking vistas of the Mackinac Bridge and the Straits of Mackinac. The park comprises a campground, accommodations for overnight stays, picnic areas, observation platforms, a playground, and a waterfront section along Lake Huron. The North Country Trail traverses the park, with a part of it running along a 1-mile hiking trail within the park. This park is a prominent location on the Northern Huron Birding Trail and is particularly renowned during the spring and fall seasons when migratory birds travel across the narrow straits connecting the Upper and Lower Peninsulas. Its strategic location also makes it a convenient base for exploring other nearby attractions, including Mackinac Island, Mackinac State Historic Parks, the Soo Locks, and Tahquamenon Falls. Within Straits State Park, you'll find the Father Marquette National Memorial, which tells the story of the 17th-century missionary-explorer and the interactions between French and Native American cultures in the North American wilderness. The Michigan History Center provides historical interpretation. The memorial features an outdoor interpretive trail, picnicking areas, and a panoramic viewpoint of the Mackinac Bridge. The site is open from Memorial Day through Labor Day and is located within the park, just west of I-75 off U.S. 2. The park offers a limited stretch of rocky shoreline along Lake Huron. Additionally, the Mackinac Bridge Authority shoreline property adjacent to the park is open to the public. Visitors can explore the Lake Huron shoreline, with carry-in access available from the end of the road to the lower campground, offering a few parking spaces. When conditions permit, roadways and campground loops are groomed for classic cross-country skiing. They are groomed for cross-country skiing on one side with packed snow on the other. It's essential to avoid groomed cross-country ski tracks. An observation platform in the day-use area provides unique views of the Straits of Mackinac and the Mackinac Bridge. Another observation platform, offering a view of the Mackinac Bridge, is located along the park's hiking trail, approximately 100 yards from the trailhead. In the day-use area, picnic areas are situated near both the playground and the overlook platform. Picnic tables and charcoal grills are available on a first-come, first-served basis. Modern restrooms are found in the day-use area. The day-use area also features a sandy-surfaced playground with slides, swings, and a sand digger. Sanitation stations are present in both the upper and lower campground loops, offering potable water and in-and-out lanes. For those not camping at Straits State Park, the sanitation station in the upper campground loop is accessible. Along the Lake Huron shoreline, pets are allowed. They must be kept on a 6-foot leash and under the owner's immediate control at all times. All pet waste must be disposed of in trash receptacles. The campground is divided into three loops: the upper loop, lower east loop, and lower west loop. It offers a variety of site options, with the potential for some sites to have views of the Mackinac Bridge and the Straits of Mackinac, even if set back from the water. Modern toilet and shower facilities, as well as sanitation stations, are available seasonally. The upper campground loop is situated atop a bluff and generally provides larger, more open sites, including some pull-through options. All sites in the upper loop offer 20/30-amp electrical service, with some sites featuring 50-amp service. The lower campground loops typically offer smaller sites best suited for small trailers and tent camping, although there are larger sites available. Toilet and shower buildings in these loops are accessible and are usually open later in the season, from mid-May to mid-October. Nonwaterfront sites in the lower campground loops provide 20/30-amp electrical service, with some offering 50-amp service. Waterfront sites along the Mackinac Bridge offer scenic views but are considered semi-modern as they lack electric hookups. However, these sites have access to modern toilet and shower facilities during the season. Note that generators and power cords are not allowed on waterfront sites. There are two accessible mini cabins located in the park's lower east campground loop. Each cabin accommodates four people and features two sets of single bunk beds, one with a full-size bed as the lower bunk. The cabins are equipped with a table and chairs, mini refrigerator, electric lighting, and electrical outlets. Fans and heating are not provided. Outdoors, there is a picnic table, a fire pit, and a charcoal grill. An accessible modern toilet and shower facility is located nearby within the campground. Guests must bring their own linens, and pets are not allowed in the cabins. For youth groups of up to 50 individuals, two tent-only, rustic campgrounds are available. The Hollow youth-group-use campground is located behind a bluff, separate from the surrounding day-use area. The Ball Diamond youth-group-use campground is more open and situated adjacent to the day-use area. In the day-use area, a modern restroom is accessible with toilets and cold running water, including an outdoor spigot for filling water containers. Campers are also welcome to use the toilet and shower buildings in the modern campground during the season. Reservations can be made by calling the park office at 906-643-8620. The Straits State Park Main Trail is a half-mile linear trail (1-mile roundtrip) suitable for hiking, cross-country skiing, and snowshoeing. This trail offers magnificent views of the Straits of Mackinac and the Mackinac Bridge as it winds through the park. The trail begins at the viewing platform in the day-use area, featuring another observation platform approximately 100 yards from the trailhead, and concludes at a viewing area in the upper campground loop.

The trail is characterized by steep, hilly, rocky terrain with some challenging slopes. A section of the trail coincides with the North Country Trail, and occasionally, there are lantern-lit hikes offered during the winter season.

DATE(S) VISITED .... ☐ SPRING ☐ SUMMER ☐ FALL ☐ WINTER

LODGING .... ☐ ☀ ☐ ☁ ☐ 🌧 ☐ 🌫 ☐ ❄

WHO I WENT WITH .... FEE(S) .... PARK HOURS .... TEMP:........

WILL I RETURN? YES / NO   RATING ☆ ☆ ☆ ☆ ☆

PASSPORT STAMPS

STURGEON POINT STATE PARK

COUNTY	ESTABLISHED	AREA (AC/HA)
ALCONA	1960	76 / 31

Sturgeon Point State Park is situated 5 miles north of Harrisville on the shores of Lake Huron. It was initially established to serve as a warning to mariners about a reef that extends 1.5 miles into the lake. The Sturgeon Point Lighthouse, built in 1869, is a historic representation of a Cape Cod-style Great Lakes lighthouse and is often considered a counterpart to the Tawas Point Lighthouse. The lighthouse stands at a height of 70 feet with a base diameter of 16 feet, and it features a 3.5-order Fresnel lens crafted in Paris, France. The U.S. Coast Guard continues to maintain the light. Both the lighthouse tower and the keeper's house have been transformed into a maritime museum, welcoming visitors from Memorial Day through mid-September. While the museum is open seasonally, the park grounds are accessible throughout the year, and there is available parking. For directions, take U.S. 23 north for approximately 3 miles from Harrisville, then turn right onto Lakeshore Drive. Continue for about 1 mile until you reach Point Road. Turn east onto Point Road and proceed for approximately 1 mile until you see the gravel road on the left leading to the lighthouse parking area. From there, it's a short walk to the lighthouse. The park boasts about half a mile of sandy Lake Huron shoreline, and picnic tables are available near the lighthouse on a first-come, first-served basis. The Alcona Historical Society's gift shop is generally open on the weekends during the same period, Memorial Day through mid-September. Visitors can explore a variety of maritime- and lighthouse-related items and gifts, including clothing and prints.

DATE(S) VISITED .... ☐ SPRING ☐ SUMMER ☐ FALL ☐ WINTER

LODGING .... ☐ ☼ ☐ ☁ ☐ ☂ ☐ ☁ ☐ ❄

WHO I WENT WITH .... FEE(S) .... PARK HOURS .... TEMP:.........

WILL I RETURN? YES / NO   RATING ☆ ☆ ☆ ☆ ☆

PASSPORT STAMPS

TAHQUAMENON FALLS STATE PARK

COUNTY	ESTABLISHED	AREA (AC/HA)
CHIPPEWA, LUCE	1947	46,179 / 18,688

Tahquamenon Falls State Park, located in Michigan's Upper Peninsula, spans nearly 50,000 acres and stretches over 13 miles. The park offers multiple campgrounds, accommodations for overnight stays, a boating access site, an extensive trail network exceeding 35 miles, and various overlooks to observe the Upper and Lower Falls. For the convenience of visitors, there is a shuttle service available between the Upper and Lower Falls, subject to a fee. The shuttle schedule varies depending on the season, so it's recommended to contact the park directly for the most up-to-date schedules. The Upper Falls, an impressive 200 feet wide, ranks among the largest waterfalls east of the Mississippi River. The river's characteristic amber color is a result of tannins released from the cedar, spruce, and hemlock trees in the surrounding swamps. The soft water agitated by the falls creates abundant foam, which is another distinctive feature of the river. Only 4 miles downstream is the Lower Falls, which consists of five smaller cascading falls around an island. These falls can be viewed from the riverbank and from the accessible Ronald A. Olson Island Bridge, which is named in honor of the DNR Parks and Recreation Division chief. Alternatively, visitors can rent rowboats from a park concession to get a closer look. Drone use is prohibited in the park. The North Country Trail, stretching 16 miles within the park, offers a path connecting the Upper and Lower Falls. Special thanks to the North Country Trail Association Hiawatha Shore-to-Shore Chapter for its contribution. The park is home to a diverse range of wildlife, including black bears, coyotes, otters, deer, foxes, porcupines, beavers, and numerous bird species like spruce grouse, pileated woodpeckers, bald eagles, and various waterfowl and songbirds. On occasion, moose can be spotted feeding in the park's wet areas, particularly along M-123 between Paradise and the Lower Falls. Boat rentals are available at the Lower Tahquamenon Falls Café & Gift Shop, offering rowboats for rent from Memorial Day weekend through mid-October, depending on river levels and conditions. Reservations are not mandatory. An accessible paved boat launch is located at the Rivermouth area, across the road from the Rivermouth Campground, with limited parking available. Additionally, there is a canoe/kayak launch in the Lower Falls day-use area. The Tahquamenon River provides 17 miles of paddling opportunities, stretching from the Lower Falls to the Rivermouth area. Carry-in access sites are available both at the Lower Falls day-use area and at the Rivermouth modern campground. The river's current is generally suitable for both upstream and downstream travel. The

Tahquamenon River, running through the park, is home to various fish species, including brown trout, walleye, muskie, northern pike, yellow perch, smallmouth bass, and more. There are accessible shore fishing locations in the Rivermouth Pines Campground, and a fishing pier can be found at the Rivermouth boating access site, located across the road from the Rivermouth Campground. Cross-Country Skiing is a popular activity in the park, with 4 miles of regularly groomed, single-track classic cross-country ski trails integrated into the hiking trail system in the Upper Falls day-use area. These trails include the 1-mile Lantern Loop and the 3.8-mile Giant Pines Loop. The park also allows backcountry skiing, encouraging visitors to explore off-trail throughout the park. Please ensure that pets remain off groomed ski tracks and avoid walking on groomed ski trails. Restrooms are available in the Lower Falls and Upper Falls day-use areas, and the restrooms in the Upper Falls day-use area are ADA-accessible. The park features numerous observation platforms for viewing the Lower and Upper falls. The first accessible viewing area is located just 100 yards from the parking lot at the Lower Falls, and additional viewing areas are situated along a half-mile accessible boardwalk. The falls are also visible from the all-accessible Ronald A. Olson Island Bridge, or visitors can rent a rowboat from a park concession to get a closer look. In the Upper Falls day-use area, there are three accessible viewing platforms along a paved pathway a third of a mile from the parking area. Hunting is allowed within the state park, except in areas designated as closed to hunting, which are clearly marked around campgrounds and visitor areas. For inquiries regarding special rules, concerns, or considerations, please contact the park office at 906-492-3415. Throughout the summer months, professional interpretive naturalists conduct daily nature-based programs in various locations within the park, providing educational and informative experiences. Accessible picnic areas are available at Whitefish Bay Picnic Area and in the Lower and Upper Falls day-use areas, complete with picnic tables and charcoal grills that are available on a first-come, first-served basis. There is a non-accessible picnic area with picnic tables and charcoal grills at the Stables, situated between the Upper and Lower falls. This picnic area has no electricity, and restrooms are a short walk away. Reservations for the picnic shelter in the Lower Falls day-use area, which includes picnic tables and a group charcoal grill, can be made up to 12 months in advance at MIDNRReservations.com or by calling 1-800-447-2757. Sanitation stations are available at the Lower Falls Modern Campground and Rivermouth Modern Campground, open seasonally from mid-May to mid-October. Each of these stations offers potable water and two lanes. Leashed pets are allowed on all trails, including viewing platforms, provided they are kept on a 6-foot leash and under their owner's immediate control. All pet waste must be disposed of in the provided trash receptacles. Snowmobiling is allowed only on designated trails within the park. Off-trail or backcountry snowmobiling is not permitted in open land areas. Trail 45, also known as Charcoal Grade Trail, traverses the park and follows the M-123 Scenic Byway. This 44-mile multi-use trail runs from Newberry to Paradise and was originally a snowmobile trail. Parts of the trail are open year-round for various uses, from snowmobiling to ORV/ATV riding, hiking, biking, and walking. Snowmobile parking and trail access are available in the Lower Falls and Upper Falls day-use areas. Additionally, the park offers 9 miles of marked snowshoe trails in the Lower Falls and Upper Falls day-use areas. Visitors are encouraged to explore the park through backcountry snowshoeing, with off-trail exploration welcomed. The Lower Falls Modern Campground is divided into two loops, Hemlock and Portage, with all sites offering 30-amp electrical service, and some sites providing 50-amp service. A sanitation station is available during the season, along with recycling facilities. The Hemlock campground loop, situated approximately a mile away from the Lower Falls, remains open year-round. This campground is generally more shaded compared to the Portage loop and offers access to the park's hiking trails. It is known for having the best cellphone service in the Lower Falls area. During the winter season, certain portions of this campground are reservable for semi-modern camping. The Portage campground loop is located near the river, about a quarter-mile from the Lower Falls. This loop features a modern toilet and shower building that is ADA-accessible, along with some accessible campsites. Some sites in this loop offer views of the river, and the area is generally sunnier and more open compared to the Hemlock loop. The North Country Trail is accessible from this campground. During the winter, the Portage loop is open for hike-in camping. To locate this campground for mapping purposes, use the physical address: 6999 N. Lower Campground Lane, Paradise, MI 49768. The Rivermouth Modern Campground is a wooded area featuring two loops with a variety of campsite types, including some accessible, paved, and pull-through sites. Campers can enjoy strolling along the river, amidst blueberry bushes and wildflowers, beneath towering red pine trees. Bicycling is a popular way to get around the campground, to reach the playground, and to access the accessible fishing platform in the adjacent Rivermouth Pines Campground. Each campsite offers 30-amp electrical service, and some provide 50-amp service. There's also a nearby boat launch, and kayaks are available for rent on a first-come, first-served basis from the Rivermouth Campground office. A sanitation station and recycling facilities are accessible. The campground is situated 5 miles south of Paradise, and for mapping purposes, use the physical address: 32130 W. South River Road, Paradise, MI 49768. The Rivermouth Pines Campground, located along the Tahquamenon River, offers picturesque sunset views of the river. The campsite area is shaded by overhead red pine trees and features a mostly open understory with a sandy surface, making it ideal for tent camping, van camping, or compact campers. The campground provides an accessible fishing platform, and visitors can often spot bald eagles, waterfowl, and beavers. Bicycling is a popular way to get around, whether it's to access the playground or the seasonal restrooms at the nearby Rivermouth Modern Campground. Each campsite is equipped with 30-amp electrical service, and some offer 50-amp service. There's also a nearby boat launch, and kayaks are available for rent on a first-come, first-served basis from the Rivermouth Campground office. The campground is considered seasonally semi-modern, with water spigots generally available from mid-May through the second Sunday in October, weather permitting. Vault toilets can be found throughout the campground. In-season, campers also have access to the nearby restroom and shower facilities at the Rivermouth Modern Campground, which is about a 10-minute walk or a short drive away. However, when the restrooms in the nearby modern campground are closed for the season and the water spigots have been turned off, the campground transitions to a rustic mode, and campers must either bring in their own water or obtain it at the park headquarters, located between the Lower Falls and Upper Falls. Generators are not permitted in the Rivermouth Pines Campground. To locate this campground for mapping purposes, use the physical address: 32130 W. South River Road, Paradise, MI 49768. The Rivermouth Pines Camper Cabin is positioned within the Rivermouth Pines Campground, offering serene views of the Tahquamenon River. This accessible two-bedroom cabin can accommodate up to seven people and features electrical outlets, lighting, and a wall-mounted heating unit in each bedroom for comfort. One bedroom has two sets of single bunk beds, while the other contains a full-size bed with a single bunk above. The cabin also includes a small living area equipped with a mini refrigerator, microwave, coffee maker, table, and chairs. Outdoors, there's a picnic table, fire pit, and charcoal grill. Please note that you'll need to bring your own linens, and pets are not allowed. The cabin doesn't have restrooms or running water. Vault toilets can be found throughout the Rivermouth Pines Campground, and a modern toilet and shower facility in the nearby Rivermouth Modern campground is accessible during the season, located within about a 10-minute walk or a short drive. Water spigots within the campground are available seasonally, generally from mid-May through the second Sunday in October, weather permitting. When the restrooms in the nearby modern campground are closed for the season, and water spigots have been turned off, the campground transitions to rustic mode, and campers must either bring their own water or obtain it at the park headquarters, located between the Lower Falls and Upper Falls. To locate this campground for mapping purposes, use the physical address: 32130 W. South River Road, Paradise, MI 49768. The Tahquamenon Falls Lodge is conveniently situated between the Upper and Lower falls and provides easy access to snowmobile trails. This spacious lodge can sleep up to eight people and offers three bedrooms and two bathrooms. On the first floor, you'll find a full bathroom, a bedroom with a queen-sized bed, a kitchen, and a living area. The fully equipped kitchen includes a stove, refrigerator, microwave, coffee maker, pancake griddle, pots and pans, silverware, bakeware, plates, and cups. The second floor contains a half bathroom, a bedroom with two sets of single bunk beds, and another bedroom with two single beds. Other amenities include games, books, and an outdoor area featuring a picnic table, charcoal grill, and fire ring. The downstairs and deck are wheelchair-accessible. Linens, blankets, bath towels, and dish towels are provided. Pets are not allowed. During the period from Memorial Day weekend through Labor Day, the lodge is only available for weekly reservations, with a minimum stay of six nights and a Saturday check-in and Friday check-out. For the rest of the year, the lodge has a minimum rental duration of four nights. Reservations can be made by calling the park office at 906-492-3415, and they can be made up to one year in advance. The lodge is located near the main park office at the following address: 41382 W. M-123, Paradise, MI 49768. This open area in the Rivermouth Pines Campground is designed for groups of up to 50 people with tents. The site features a vault toilet and a fire ring with bench seating. For reservations, please contact the park office at 906-492-3415. The Rivermouth Pines Campground is seasonally semi-modern, with water spigots generally available from mid-May through the second Sunday in October, weather permitting. Campers are encouraged to fill their water jugs near site #132. During the season, campers also have access to the nearby restroom and shower facilities at the Rivermouth Modern Campground, which is located about a 10-minute walk or a short drive away. However, when the restrooms in the nearby modern campground are closed for the season and the water spigots have been turned off, the campground shifts to a rustic mode, and campers must either bring their own water or obtain it at the park headquarters, situated between the Lower Falls and Upper Falls. Generators are not allowed in the Group Use Area. To locate this area for mapping purposes, use the following physical address: 32130 W. South River Road, Paradise, MI 49768. Tahquamenon Falls State Park offers three backcountry campsites available for reservations, and they are situated along or near the North Country Trail. Each campsite includes a picnic table, fire ring, and a latrine (an open-air toilet seat on a wooden box over a hole in the ground). Hike-in distances to these campsites vary, ranging from 1 to 5 miles, depending on your chosen site and parking location. Please reach out to the park office at 906-492-3415 for detailed information and route options. Reservations are mandatory and can only be made at the park. On the day of your reservation, you'll need to check in at the park office and provide information regarding the parking location for your vehicle overnight. Hikers on the North Country Trail with uncertain arrival dates can call the park office for same-day reservations, and a reservation phone number is available at the campsite. Park staff will guide you to an available campsite, and an email confirmation receipt will be provided. The Clark Lake Loop is a 5.2-mile trail open to hiking, cross-country skiing, and snowshoeing, starting at the parking lot on Clark Lake Road. This trail provides scenic views of Clark Lake and passes through pine forests. Along the way, you'll encounter areas with silver and green lichens, ferns, blueberries, jack pine uplands, and moss-covered lowlands. The trail can easily connect to the Wilderness Loop if you wish to extend your hiking adventure. Keep in mind that this area is inhabited by bears and moose. Emerson Trail: This 1-mile trail, located near the Rivermouth campgrounds, is still under development. It runs along Tahquamenon Bay, where the Tahquamenon River flows into Lake Superior, passing through black spruce and shrub swamp areas. The trail follows the route leading to the abandoned sawmill town of Emerson. The final 200 feet leading to Whitefish Bay can be challenging to navigate but not impossible. This trail is an excellent location for birdwatching, particularly during spring migration, and is known for hosting songbirds and grouse. The Giant Pines Loop is a 3.8-mile hiking trail that offers visitors the chance to experience hemlock forests, bubbling streams, and the local wildlife. The trail also features two giant white pine trees, which have stood since the logging era of the late 1800s, giving the trail its name. You can access the trail from the Upper Falls day-use area or at the Stables picnic area. In the winter, the trail is groomed for cross-country skiing and is partially included in the lantern-lit cross-country ski and snowshoe program, which is typically available every Saturday in February. The Nature Trail serves as an alternative half-mile route from the Upper Falls viewing area back to the parking lot. This forested trail is an excellent spot for birdwatching during spring migration and becomes a lush carpet of ferns during the summer. The Nature Trail is integrated into the lantern-lit cross-country ski and snowshoe program, typically offered every Saturday in February. The River Trail is known as one of the most scenic trails in the park and spans 4 miles, connecting the Upper and Lower falls. The trail passes through an old-growth forest, featuring American beech, sugar maple, eastern hemlock, and yellow birch. A private shuttle service is available from Memorial Day weekend to Labor Day to transport hikers between the Upper and Lower falls. Please check the schedule and current fees, which are posted at park entrances, campgrounds, and shuttle stops, as the shuttle times may vary depending on the season. This trail is considered difficult due to exposed roots, hilly terrain, and numerous staircases. To ensure a safe hike, be sure to bring ample water, snacks, and insect repellent. Bicycles are not allowed on this trail, and it is not maintained during the winter months. The Wilderness Loop is a 7-mile trail accessible for hiking, cross-country skiing, and snowshoeing, with access points from the North Country Trail, Clark Lake Loop, and Giant Pines Loop. This trail passes through pine ridges, peat lands, and old-growth hemlock forests, offering a more challenging and primitive hiking experience with minimal bridges and boardwalks. The area is also home to bears and moose, so visitors should remain cautious.

DATE(S) VISITED .... ☐ SPRING ☐ SUMMER ☐ FALL ☐ WINTER

LODGING .... ☐ ☀ ☐ ☁ ☐ 🌧 ☐ 🌫 ☐ ❄

WHO I WENT WITH .... FEE(S) .... PARK HOURS .... TEMP:........

WILL I RETURN? YES / NO RATING ☆ ☆ ☆ ☆ ☆

PASSPORT STAMPS

TAWAS POINT STATE PARK

COUNTY	ESTABLISHED	AREA (AC/HA)
IOSCO	1960	183 / 74

Tawas Point State Park is located on the tip of a sandy peninsula that forms Tawas Bay along the shores of Lake Huron. It's often likened to the "Cape Cod of the Midwest" and spans 183 acres, offering a range of recreational activities. The park is a crucial rest stop for numerous migratory birds during spring and fall, drawing birdwatchers from across the Midwest. The park provides various accommodation options, including a modern campground and overnight lodging facilities. Its prime location on Tawas Bay, known for its shallow and warm waters, makes it a favored spot for swimming. The day-use area features a popular swimming beach, a picnic area, and a scenic nature trail along the picturesque Lake Huron coastline. Visitors can access the Tawas Bay Multi-Use Trails, which are part of Michigan's Iron Belle Trail, and enjoy outdoor exploration along Lake Huron or nearby historical, natural, and cultural sites on the Lumbermen's Monument Auto Tour. One of the main attractions in the park is the Tawas Point Lighthouse, a significant draw for maritime enthusiasts. While the lighthouse has undergone several renovations, it remains an authentic representation of a Victorian-era lighthouse on the Great Lakes. The Michigan History Center offers historical interpretation at this site. To reach Tawas Point, take U.S. 23, and you'll find the park just 2.5 miles southeast of East Tawas on Tawas Beach Road. The park is conveniently located, approximately one hour from the Tri-Cities area and three hours from Detroit. Tawas Bay is renowned as an excellent sailing destination due to its favorable winds and sheltered waters. It's also a prime spot for fishing, including ice fishing on Tawas Bay. There are several nearby boat launch sites, including one managed by the Department of Natural Resources (DNR) located on U.S. 23 behind the State Police post. Boats can be anchored in the bay near the campground, and there are charter boats available for those looking to explore the waters further. In 1987, the construction of an 800-foot by 25-foot limestone reef on the northern side of Tawas Bay significantly improved fishing by providing habitat for small bait fish, attracting larger predator fish such as walleye, pike, perch, and smallmouth bass. The park boasts a two-mile stretch of sandy shoreline along Lake Huron and Tawas Bay. Pets are generally not allowed on the beaches except for a designated pet-friendly area. Be aware of the beach flag warning system in designated swim areas, with red flags indicating unsafe water conditions. Do not swim near or jump off break walls or navigational channel walls and stay alert to changing conditions. The park offers access to Tawas Bay and Lake Huron's shoreline, making it convenient for paddle sports, even though there is no designated carry-in launch. Tawas Bay is a popular fishing destination for a variety of species, including perch, walleye, brown trout, lake trout, northern pike, bass, coho, and Chinook salmon. The reef constructed in 1987 has significantly enhanced fishing opportunities by providing a habitat for bait fish, attracting larger predator fish. The fishing pier at nearby East Tawas State Harbor is another favored fishing spot. The highlight of the park, the Tawas Point Lighthouse, was built in 1876 and features a Frensnel lens produced in Paris in 1880. Adjacent to the park, the Coast Guard station on Lakeview Drive is the last surviving example of the First Series Life Saving Stations constructed on the Great Lakes. Despite various renovations, it remains an authentic Victorian-era station built on the Great Lakes. In 1991, the Coast Guard built a new station outside the park and decommissioned the old one. The lighthouse is open for tours during the season, allowing visitors to climb to the top of the tower for breathtaking views of Tawas Point. Tickets are available at the museum store. When the lighthouse isn't open for tours, visitors can still explore the exterior and grounds, as well as other historic structures like an oil house and fog signal area. For more information, you can contact the lighthouse directly at 989-362-5658 or the Michigan History Center at 517-930-3806. From the park, visitors can access the Tawas Bay Multi-Use Trails, which are part of Michigan's Iron Belle Trail along Lake Huron. The trail covers about four miles from the park entrance to East Tawas City Park and continues to Tawas City and the Alabaster Bike Trail Arboretum. The trail consists of a combination of sidewalks and asphalt suitable for bicycling. While it's not groomed, the paved path connecting the day-use area and campground is not plowed in winter, making it suitable for cross-country skiing. The park offers food and drink concessions located outside the beach house in the day-use area on the Lake Huron side of the point. In the day-use area, you'll find a picnic area with picnic tables and charcoal grills available on a first-come, first-served basis. There's also a pavilion for larger groups accommodating up to 75 people in the day-use area, equipped with picnic tables, a large charcoal grill, and three 110-amp electrical outlets. The shelter is screened and separated from the restrooms by a partition wall, and restrooms are accessible to the public during rentals. You can make shelter reservations up to 12 months in advance at MIDNRReservations.com. Additionally, an accessible playground in the day-use area offers play structures, swings, and slides, with a rubberized surface and a sand and woodchip border. Horseshoe pits and a sand volleyball court are also available in the day-use area. The park's sanitation station is located near the campground entrance, providing potable water and two lanes. Modern restrooms are situated in the day-use area beach house on the Lake Huron side of the point, and a vault toilet is near the lighthouse and the first parking lot in the day-use area. For pet owners, there's a designated pet-friendly shoreline area enclosed by fencing on Tawas Bay between the campground and the lighthouse. Pets are allowed off-leash within this designated area but must be on a 6-foot leash when entering and exiting, and they should be under the owner's immediate supervision. It's important to properly dispose of all pet waste in trash receptacles. This is the only shoreline area in the park where pets are allowed, as they are generally prohibited on all other beach areas and the Sandy Hook Trail. The modern campground is located along the Tawas Bay side of the point and boasts a designated swimming beach known for its warm and shallow waters. You can find some sites with water views, pull-through access, or ADA accessibility. Each site provides 20/30-amp electrical service, and there's a sanitation station available. Recycling facilities are also on-site. Within the modern campground, there are two accessible cabins with beach views and direct beach access. These cabins feature two bedrooms, a living room, seating, electric outlets, ceiling fans, lights, a refrigerator, microwave oven, coffee maker, and electric heaters for winter use. Restrooms with showers and running water are located nearby within the modern campground and are open year-round. The Tawas Bay cabin can accommodate six people and includes two full-size beds, a twin bed, and a pullout sofa. The Fox Den cabin also sleeps six people and features two twin bunk beds and a full-size futon. Each cabin has a picnic table, fire pit, and charcoal grill. You must provide your own linens and cooking supplies, and pets are not allowed. Additionally, there are two mini cabins in the modern campground, each accommodating up to six people. Each mini cabin offers a single room furnished with two sets of bunk beds (two full beds and two twin beds). The cabin includes a counter, two stools, a ceiling fan with light, electric wall heater, small refrigerator, microwave, coffee pot, electric outlet, and a vacuum cleaner. Outside, there's a small deck, picnic table, and fire ring. Restrooms with showers and running water are located nearby within the modern campground, and they are open year-round. Just like with the larger cabins, you must provide your own linens and cooking supplies, and no pets are allowed. The park also features a yurt situated within the modern campground. This 16-foot diameter structure offers accommodation for up to six people and is equipped with two sets of bunk beds (two full beds and two twin beds), a table and chairs, lighting, a small refrigerator, microwave, coffee pot, and electric heater. Outside, there's a deck, picnic table, and fire pit. Restrooms with showers and running water are located nearby within the modern campground. You must provide your own linens and cooking supplies, and pets are not allowed. The yurt is available for booking from April to November. For nature enthusiasts, the Sandy Hook Nature Trail is a 1.5-mile interpretive trail loop suitable for hiking, cross-country skiing, and snowshoeing. The trail commences in the day-use area and meanders through the sandy dunes along the beach, providing scenic views of Tawas Bay and the Lake Huron coast, and it leads to the U.S. Coast Guard's Fog Horn at the tip of the sandy point. Expect to spend about 90 minutes exploring the natural features along this predominantly sandy trail with some boardwalk sections. The trail passes by the Tawas Point Lighthouse and is particularly popular among birdwatchers, as the park hosts the Tawas Point Birding Festival and is a significant stopover site for birds migrating across Saginaw Bay. Note that bicycles and pets are not allowed on this trail. The self-guided Lumbermen's Monument Auto Tour is a 68-mile route that follows the Au Sable River corridor. It provides information about various historical, natural, and cultural features in the area. The tour includes several monuments, scenic overlooks, popular backwater recreation sites, and birding hotspots. You can obtain brochures and additional information at the park office.

DATE(S) VISITED .... ☐ SPRING   ☐ SUMMER   ☐ FALL   ☐ WINTER

LODGING .... ☐ ☀ ☐ ☁ ☐ 🌧 ☐ ⛅ ☐ ❄

WHO I WENT WITH .... FEE(S) .... PARK HOURS .... TEMP:.........

WILL I RETURN? YES / NO   RATING ☆ ☆ ☆ ☆ ☆

PASSPORT STAMPS

THOMPSON'S HARBOR STATE PARK

COUNTY	ESTABLISHED	AREA (AC/HA)
PRESQUE ISLE	1988	5,109 / 2,068

Thompson's Harbor State Park is situated in the northeastern part of Michigan's Lower Peninsula, just north of Alpena. It runs along approximately seven and a half miles of Lake Huron shoreline, providing a pristine and natural setting for hikers to explore the park's extensive six-mile trail system. The park now offers two basic cabins for visitors. Cedar Haven Cabin - This cabin accommodates 4-6 individuals and is equipped with two bunk beds, a pull-out couch, a gas stove, gas lanterns, an outdoor hand pump for water, and a vault toilet. It includes gas lighting, a dining table with four chairs, a propane stove, and a cooktop. Please note that no linens or kitchen supplies are provided. The cabin is located more than a mile away from the beach. Stone Path Cabin - This rustic, stick-built cabin can also house 4-6 people and features two bunk beds, a pull-out couch, a gas stove, gas lanterns, an outdoor hand pump for water, and a vault toilet. It is equipped with a dining table and four chairs, a propane stove, and a cooktop. Similar to the other cabin, it does not come with linens or kitchen supplies. This cabin is also located more than a mile from the beach. The main trail within Thompson's Harbor State Park spans a length of 5.2 miles and is divided into two interconnected loops. It offers stunning views of Lake Huron and takes hikers through a unique landscape primarily composed of limestone terrain. Throughout the hike, visitors may have the opportunity to witness an abundance of Dwarf Lake Iris, as this area is known for hosting the largest population of this flower species globally. The park is also home to over 100 bird species, as well as wildlife like coyotes, deer, and possibly black bears. The Main Trail in Thompson's Harbor State Park is perfect for those seeking adventure and allows activities such as hiking, mountain biking, and cross-country skiing, weather permitting.

DATE(S) VISITED .... ☐ SPRING ☐ SUMMER ☐ FALL ☐ WINTER

LODGING .... ☐ ☀ ☐ ☁ ☐ 🌧 ☐ ⛆ ☐ ❄

WHO I WENT WITH .... FEE(S) .... PARK HOURS .... TEMP:.........

WILL I RETURN? YES / NO   RATING ☆ ☆ ☆ ☆ ☆

PASSPORT STAMPS

TWIN LAKES STATE PARK

COUNTY	ESTABLISHED	AREA (AC/HA)
HOUGHTON	1964	175 / 71

Twin Lakes State Park is situated in Michigan's Copper Country, and it encompasses 175 acres. The park features a modern campground located on the southwest shore of Lake Roland, offering direct access to various trails, including the Bill Nicholls Trail. Popular activities within the park include fishing, boating, and swimming. Notably, Twin Lakes State Park is one of the few ORV-friendly locations, with an extensive network of ORV trails nearby and allowing ORV operation to and from the park. The park serves as an excellent base camp for exploring numerous local attractions, including Fort Wilkins State Historic Park, copper mines, the Keweenaw National Historic Park in Calumet, and the Bill Nicholls Snowmobile Trail that runs parallel to M-26 northwest of the park. Lake Roland stands out as one of the warmest inland lakes in the Upper Peninsula, providing an ideal environment for swimming and various water sports. The twin lakes, Lake Roland and Lake Gerald, offer anglers the opportunity to catch one of the sixteen different fish species found in these lakes. A 1.5-mile nature trail equipped with two scenic overlooks offers breathtaking views of Lake Superior on clear days. Additionally, the nature trail is suitable for cross-country skiing, although the trails are not groomed. In the day use area adjacent to the campground, you'll find a 500-foot beach, a boat launch, playground equipment, horseshoe pits, and a volleyball net. The park offers one ADA accessible open shelter and one enclosed shelter, both of which are available for rent. Reservations for these shelters can be made up to a year in advance through 1-800-447-2757 or the website www.midnrreservations.com. The modern campground at Twin Lakes State Park provides 62 camp sites. Moreover, there's a mini cabin capable of accommodating four individuals. This cabin features electric lights, electric heat, and a hot plate. Formerly serving as the park supervisor's residence, the Twin Lakes Lodge is nestled amidst wooded surroundings and can sleep up to six people across three bedrooms, each equipped with a queen-size bed. The lodge also offers one and a half modern bathrooms, a kitchen, a family room with a television and VCR/DVD player, and a dining area. The well-equipped kitchen includes a refrigerator, stove, microwave, coffee maker, toaster, various cookware, bakeware, utensils, and dinnerware. Outside the lodge, guests will find a picnic table, gas grill, and fire pit. An exceptional advantage of this location is its proximity to the Bill Nichols Multi-Use Trail, designed for snowmobiles and ORVs. This area also serves as an ideal base camp for those interested in fishing, hunting, swimming, golfing, cross-country skiing, hiking, or simply seeking a peaceful wooded setting. Linens are provided in the lodge, but guests are expected to clean up before leaving. Please note that pets and smoking are not allowed. The Bill Nicholls Trail extends for 41 miles from Mass City to Houghton in the Copper Country of the Upper Peninsula. This trail offers opportunities to observe wildlife and explore remnants of the copper mining history that once dominated the region in the 1800s. The trail follows the path of the Copper Range Railroad, making it an excellent choice for history enthusiasts. The trail varies in difficulty, passing through pine and hardwood forests and near Twin Lakes State Park. While hiking, horseback riding, biking, and cross-country skiing are allowed on all segments of the pathway, some sections permit motorized vehicles (ATVs & Snowmobiles). Twin Lakes Nature Trail, located within Twin Lakes State Park in the Upper Peninsula, spans 1.5 miles and features several scenic overlooks that offer spectacular views of Lake Superior on clear days. The trail accompanies a 175-acre campground on the southwest shore of Lake Roland, as well as a day-use area with a large beach, fishing spots, and picnic areas. The Twin Lakes Nature Trail allows for both hiking and cross-country skiing.

DATE(S) VISITED .... □ SPRING   □ SUMMER   □ FALL   □ WINTER

LODGING .... □ ☼   □ ☁   □ 🌧   □ 🌫   □ ❄

WHO I WENT WITH .... FEE(S) .... PARK HOURS .... TEMP:.........

WILL I RETURN? YES / NO   RATING ☆ ☆ ☆ ☆ ☆

PASSPORT STAMPS

VAN BUREN STATE PARK

COUNTY	ESTABLISHED	AREA (AC/HA)
VAN BUREN	1966	400 / 160

Van Buren State Park is situated along the picturesque Lake Michigan shoreline. The park features impressive high dune formations, a well-equipped modern campground, a beautiful one-mile stretch of sandy beach, serene woodland trails, and a convenient day-use area. Within the day-use area, visitors can take advantage of picnic tables and grills, a picnic shelter, and two modern restroom buildings. Lake Michigan provides an idyllic setting for swimming and sunbathing, particularly around the designated swim area located just west of the middle day-use parking lot. This section also includes a modern restroom, accessible parking area, and a beach mat (although it's not considered accessible due to the steep grade to the water). Beachgoers should pay attention to the beach flag warning system in designated swim areas, with red flags signaling unsafe water conditions. In addition, there is a beach house situated in the day-use area, offering restrooms and vending machines. For those looking to explore further, the Van Buren State Park Spur Trail, which begins within the park, provides a scenic four-mile paved route leading to the City of South Haven. Along this route, visitors can access the Van Buren Trail State Park, a trail with a gravel surface that spans about 14 miles and connects to the City of Hartford in the south. Moreover, the Kal-Haven Trail State Park joins in South Haven, extending for an additional 33.5 miles. The picnic area, conveniently located in the day-use area, boasts picnic tables and charcoal grills available on a first-come, first-served basis. Modern restrooms are nearby, and there's also a picnic shelter in the day-use area, featuring picnic tables, charcoal grills, an electrical outlet, and a modern restroom. Reservations for the shelter can be made up to a year in advance at MIDNRReservations.com. Families with children will appreciate the two small play areas in the day-use area, complete with swings and a slide. Notably, alcoholic beverages are prohibited in the park's day-use areas and designated swim beach from April 1 through Labor Day unless written authorization has been granted by the park manager through an event permit. For nature enthusiasts, Van Buren State Park offers weekly nature-based programming led by seasonal naturalists during the period between Memorial Day and Labor Day. Hunting is permitted within the state park; however, it is advisable to call the park directly to inquire about any specific rules, concerns, or considerations regarding hunting activities. The park welcomes pets along the entire length of the Lake Michigan shoreline, excluding the designated swim area, and in the park's pet-friendly beach area. Access to the pet-friendly beach area, located south of the designated swim area, is available via the dog beach access trails just west of the picnic shelter. The remainder of the shoreline, north of the designated swim area, can only be accessed through the primary "beach walk," situated just west of the middle parking lot. Pet owners are reminded to keep their pets on a 6-foot leash and under immediate control. Additionally, all pet waste must be properly disposed of in provided trash receptacles. The modern campground at Van Buren State Park is organized into five loops. Campsites are generally spacious and come in a mix of shaded and sunny spots. Campers can conveniently access the day-use area along the Lake Michigan shoreline via a central walking path located within the campground. The campground features two modern restroom/shower buildings and a children's play area. The park also offers a youth group use area, distinct from the modern campground and intended for use by youth organizations accompanied by adults. Eligibility as a youth group is determined by a youth-to-adult ratio of 4:1. In most cases, youth participants should be 16 years of age or younger, although high school-sponsored groups may include youths up to 18 years of age. The campground area comprises two adjoining rustic sites with a combined capacity for 50 people. Each site is equipped with picnic tables, fire pits, vault toilets, and potable water. To make a reservation, please contact the park office at 269-637-2788. To further explore the surroundings, visitors can access the Van Buren State Park Spur Trail, a scenic four-mile paved pathway leading to the City of South Haven. Along this route, one can connect with the 14-mile-long Van Buren Trail State Park, which features a gravel surface and extends to the City of Hartford in the south. Additionally, the Kal-Haven Trail State Park is accessible from South Haven, providing an extra 33.5 miles of trail for outdoor enthusiasts. The Van Buren Trail State Park is a linear, multi-use trail established along a former railroad right-of-way. It connects the cities of Hartford and South Haven, situated off the Lake Michigan coast. The trail meanders through open farmland, blueberry fields, dense brush, and wooded areas, offering opportunities to spot native wildlife like deer, rabbits, foxes, and eagles. These natural attractions make the trail popular among birders and nature enthusiasts. Within the Van Buren Trail State Park, a two-mile section of the trail between the city of South Haven and 16th Avenue features a paved surface suitable for bicycles. However, a 12-mile undeveloped portion of the trail between 16th Avenue and the city of Hartford offers an unimproved gravel surface more suitable for mountain biking. The undeveloped trail traverses through long stretches of grass and sand, occasionally passing over rough ballast stones and winding through areas of pine and hardwood trees. Visitors have two primary starting points for their trail adventure. To begin from the grass-covered parking lot in Hartford, simply take the Hartford exit off Interstate 94, head north two blocks past the first stoplight, and turn left onto Prospect Street. After another two blocks, you'll reach your destination. For those starting in South Haven, the trailhead is accessible by taking Lagrange Street to Aylworth Avenue, proceeding west to Kalamazoo Street, and then heading south on Kalamazoo to Lovejoy Avenue. The trail can be found just 0.1 mile to the west on the south side of the street.

DATE(S) VISITED .... □ SPRING □ SUMMER □ FALL □ WINTER

LODGING .... □ ☀ □ ☁ □ 🌧 □ 🌫 □ ❄

WHO I WENT WITH .... FEE(S) .... PARK HOURS .... TEMP:.........

WILL I RETURN? YES / NO   RATING ☆ ☆ ☆ ☆ ☆

PASSPORT STAMPS

VAN RIPER STATE PARK

COUNTY	ESTABLISHED	AREA (AC/HA)
MARQUETTE	1956	1,100 / 445

Van Riper State Park is situated 35 miles to the west of Marquette, accessible from U.S. 41. Covering an expansive 1,100 acres, the park boasts 1.5 miles of scenic waterfront along both Lake Michigamme and the Peshekee River. This park offers an array of attractions, including a designated swim beach, a bicycle pump track, an accessible playground, hiking trails, picnic areas, a paved trail leading to the historical town of Champion, and more. Visitors particularly appreciate the park's designated swim beach, known for its fine sandy shoreline and more moderate water temperatures compared to Lake Superior. The Blueberry Ridge Pathway, located just 35 miles away in Marquette, is among the Upper Peninsula's most renowned trails for cross-country skiing and hiking. The park's waterfront extends along 1.5 miles of Lake Michigamme and the Peshekee River. There's a designated swim area in the park's day-use section, while paddling is a popular activity on Lake Michigamme and the Peshekee River. The park provides an accessible boat launch on Lake Michigamme, making it convenient for boaters. Additionally, fishing enthusiasts will find Lake Michigamme and the Peshekee River ideal for their favorite pastime. You'll also discover a beach house in the day-use area near Lake Michigamme, featuring modern restrooms, changing rooms, and a laundry facility. A paved trail runs parallel to U.S. 41, connecting the park with the historic town of Champion. Within the day-use area, there are two bicycle pump tracks, designed as looped sequences of rollers and berms to maximize momentum and reduce the need for pedaling. Snowmobile Trail No. 8 passes through the park, although snowmobiles are not allowed on park trails. Hunting is permitted within the state park; however, it's advisable to contact the park directly for information on specific rules, concerns, or considerations related to hunting activities. The picnic area in the day-use section offers picnic tables and charcoal grills, available on a first-come, first-served basis. You'll also find a picnic shelter located between the designated swim beach and the modern campground, equipped with picnic tables, charcoal grills, and electrical service (available by reservation only). This shelter even features a fireplace, although firewood is not provided. Reservations for the shelter can be made up to 12 months in advance at MiDNRReservations.com. Near the designated swim beach, there's an accessible playground, featuring slides, bridges, a net, and other interactive features, all set on a rubberized surface for ease of access to visitors of varying mobility levels. Furthermore, the day-use area includes two other small playgrounds near the modern campground. The park's sanitation station is located near the entrance of the modern campground, with potable water available and two lanes for your convenience. Van Riper State Park welcomes pets along the entire length of the Lake Michigamme and the Peshekee River, with the exception of the designated swim beach. It is essential to keep pets on a 6-foot leash and under the owner's immediate control at all times. Additionally, it's crucial to properly dispose of all pet waste in provided trash receptacles. The modern campground at Van Riper State Park is divided into two loops and offers many campsites with views of Lake Michigamme. While the sites are generally smaller in size, most benefit from ample shade. Visitors often describe the campground as family-friendly. The rustic campground features a range of sites set amid the woods near the modern campground. These sites vary, with some providing a more secluded setting, while others are more open and sunny. For a more unique experience, consider the Cully Gage camper cabin, situated on the shores of Lake Michigamme. This three-room cabin accommodates up to six guests and is furnished with a bunk bed (sleeping two) and a dresser in each bedroom, as well as a futon (sleeping two) in the main living area. The cabin's interior boasts hardwood floors, electric heating, and a ceiling fan. You'll find a dining table and chairs, a futon, a mini refrigerator, a microwave, and a coffee maker. Outdoors, there's a picnic table, a log swing, a charcoal grill, and a fire ring (please note that firewood is not provided). A vault restroom is located nearby. Guests must bring their linens and cookware. The park also offers two mini cabins, each capable of accommodating four guests. These cabins include a bunk bed, a full-size futon, electrical outlets, a mini refrigerator, a microwave, an electric fireplace, and a table with chairs. Outside, you'll find a picnic table, a fire ring, an awning, and a deck area. Guests should provide their linens and cookware. Mini cabin #2 is pet-friendly. Up to two pets (cats and dogs only) are allowed. The Peshekee River rustic cabin, located on the banks of the Peshekee River, is available year-round. The cabin accommodates up to six guests and features bunk beds, a table with four chairs, a small kitchen counter with cabinets, and a woodstove for heating (with wood provided for heating from September 15 to June 1). The cabin has no electricity or water. Outdoors, there's a picnic table, a charcoal grill, and a fire ring (wood not provided). A vault toilet and hand pump for water are located nearby. Just like with the other cabins, guests need to bring their own linens and cookware. The cabin is also pet-friendly. Up to two pets (limited to cats and dogs) are allowed. For those interested in hiking, the park offers several trails. Main Trail: This half-mile route takes you through rugged wooded terrain steeped in old mining history. You'll also come across an old beaver pond along the way. Bug spray might be a good idea, as the trail is rich in natural beauty. Old Wagon Road Trail: Covering 1.5 miles, this trail guides you through varying and moderately challenging terrain. If you look closely, you can spot the bases of old power poles that once lined the trail. To create a longer loop with scenic overlooks of the Peshekee River, you can combine this trail with the River Trail. The trailhead is located along U.S. 41 across from the park's main entrance. You can also explore the .25-mile Miners Loop, a spur trail that can be added to your route. Overlook Trail: This 1.5-mile loop trail offers stunning ridge-top vistas of the Peshekee River and Lake Michigamme. You can access the trailhead along Martin's Landing Road, which you can find by turning off of Peshekee Grade County Road 607. River Trail: The 1.5-mile River Trail can easily be combined with the Old Wagon Road Trail to create a longer loop. This hike takes you through deep pine forests, offering views of the Peshekee River and several small climbs along the way. The trailhead is located in the group-use campground or along Martin's Landing Road, accessible by turning off of Peshekee Grade County Road 607. If you're seeking a unique winter experience, you can also explore the park's winter lantern-lit snowshoe event.

WARREN DUNES STATE PARK

COUNTY	ESTABLISHED	AREA (AC/HA)
BERRIEN	1930	1,500 / 607

Warren Dunes State Park, a sprawling 1,500-acre recreational area located along the stunning Lake Michigan shoreline, offers a plethora of activities. Its defining feature is the rugged dune formation, rising 260 feet above the lake, which provides breathtaking vistas and serves as an ideal location for hang gliding (permit required). The park boasts three miles of pristine Lake Michigan shoreline, six miles of hiking trails, and two popular campgrounds. Serving as the unofficial western gateway to Michigan's state park system, the park is renowned for its extensive network of lushly forested dunes, vast open dunes, and interdunal wetlands. Additionally, the park attracts a diverse range of bird species as it lies on a key bird migration route. Visitors can relish three miles of sandy Lake Michigan shoreline, complete with a designated swim area situated in the day-use section. Three accessible walkways, each around 100 feet in length, connect the day-use area's sidewalk with the water. Please note that these walkways may not reach the water's edge entirely. The park also provides two beach/aqua wheelchairs available for loan at the ranger station. Visitors should be mindful of the beach flag warning system in designated swim areas; red flags indicate hazardous water conditions, signaling that swimming or entering the water is unsafe. Lake Michigan is popular for paddling, and Third Coast Surf offers rentals at the north end of beach parking lot 2, offering stand-up paddleboards, kayaks, and paddleboats. These rentals are available from mid-May through Labor Day, with hours of operation from 1 to 6 p.m. on weekdays and noon to 6 p.m. on weekends. From May through Labor Day weekend, four food trucks can be found in the beach parking lot. Additionally, these food trucks are often open during nice weekends in September. Seasonal naturalists offer weekly nature-based programming from Memorial Day through Labor Day. While hunting is permitted in the state park, it's advisable to contact the park directly for information on specific regulations, concerns, or considerations regarding hunting activities. The park features five picnic areas along the main entrance road leading to the beach area. Moreover, there's a picnic shelter located near the campground, equipped with picnic tables, charcoal grills, electrical service (reservations only), and vault toilets. You can make shelter reservations up to 12 months in advance at MiDNRReservations.com. The day-use area on the beach boasts three accessible bathroom buildings, each featuring two-foot showers and bottle fillers. Pets are welcome north of the northernmost swim buoy at the beach, which provides 2.5 miles of shoreline open to pets. Keep in mind that pets must be on a 6-foot leash and under their owner's immediate control at all times. Proper disposal of pet waste in designated trash receptacles is essential. It's important to note that alcoholic beverages are not allowed in the park from April 1 through September 30, unless written authorization is granted by the park manager through an event permit. The park's modern campground is divided into two loops, offering a variety of site types and sizes, including shaded and sunny spots, with some nestled in wooded areas. Recycling facilities are available for campers. The semi-modern campground provides a more rustic camping experience within a serene atmosphere. Most sites are sunny and open, although a few are tucked away in wooded, private locations. This area does not offer electrical service. Vault toilets are centrally situated in the campground, while three modern toilet and shower buildings can be found at the nearby Mt. Randall modern campground, just a five-minute walk away. Campers can also use the recycling facilities here. The park features a Youth Group Use Campground designed for groups of up to 100 people. This rustic group campground encompasses six sites, each furnished with a picnic table and fire pit, and a hand pump for water. To reserve the group camp area, please call 269-426-4013. Warren Dunes State Park offers three rustic cabins in the Mt. Randall campground. Each cabin can accommodate up to six people and includes two full-size beds and two single bunk beds. The interior is equipped with a table, bench seat, and ceramic heater. Outdoor amenities comprise a small deck, picnic table, fire pit, and a waist-high cook grill (only for cooking purposes). These cabins have electricity, but guests need to provide their own linens and cookware. All three cabins, Pine (site #5), Oak (site #51), and Hemlock (site #65), are located in the first loop. Pine and Hemlock cabins enjoy a more open setting, while Oak cabin offers a shaded environment with trees. For hikers, the park offers various trails. Blue Jay Trail (marker #14): This trail spans through dunes and wooded areas, covering 0.75 miles. It effortlessly connects with the Red Squirrel (marker #13) and White Tail (marker #6) trails as you head away from the lakeshore. The trail starts at the picnic shelter. Cross-Country Ski Trail: This 3-mile loop winds through a beautiful wooded area behind the Great Warren Dunes, passing through the campground and returning to the park. The trail begins at trail marker #2, located near the picnic shelter. Golden Rod Loop: Starting at the Flora Lane Trailhead alongside the Golden Rod Loop, this 0.33-mile trail meanders through the park's dune forests, offering glimpses of majestic Lake Michigan. The trail starts at marker #12 in the Floral Lane parking lot. Mt. Randall Loop (marker #3): Spanning 1.5 miles, this loop provides scenic views of Lake Michigan, a wooded forest area, and dune climbs that lead to the shoreline. Visitors should be prepared for various terrain changes, from flat, wooded sections to dune climbs that may vary in difficulty from year to year. The trail starts at marker #3 at site #37 in the Mt. Randall campground and intersects with Shoreline Trail #1. Nature Trail: A 1-mile trail that follows a ridge overlooking the Lake Michigan shoreline, with picturesque views of the Great Warren Dunes area, the Great Lakes shoreline, and a forest on the other side. The trail begins at marker #1 and is most easily accessible from marker #2 (by the picnic shelter) or the northern beach parking lot. Red Squirrel Trail (marker #5): Beginning at marker #5, this trail offers easy access from marker #9 at the Floral Lane parking lot. It meanders through a wooded area with a gentle incline. It can be combined with other park trails for a longer hike. White Tail Trail (marker #6): Accessible from marker #9 at the Floral Lane parking lot, this trail provides picturesque views of Lake Michigan. It can be combined with most of the park's other trails for an extended hike. Yellow Birch Loop: This 1.2-mile loop incorporates a well-known boardwalk that crosses a wetland area. It begins at the Flora Lane trailhead alongside the Golden Rod Loop, specifically at marker #10 in the Floral Lane parking lot.

DATE(S) VISITED .... ☐ SPRING ☐ SUMMER ☐ FALL ☐ WINTER

LODGING .... ☐ ☀ ☐ ☁ ☐ 🌧 ☐ 🌬 ☐ ❄

WHO I WENT WITH .... FEE(S) .... PARK HOURS .... TEMP:.........

WILL I RETURN? YES / NO   RATING ☆ ☆ ☆ ☆ ☆

PASSPORT STAMPS

WARREN WOODS STATE PARK

COUNTY	ESTABLISHED	AREA (AC/HA)
BERRIEN	1949	311 / 126

Warren Woods State Park, a 311-acre natural sanctuary located just a short 7-minute drive from Warren Dunes State Park, stands as a hidden treasure waiting to be explored. The park is graced with a towering beech and majestic maple forest and is crisscrossed by the meandering Galien River, making it a captivating haven for nature enthusiasts. Visitors can traverse a tranquil, 1-mile trail that traces the picturesque course of the river, with the added bonus of a charming bridge that spans the river. The Galien River winds its way through the park, creating an ideal setting for fishing.

DATE(S) VISITED .... ☐ SPRING ☐ SUMMER ☐ FALL ☐ WINTER

LODGING .... ☐☀ ☐☁ ☐🌧 ☐⛅ ☐❄

WHO I WENT WITH .... FEE(S) .... PARK HOURS .... TEMP:.........

WILL I RETURN? YES / NO   RATING ☆ ☆ ☆ ☆ ☆

PASSPORT STAMPS

WATKINS LAKE STATE PARK AND COUNTY PRESERVE

COUNTY	ESTABLISHED	AREA (AC/HA)
WASHTENAW	2017	1,122 / 454

Watkins Lake State Park and County Preserve is a unique natural area managed in partnership by the Washtenaw County Parks and Recreation Commission and the Department of Natural Resources (DNR). This park is renowned for its peaceful and serene ambiance, offering visitors a picturesque lake, a 5-mile walking trail, excellent bird-watching opportunities, and numerous other attractions. The park's landscape comprises rolling terrain with a mix of open meadows, diverse hardwood forests, wetland areas, and the standout feature, Watkins Lake. The park also holds historical significance, as it has connections to the Underground Railroad. The original landowners, Royal and Sally Carpenter Watkins, played a vital role in this historic network. To protect its essential bird habitat, Watkins Lake and the surrounding area are designated as a waterfowl refuge. As a result, the park is closed to the public from February 15 to May 15 and from September 1 to January 1. The refuge area is indicated in red on the park map, but visitors can still engage in wildlife viewing along Arnold Road throughout the year. Furthermore, Watkins Lake State Park and County Preserve has earned recognition for its association with the National Underground Railroad Network to Freedom. This designation is bestowed upon places with significant historical ties to the Underground Railroad, a network through which enslaved African Americans sought freedom by escaping their bondage. The park offers 5-mile trail is an out-and-back rail-trail that traverses the park's diverse landscapes. It offers picturesque lake views and takes you through prairie grasses, rolling hills, forested areas, and wetlands. This part of the park is open year-round, although certain sections may be open to hunting during specific times of the year. The trailhead is conveniently located in the parking lot off Arnold Road, and plans are in place to expand the trail from Manchester to Brooklyn. The park offers an observation hill, located at the north end of Watkins Lake, which provides a scenic overlook of the lake. There are also a few picnic tables along the lake's shoreline. Hunting is permitted within the state park, although visitors are encouraged to contact the park directly for information about specific rules, concerns, or considerations. Within a 10-mile radius of the park, there are two other state parks that offer distinct recreational experiences. Hayes State Park provides camping, a swimming beach, a recreational lake, concessions, hiking trails, and more. Cambridge Junction Historic State Park features the Walker Tavern Historic Site, a farmer's market, a reconstructed 1840s barn, vintage baseball games, and other historical attractions.

DATE(S) VISITED .... ☐ SPRING ☐ SUMMER ☐ FALL ☐ WINTER

LODGING .... ☐ ☀ ☐ ☁ ☐ 🌧 ☐ 🌫 ☐ ❄

WHO I WENT WITH .... FEE(S) .... PARK HOURS .... TEMP:.........

WILL I RETURN? YES / NO   RATING ☆ ☆ ☆ ☆ ☆

PASSPORT STAMPS

WELLS STATE PARK

COUNTY	ESTABLISHED	AREA (AC/HA)
MENOMINEE	1925	700 / 283

Wells State Park, situated about 30 miles south of Escanaba on the shores of Green Bay, spans 700 acres of natural beauty. The park offers a 3-mile shoreline featuring a stunning sandy beach for swimming, a spacious picnic area, a modern campground, and rustic cabins. Founded in 1925, the park was a generous donation to the State of Michigan from the descendants of John Walter Wells, a prominent lumberman and former mayor of Menominee. Many of the park's structures, landscape features, and water and sewage systems were constructed by the Civilian Conservation Corps during the 1930s and 1940s. Wells State Park welcomes visitors year-round, even when the campground is closed, providing opportunities for winter activities such as cross-country skiing, snowshoeing, and ice fishing. Nearby Cedar River offers a modern boat ramp and charter fishing services. The region surrounding the park provides excellent fishing opportunities, including species like smallmouth bass, pike, walleye, panfish, trout, and salmon. Some of the best brown trout fishing in Michigan can be experienced nearby, especially in early April. Menominee County is known for its abundant deer population, making it an appealing destination for deer hunting enthusiasts. Public land for hunting large and small game is readily available in the surrounding areas. The park's day-use area, conveniently located near the campground, features a large picnic area with two picnic shelters, horseshoe courts, picnic tables, charcoal grills, and a spacious playground. Two volleyball courts and a sandy beach add to the recreational offerings within the park. Visitors can rent the two picnic shelters, which can be reserved up to a year in advance by contacting 1-800-447-2757 or visiting www.midnrreservations.com. For hikers, Wells State Park offers six miles of hiking trails, which also include three rustic trailside shelters for rest along the way. These trails are open year-round, providing opportunities for cross-country skiing during the winter months, although they are not groomed. The park's seasonal naturalists offer weekly nature-based programs from Memorial Day through Labor Day. The modern campground at Wells State Park provides 150 campsites for visitors to enjoy. Wells State Park also features five rustic cabins situated on the picturesque Green Bay shoreline. Poverty cabin: Accommodates 8 people in a one-room cabin with sleeping, kitchen/dining area, gas range, bunk beds, nightstands, dresser, gas heater, dining table, chairs, screened door and windows. No linens, kitchen supplies, or electricity are provided. Nearby vault toilet and hand pump for water. Picnic tables and a small charcoal grill outside.

Cabin open year-round until road access is restricted due to snow. Rock cabin: Accommodates 10 people in a one-room cabin with similar amenities to the Poverty cabin. Cabin open year-round until road access is restricted due to snow. St. Martin cabin: Accommodates 9 people in a three-room cabin with gas range, 7 bunk beds or double beds, dresser, benches, gas heater, dining table, and chairs. Cabin open year-round until road access is restricted due to snow. Washington cabin: Accommodates 12 people in a one-room cabin with gas range, bunk beds, dresser, nightstands, benches, gas heater, dining table, and chairs. Cabin open year-round until road access is restricted due to snow. Summer cabin: Accommodates 9 people in a one-room cabin with gas range, bunk beds, double beds, dresser, gas heater, dining table, chairs, and two picnic tables outside. Cabin open year-round until road access is restricted due to snow. Wells State Park also boasts the historic Baystone Lodge, located approximately 30 miles northeast of Menominee or 40 miles south of Escanaba. The lodge is positioned near the beach and day-use area, offering a wide range of recreational activities, including swimming, fishing, hunting, picnicking, horseshoes, volleyball, hiking, and groomed/tracked cross-country skiing. This lodge was originally constructed in the 1940s by the Civilian Conservation Corps and served as the park manager's residence. Today, it is available for rent and is an ideal venue for family gatherings, weddings, and special events. The lodge accommodates 12 people, includes a fully-equipped kitchen, and provides outdoor amenities such as a gas grill, fire pit, and picnic table. Linens and kitchen supplies are not provided, and visitors are responsible for cleaning the unit before departure. The lodge is a smoke-free and pet-free facility, and a Recreation Passport is required for all vehicles while staying there. To make a reservation, you can call Wells State Park at 906-863-9747. Wells State Park also offers the Cedar River Trail, a 7-mile trail with three distinct loops: Timber Loop, Evergreen Loop, and Ridgewood Loop. These trails provide breathtaking views of Green Bay, sandy beaches, and rustic cabins. The Cedar River Trail is open year-round for hiking and cross-country skiing.

DATE(S) VISITED .... ☐ SPRING ☐ SUMMER ☐ FALL ☐ WINTER

LODGING .... ☐ ☀ ☐ ☁ ☐ 🌧 ☐ 🌨 ☐ ❄

WHO I WENT WITH .... FEE(S) .... PARK HOURS .... TEMP:.........

WILL I RETURN? YES / NO   RATING ☆ ☆ ☆ ☆ ☆

PASSPORT STAMPS

WILDERNESS STATE PARK

COUNTY	ESTABLISHED	AREA (AC/HA)
EMMET	1927	10,512 / 4,254

Wilderness State Park, situated only 11 miles west of Mackinaw City, encompasses 26 miles of stunning Lake Michigan shoreline, over 20 miles of scenic trails, a designated beach for swimming and pets, and distinctive camping experiences. The park is also recognized as a dark sky preserve, providing exceptional views of the night sky, and it's conveniently located just 9 miles away from Headlands Dark Sky Park, which is an Emmet County park. Certain areas of the park offer vistas of the 170-year-old Waugoshance Lighthouse when looking west toward the Straits of Mackinac, while gazing east reveals the majestic Mackinac Bridge. The landscape within the park is characterized by a blend of dense coniferous forests, mature hardwood forests, interspersed with open meadows, and carpets of wildflowers in the spring. There are numerous small ponds scattered amidst coniferous wetlands. Visitors are advised to heed trail signage and carry a map for navigation. You can relish 26 miles of sandy shoreline along Lake Michigan, including the presence of Temperance and Waugoshance islands situated near the tip of Waugoshance Point. A designated swimming area is available near the picnic area, located just east of the park's headquarters building. This area is equipped with accessible parking, a vault toilet, and a walkway to the water. Another designated swimming area is situated in the west loop of the modern campground. A beach wheelchair is accessible for borrowing from the campground host at campsite #416. For safety, visitors are urged to observe the beach flag warning system in designated swimming areas; red flags indicate unsafe water conditions, and swimming or entering the water should be avoided. A boat launch offers access to Lake Michigan at Big Stone Bay, along with an ADA-accessible vault toilet. Please note that the site may not be usable due to high water conditions. The southside of Waugoshance Point is a popular spot for smallmouth bass fishing and fly fishing for carp. Paddling is a common activity, with a recommendation for paddlers to remain in Big Stone Bay. Nebo Trail, South Boundary Trail, Swamp Line Trail, and Sturgeon Bay Trail are two-track trails open to bicyclists. Additionally, many visitors enjoy cycling along Waugoshance Point Road. It's important to note that all single-track trails are off-limits to both bicycles and mountain bikes. Hunting is permitted within the state park; however, it's advisable to contact the park directly for specific regulations, concerns, or considerations. The park offers seasonal naturalists who provide weekly nature-based programs from Memorial Day through Labor Day. A picnic area is conveniently located just east of the headquarters building, featuring picnic tables and charcoal grills. The park's sanitation station is situated across from the headquarters building, offering potable water and three lanes. Wilderness State Park provides two pet-friendly beaches: one is located just east of the headquarters building (adjacent to the picnic area and accessed via a small path), and the other is situated on the west end of the East Lake Lakeshore Campground. The majority of the park's shoreline allows pets from September through March; however, the shoreline, excluding the designated pet-friendly areas, is off-limits to pets from April through August to safeguard the endangered piping plover habitat. Pets must remain on a 6-foot leash and under the immediate control of their owner. Proper disposal of pet waste in designated trash receptacles is required. The East Lakeshore campground, comprising sites #301-365, offers most sites with a view of the shoreline. This campground features a modern shower and toilet building with accessibility features, beach access, a dishwashing station, walkways, and four ADA-accessible sites equipped with concrete pads. All sites provide 20- and 30-amp electrical service, with 13 sites also offering 50-amp service. The campground underwent remodeling in 2022, and modern restrooms are available from mid-May through mid-October. The West Lakeshore campground, encompassing campsites #401-471, is located along the Lake Michigan shoreline, with most sites offering shoreline views. This campground provides accessible facilities, including a shower and toilet building, beach access, walkways, and four barrier-free sites. All sites offer 20- and 30-amp electrical service, and 19 sites have 50-amp service. The campground underwent remodeling in 2019, and modern restrooms are available from mid-May through mid-October. The Pines Loop, which consists of campsites #501-599, is situated on the opposite side of the county road from the East and West Lakeshore campgrounds. The majority of these sites are generously sized and shaded by various deciduous and coniferous trees. This loop offers direct access to the trail system. All sites feature 20- and 30-amp electrical service. Modern restrooms are accessible from mid-May through mid-October, with specific dates available by contacting the park. There are 18 full-hook-up campsites (sites #201-218) located along the Lake Michigan shoreline. These sites provide 20-, 30-, and 50-amp service, although there are no modern bathrooms or vault toilets associated with the campsites. One of the sites is barrier-free. Campers must have self-contained units. The park includes two backcountry (or primitive) campsites, namely the East Boundary campsite, located along the North County Trail, and the O'Neal Lake campsite, situated along the water. These campsites are site-specific, meaning campers stay at the registered site, and each is equipped with a metal fire ring. Bear bags must be suspended at least 12 feet above the ground and at a distance from trees to prevent animals from reaching or jumping on them. Bear poles are provided. Reservations for these sites can be made by calling the park at 231-436-5381. Three rustic bunkhouses, constructed by the Civilian Conservation Corps in the late 1930s, are located near the Pine Campground. Each one-room bunkhouse accommodates 24 individuals in 12 bunk beds and is furnished with a cafeteria-style folding table, 12 chairs, and a wood stove (wood is provided during colder months for heating). These bunkhouses have electricity but no running water; however, water is available in the nearby campground from May through mid-October and at the park headquarters during winter. They also include lighting, a ceiling fan, and outlets but lack a refrigerator. Visitors must provide their own linens, towels, cookware, plates, and utensils. Outside, there is a fire pit, picnic table, and a large charcoal grill. Vault toilets are nearby. Guests are responsible for cleaning the cabin, toilets, and the surrounding area before checking out. All garbage must be removed to the dumpsters located along the drive to the bunkhouses. Limited parking is available year-round. The park offers six rustic cabins. Big Stone Bay cabin, featuring four bunk beds, sleeps eight guests. It is located in a mixed conifer forest along the Straits of Mackinac. The cabin offers scenic views of the Mackinac Bridge to the east and Michigan's Upper Peninsula to the north. A short walk from the cabin leads to a cobblestone and gravel shoreline where visitors can enjoy fossil hunting. This cabin is accessible by a .75-mile hike from the winter parking lot, making it the closest cabin to reach. Caps Cabin, with four bunk beds, sleeps four individuals. It is situated on a forested bluff, approximately 100 yards from the Straits of Mackinac shoreline. This eight-person cabin is surrounded by pine, spruce, and balsam trees, providing a tranquil setting. Visitors can enjoy views of the Mackinac Bridge, Michigan's Upper Peninsula, and Waugoshance and White Shoals lighthouses when strolling to the shoreline. The cabin is located 1.5 miles from the winter parking lot. Nebo cabin, accommodating five guests, has two bunk beds and one single bed. Nestled on top of a ridge in a red pine forest, this five-person log cabin offers a remote setting and ridge-valley topography that appeals to hikers and hunters. The cabin is located 2 miles from the winter parking lot and sits along the park's designated cross-country ski trail, allowing winter access via cross-country skiing or snowshoeing. Station Point cabin, with two bunk beds, sleeps four guests. This cabin is located along the shoreline of the Straits of Mackinac, offering stunning lake views through a large window. Visitors can observe the Mackinac Bridge, Michigan's Upper Peninsula, and Waugoshance and White Shoals lighthouses. During the summer, this four-person log cabin provides improved surface parking and walkways, a hand pump for water, a picnic table, fire ring, grill, and an ADA-accessible vault toilet. It's 2 miles from the parking lot to the cabin in the winter. Sturgeon Bay cabin sleeps five individuals and features two bunk beds and one single bed. Located near Sturgeon Bay, this cabin provides a remote setting with marshy shoreline and a cedar-dominated forest. The cabin is particularly appealing to wildlife enthusiasts, and during certain hunting seasons, the cabin gate may be opened for park visitors to access the area southeast of the cabin. In the winter, it is 3.5 miles from the parking lot to the cabin, making it one of the park's more remote winter camping options. Waugoshance cabin, accommodating eight guests, features four bunk beds. The large north-facing window offers a direct view of the Straits of Mackinac, providing an opportunity to observe wildlife in the dunes as freighters pass in the background. The cabin's sandy shoreline with gravel along the water's edge is perfect for sun lovers and rock hunters. Visitors can view the Mackinac Bridge, Michigan's Upper Peninsula, and Waugoshance and White Shoals lighthouses from the shoreline. This cabin is located 2.5 miles from the winter parking lot, making it a suitable choice for more adventurous campers. Within Wilderness State Park, you'll find 25 walk-in campsites numbered from #101 to #125. To access these sites, you'll need to take a short walk ranging from 15 to 150 yards along the Lake Michigan shoreline. These sites are quite spacious and work well, especially if you're camping with another group. Two of these sites are barrier-free, and each site allows for two parking spots. Additionally, there's a Youth Group Campground designed for youth groups of up to 72 people. Each site at this rustic group campground provides a picnic table, fire pit, and a hand pump for water. To reserve this group camp area, please contact 231-436-5381. If you're looking to explore the park's trails, here's a summary of some of the trails and their features. Big Stone Trail: This trail connects the park's full-hookup campsites and walk-in tent sites. It runs alongside Big Stone Creek, offering opportunities for wildlife viewing. The trail is considered low-intensity due to its minimal elevation changes, with an accessible trailhead near the Pines Campground. East Old Boundary Trail: Located on the park's eastern side, this 2.2-mile trail passes through different ecosystems, making it popular for bird watchers and wildflower enthusiasts. The trail features gradual elevation changes and is considered low-intensity. East Ridge Trail: A 1.4-mile trail that offers opportunities for wildlife viewing, especially around the wild blueberry and huckleberry patch. With some elevation changes, protruding rocks, and roots, it's rated as an intermediate-intensity trail. Hemlock Trail: A 0.6-mile trail that leads to the top of Mount Nebo. The trail has two paths to the top, one with a steep incline and the other with a gradual incline. It's named after the large hemlock trees in the area and is cooler due to the dense tree canopy. The trail offers high-intensity hikes due to elevation changes. Nebo Trail: Running north and south, it intersects with various other trails, creating loop options. The trail passes through conifer and red pine forests with gradual elevation changes, making it a low-intensity trail. During winter, it's part of the designated cross-country ski trail. North Country National Scenic Trail: Part of this long-distance trail passes through the park, with 8 miles of trail. It enters from the southern boundary, follows several trails through different ecosystems, and exits the park after about 1 mile of divergence. O'Neal Lake Trail: This is the park's most remote trail, passing through a variety of landscapes. The trail offers intermediate to high-intensity hikes due to elevation changes and remoteness. Pondside Trail: A short 0.35-mile trail encircling Goose Pond, ideal for combining with other nearby trails for a longer hike. Interpretive posts along the trail provide information about the area. Red Pine Trail: This 1.2-mile trail winds through forest lowlands, gradually rising in elevation through conifer forests. It forms a loop with other trails, allowing you to experience various ecosystems, but insect repellent is recommended for wildlife and flower viewing. South Boundary Trail: Covering 2 miles, this trail passes through lowlands and wetlands and provides opportunities for observing a variety of wildlife, especially during certain seasons. Some sections of the trail may be wet, so waterproof footwear is recommended. Sturgeon Bay Trail: Despite its name, this trail doesn't offer direct bay views but passes through mixed forests, wetlands, and creeks. It's remote, and you may spot songbirds, waterfowl, eagles, beavers, and deer. It's considered intermediate due to some wet areas. Swamp Line Trail: A 2-mile trail winding through cedar and aspen tree stands and a small creek. It offers opportunities for wildlife and wildflower viewing, with a low-intensity rating. Wiikenhs Trail: This trail stretches through hardwood and conifer forests and is popular for its abundance of flowers. You can easily access this trail from multiple campgrounds and other trails, and it's rated as a low-intensity trail.

PASSPORT STAMPS

WILLIAM G. MILLIKEN STATE PARK AND HARBOR

COUNTY	ESTABLISHED	AREA (AC/HA)
WAYNE	2004	31 / 13

William G. Milliken State Park and Harbor is situated at the heart of Detroit, just east of downtown, adjacent to a section of Detroit's Riverwalk. This location offers easy access for various outdoor activities such as fishing, biking, walking, and rollerblading. The park is divided into three distinct areas: the harbor, the picnic shelter area, and the popular berm area. Recent renovations have improved the berm section by adding an accessible walkway, handrails, and new plantings of trees, shrubs, and grass. The berm is a favored spot for picnics and wildlife observation. At the top of the berm, visitors can enjoy views of the Detroit River and neighboring Canada using two new spotting scopes provided by the Detroit River International Wildlife Refuge and Enchroma. These scopes offer enhanced color views for visitors who are color blind. Additionally, there's an accessible walkway and handrails in the berm area. The state harbor within the park offers 52 boat slips, along with amenities like showers, a laundry facility, grilling areas, and picnic tables. The harbor is also home to a 63-foot lighthouse, which is a scaled-down replica of the Tawas Point State Park lighthouse. Along the Detroit River's shoreline, there are ample opportunities for fishing, including species like bass, walleye, and catfish. Conveniently, the park is in close proximity to the Outdoor Adventure Center, Belle Isle Park, and numerous other significant downtown Detroit attractions.

DATE(S) VISITED .... ☐ SPRING ☐ SUMMER ☐ FALL ☐ WINTER

LODGING .... ☐ ☀ ☐ ☁ ☐ 🌧 ☐ 🌦 ☐ 🌙

WHO I WENT WITH .... FEE(S) .... PARK HOURS .... TEMP:.........

WILL I RETURN? YES / NO RATING ☆ ☆ ☆ ☆ ☆

PASSPORT STAMPS

WILSON STATE PARK

COUNTY	ESTABLISHED	AREA (AC/HA)
CLARE	1920	36 / 15

Wilson State Park is located on 36 acres of wooded land on the northern edge of Budd Lake in Clare County. In the late 1800s, this area was originally occupied by the Wilson Brothers Sawmill and Company Store. The park offers a range of features, including a modern campground, a playground, picnic areas, and opportunities for various outdoor activities such as fishing, paddling, and day trips. Hunting is not permitted within Wilson State Park, but there are extensive state-owned lands open to hunting just a few miles away. These surrounding hunting areas are popular for game animals such as grouse, woodcock, squirrel, rabbit, deer, and bear. During the winter, the park becomes a hub for activities like ice fishing, snowmobiling, and cross-country skiing. Additionally, the annual Frost Bite Open Golf Tournament is held on Budd Lake, offering a unique golfing experience. Snowsnake Mountain provides opportunities for downhill skiing, and visitors can also enjoy winter hiking. The Clare County Fairgrounds, located across from the park, host various events during the summer months, including the County Fair, Michigan Bow Hunters Rendezvous, Monster Truck Show, and the Exhibitor's Exposition. Other local activities include miniature golf, arcade games, batting cages, go-karts, canoeing on the Muskegon River, golfing, biking, and nature observation. Budd Lake, covering 175 acres, is renowned for its excellent fishing opportunities. The lake is home to a variety of fish species, including muskellunge, bass, panfish, perch, and walleye. In addition to fishing, pleasure boating and water-skiing are popular activities on Budd Lake. The park provides a modern concrete launch ramp on the lake's southern end, and mooring is permitted along the shoreline. The park's day use area boasts a sandy beach with a pavilion and a picnic shelter. Visitors can use fire pits and grills in this area. Shelters can be reserved up to a year in advance by calling 1-800-447-2757 or visiting www.midnrreservations.com. The modern campground at Wilson State Park offers 158 camp sites. The Modern Lodge features a half bath and a 3/4 bath, one queen-sized bed, a set of bunk beds, a queen-sized futon, stove, refrigerator, microwave, toaster, coffee maker, cooking utensils, TV with DVD player, and a gas log fireplace. It accommodates six guests, and guests should bring their own bedding. To make a reservation or learn more about this lodge, please call 989-386-4067 (from December to April 15) or 989-539-3021 (from April to November 30). The Mini Cabin provides sleeping arrangements for four with bunk beds, a table with four chairs, a fire circle, cooking grill, picnic table, and a concrete patio.

DATE(S) VISITED .... ☐ SPRING ☐ SUMMER ☐ FALL ☐ WINTER

LODGING .... ☐ ☀ ☐ ☁ ☐ 🌧 ☐ 🌫 ☐ ❄

WHO I WENT WITH .... FEE(S) .... PARK HOURS .... TEMP:.........

WILL I RETURN? YES / NO RATING ☆ ☆ ☆ ☆ ☆

PASSPORT STAMPS

YOUNG STATE PARK

COUNTY	ESTABLISHED	AREA (AC/HA)
CHARLEVOIX	1921	563 / 228

Young State Park is positioned on the eastern shoreline of the picturesque Lake Charlevoix, just beyond Boyne City. Covering 563 acres, the park is a blend of gently rolling terrain, lowlands, and cedar swamp. Its facilities include three modern campgrounds, accommodations for overnight stays, a boat launch, a popular swimming beach, picnic areas, a network of 6.5 miles of trails, and more. Originally established in 1921, the park's day-use building was constructed by the Civilian Conservation Corps during the 1930s. Visitors to the park have access to the Boyne City to Charlevoix Trail, which is soon to be completed. This nonmotorized 14-mile trail will connect the cities of Charlevoix, Petoskey, and Harbor Springs. The park is beautifully located on the shores of Lake Charlevoix, Michigan's third-largest inland lake. The park's day-use area features a designated swim area with an accessible walkway to the water. A boat launch situated at the Terrace Campground offers access to Lake Charlevoix, although parking is limited. The skid pier is accessible. Lake Charlevoix is a favored destination for anglers, and Mirror Pond within the day-use area provides a suitable fishing site for children. Explorer guides conduct weekly learn-to-fish programs. A fishing pier is also available on Mirror Pond. Paddling is a popular activity on Lake Charlevoix, particularly in the mornings and evenings. Young State Park is also a gateway to the Boyne City to Charlevoix Trail, offering a 14-mile nonmotorized route connecting Charlevoix, Petoskey, and Harbor Springs. A day-use building near the beach houses the Lake to Lake Rentals store, which sells snacks, ice cream, and souvenirs. The park's day-use area is equipped with picnic tables and charcoal grills available on a first-come, first-served basis. Modern restrooms are located within the day-use building near the beach. The park features a sanitation station along the entrance road, providing potable water and two lanes for convenience. Visitors can enjoy a three-basket course at the sports field, along the entrance road. Discs for disc golf can be borrowed at the campground host site (for campers only), and the course remains open year-round. Pets are permitted in the area southeast of the boat launch. However, pets must always be on a 6-foot leash and under the owner's immediate control. All pet waste should be properly disposed of in trash receptacles. The Oak modern campground is shaded by large oak trees and features a paved walkway connecting it to the day-use area. An overflow parking lot is available on a first-come, first-served basis, providing storage for boats. The campground offers recycling and refuse disposal, and a self-serve station near the campground entrance road sells firewood. The sites have either 20- or 30-amp electrical service, with a few offering 50-amp service. Some sites are located along the Lake Charlevoix shoreline, providing direct water access. A modern toilet and shower building is centrally located within the campground. This campground has accessible potable water. The Spruce modern campground, divided into four loops, is ideal for larger groups due to its open campsite layouts. This campground is conveniently situated near Lake Charlevoix, the sports field, and the day-use area. An overflow parking lot provides space for boat storage and is available on a first-come, first-served basis. Recycling and refuse disposal facilities are accessible. The Terrace modern campground, named for its terraced landscape, is nestled among a mix of cedar, birch, and oak trees. It features a paved walkway connecting to the Oak campground and the day-use area. Recycling and refuse disposal facilities are available, and the campground hosts site is located within this campground. All three campgrounds are popular among boaters, as they offer access to Lake Charlevoix. Two mini cabins are available at Young State Park, with one located in the Terrace campground and another in the Spruce campground. Each cabin accommodates four people and includes a mini refrigerator and an electric wall heater. The Timberdoodle mini cabin features one double bed and three single beds, while the Sundew mini cabin includes two sets of single beds. Outdoors, visitors will find a picnic table, a fire pit, and a waist-high cooking grill. The cabins are equipped with electricity, and guests need to provide their own linens. Young State Park offers the Deer Flats Nature Trail, a 3-mile single-loop path that traverses cedar swamp terrain and low-lying woods. This trail shares a section with the White Birch Trail and includes an interpretive segment to help visitors identify tree species. The relatively easy hike is suitable for families, and the trail is accessible from various points in the park. Visitors camping in the Terrace campground can begin their hike next to the Timberdoodle mini cabin in the Terrace campground. Mountain biking is not allowed on any of the park's trails. The Spruce Trail is a 2-mile single-loop trail that runs alongside Boyne City Road and the rear of the sports field, extending from the headquarters building to the Spruce campground. The trail also traverses cedar swamp terrain and low-lying woods and offers an easy hike, perfect for families. The park does not permit mountain biking on any of its trails. Within Young State Park, the White Birch Nature Trail is a 1.5-mile path that winds past Lake Charlevoix, providing easy access to the water. The trail offers scenic views of Boyne City, Avalanche Peak, and the surrounding wilderness. The White Birch Trail is well-suited for visitors, particularly families with children, given its relatively easy terrain. The trailhead is located near the boat launch in the Terrace campground, and hiking and cross-country skiing are allowed on this pathway.

DATE(S) VISITED .... □ SPRING □ SUMMER □ FALL □ WINTER

LODGING .... □ ☀ □ ☁ □ 🌧 □ 🌫 □ ❄

WHO I WENT WITH .... FEE(S) .... PARK HOURS .... TEMP:.........

WILL I RETURN? YES / NO   RATING ☆ ☆ ☆ ☆ ☆

PASSPORT STAMPS

PHOTOS

PHOTOS

PHOTOS

PHOTOS

PHOTOS

PHOTOS

PHOTOS

Thank you for taking the time to read our book. We hope you found it enjoyable.

Your feedback is important to us, and we would greatly appreciate it if you could take a moment to share your thoughts by leaving an online review.

Your review will not only help us improve as an author but also assist other potential readers in making informed decisions.

Once again, thank you for your support and for considering leaving a review.

Write to us if you think we should improve anything in our book:

y4.publishing@gmail.com

COLORADO
STATE PARKS
BUCKET LIST
Y4

FLORIDA
STATE PARKS
BUCKET LIST
Y4

GEORGIA
STATE PARKS
BUCKET LIST
Y4

IDAHO
STATE PARKS
BUCKET LIST
Y4

INDIANA
STATE PARKS
BUCKET LIST
Y4

KANSAS
STATE PARKS
BUCKET LIST
Y4

MAINE
STATE PARKS
BUCKET LIST
Y4

MICHIGAN
STATE PARKS
BUCKET LIST
Y4

MINNESOTA
STATE PARKS
BUCKET LIST
Y4

MISSOURI
STATE PARKS
BUCKET LIST
Y4

NEW YORK
STATE PARKS
BUCKET LIST
Y4

OHIO
STATE PARKS
BUCKET LIST
Y4

PENNSYLVANIA
STATE PARKS
BUCKET LIST
Y4

TENNESSEE
STATE PARKS
BUCKET LIST
Y4

TEXAS
STATE PARKS
BUCKET LIST
Y4

UTAH
STATE PARKS
BUCKET LIST
Y4

VIRGINIA
STATE PARKS
BUCKET LIST
Y4

WASHINGTON
STATE PARKS
BUCKET LIST
Y4